Witness to the Human Rights Tribunals

Bruce Granville Miller

Witness to the Human Rights Tribunals

How the System Fails Indigenous Peoples

UBCPress · Vancouver · Toronto

© UBC Press 2023
Foreword © Sharon Venne-Manyfingers 2023

All rights reserved. No part of this publication may be reproduced, stored in a retrieval system, or transmitted, in any form or by any means, without prior written permission of the publisher, or, in Canada, in the case of photocopying or other reprographic copying, a licence from Access Copyright, www.accesscopyright.ca.

32 31 30 29 28 27 26 25 24 23   5 4 3 2 1

Printed in Canada on FSC-certified ancient-forest-free paper
(100% post-consumer recycled) that is processed chlorine- and acid-free.

Library and Archives Canada Cataloguing in Publication

Title: Witness to the human rights tribunals : how the system fails Indigenous peoples / Bruce Granville Miller.
Names: Miller, Bruce Granville, 1951- author.
Description: Includes bibliographical references and index.
Identifiers: Canadiana (print) 20220443785 | Canadiana (ebook) 20220443807 | ISBN 9780774867757 (hardcover) | ISBN 9780774867771 (PDF) | ISBN 9780774867788 (EPUB)
Subjects: LCSH: Indigenous peoples—Civil rights—British Columbia. | LCSH: Indigenous peoples—Legal status, laws, etc.—British Columbia. | LCSH: British Columbia Human Rights Tribunal. | LCSH: Law and anthropology.
Classification: LCC KEB529 .M55 2023 | DDC 342.71108/72—dc23

Canadä

UBC Press gratefully acknowledges the financial support for our publishing program of the Government of Canada (through the Canada Book Fund), the Canada Council for the Arts, and the British Columbia Arts Council.

This book has been published with the help of a grant from the Canadian Federation for the Humanities and Social Sciences, through the Awards to Scholarly Publications Program, using funds provided by the Social Sciences and Humanities Research Council of Canada.

Printed and bound in Canada by Friesens
Set in Meta and Garamond by Artegraphica Design Co.
Substantive Editor: Lesley Erickson
Copy editor: Robyn So
Proofreader: Caitlin Gordon-Walker
Indexer: Judy Dunlop
Cover designer: JVDW Designs

UBC Press
The University of British Columbia
2029 West Mall
Vancouver, BC V6T 1Z2
www.ubcpress.ca

For Rose Law Miller
1920–2021

Contents

Foreword / ix
SHARON VENNE-MANYFINGERS

Acknowledgments / xii

Introduction / 3

Part 1: Anthropology and Law

1 My Life in Anthropology and Law / 13

2 Symbolic Violence, Trauma, and Human Rights / 27

3 Thinning the Evidence, Discrediting the Expert Witness / 43

4 Entering Evidence in an Adversarial System / 72

5 Anthropologists versus Lawyers / 83

Part 2: The Tribunal

6 The British Columbia Human Rights Tribunal / 99

7 *McCue v. University of British Columbia* / 126

8 *Menzies v. Vancouver Police Department* / 160

Conclusion / 178

Case Law and Legal Materials / 193

References / 195

Index / 208

Foreword

NOTED MĀORI LAWYER Moana Jackson described the legal systems of colonizing states as the "jurisprudence of oppression" of Indigenous Peoples. In *Witness to the Human Rights Tribunals,* Bruce Miller, an observer of the police, courts, and tribunals that are "supposed to" provide safety and justice, documents in stark detail the way the legal system creates a jurisprudence of oppression. He gives the reader a ringside seat at hearings where Indigenous Peoples have tried to protect themselves. The scenes inside and outside the court system demonstrate, however, what many First Nations say: "Just us" – there is nothing in the system for us Indigenous Peoples.

Miller's careful notes transport the reader into those sterile tribunal rooms. His keen observations of the various actors, right down to the red socks worn by one of the witnesses, tell the real story. The witnesses all know each other – exchanging greetings and visiting – while the Indigenous Peoples come into a space that is not their own. Miller makes clear who is in charge – and it is not the Indigenous Peoples. In many ways, Miller has chosen to present the materials with an Indigenous story tool used in oral tradition: the volume of detail, for the listener, gives the story authenticity. As an Indigenous reader, I can put myself in the room. By giving context to the tribunal courtroom – the view out the windows, the demeanor of the various witnesses, the clothes they are wearing – Miller draws me in. He not only makes visual observations but also adds sections of transcripts to the mix. His clever use of the written version of the oral statements advances the oral component to the telling. It is a very shrewd way of writing. He brings the reader to be a witness.

In one human rights case that Miller describes, an Indigenous woman is pushed away by the police and made to feel unwanted and unsafe for asking questions about her son. In her Indigenous world, she is a mother. She has a natural instinct to ask, What is happening with my son? In the police world, she has no right to ask or interfere. It is very clear that there is the Indigenous world and the police world. In the police world, Indigenous Peoples are more than marginalized. They are ghosted. The interaction with the Indigenous woman is insignificant to police. However, the mother is traumatized. The lack of knowledge about and acknowledgement of Indigenous Peoples is at the core of systemic racism in the legal system.

Systemic racism is a part of colonization, of dehumanizing the original peoples in order to justify the theft of our lands and resources. It is not unique to Great Turtle Island. Interactions around the world tell the same stories of ongoing colonization, of using the judicial system to dehumanize Indigenous Peoples. In the state of Canada, at least twenty inquiries in the last fifty years point to systemic racism in the justice system. Those inquiries have called for more education for police and the judicial system on the rights of Indigenous Peoples. Despite those calls, horrific examples of systemic racism occur each year and lead to public inquiries. Think of Betty Ann Osborne, Donald Marshall, and Dudley George; think of the Blood Tribe inquiry, "Starlight Tours," the National Inquiry into Murdered and Missing Women, the Royal Commission on Aboriginal Peoples, the Truth and Reconciliation Commission, and many more inquiries that called for action in their reports. Those reports sit on shelves gathering dust. The system does not want to change. It is comfortable. To change, the system has to admit it is wrong.

Indigenous laws have to fit within the colonial system rather than the system accept that Indigenous laws exist side-by-side with the colonial system. To incorporate Indigenous laws into the colonial system is to destroy Indigenous laws. Miller's detailed study of the human rights complaint filed by Lorna June McCue, who was denied tenure at the University of British Columbia, is a classic case of systemic racism. In being admitted to teach in such an institution, a person is essentially told "You are privileged. We have allowed you to enter these halls as a human – but a human without a point of view." In this case, the university had signalled its desire to have an Indigenous presence in the law school. The problem for McCue, however,

X FOREWORD

was that the university wanted a human Indigenous "presence" and a symbol or two on the walls, but not an Indigenous point of view or Indigenous legal view of the world. Law schools do not accept that there are two functioning legal systems in this state: Indigenous and non-Indigenous. Law schools have incorrectly assumed that their colonial system is the only one.

In this incorrect world, McCue was forced to drag four suitcases of materials to the BC Human Rights Tribunal hearings, trying to prove her points that her work in oral history and oral telling of laws of the Indigenous Peoples constituted valid scholarly work. However, those four suitcases represented the systemic racism that is built into the tribunals and courts. As an Indigenous person, you enter into the process to prove your rights. There is no starting point that an Indigenous person has a valid point of view based on their Indigenous worldview. Rather, that point of view is immediately discounted, forcing an Indigenous person to "prove" themselves in the face of the system. The tribunal and the university were not prepared to accept that oral presentations constituted anything in their world. If the system made that admission, the tenure process would have to adapt. They are not prepared to adapt. They are comfortable in their continued oppression, in building their jurisprudence of oppression.

This book is worth reading for everyone – Indigenous and non-Indigenous alike. It shows in stark detail the barriers encountered in so-called human rights law. This law is built on the European notion of human rights – an individual against the system. In the Indigenous world, the rights of the collective are paramount. Take, for example, the original Declaration on the Rights of Indigenous Peoples, completed in 1992, that addresses collective rights of Indigenous Peoples. There was a fundamental gap in international human rights law that was filled by the original declaration. Unfortunately, the United Nations General Assembly, in their wisdom, added the individual into the document, thereby undermining and devaluing the rights of the collective. Report after report will continue to outline systemic racism because colonization knows no end, until someone takes the bull by the horns and says, "This is systemic racism and it has to be dealt with – step 1 and step 2 and so forth." Miller is putting forth ideas on overcoming the structural barriers he has witnessed. It is well worth the read to ponder on his ideas – obviously written from a point of view that hovers between two worlds.

Sharon Venne-Manyfingers

Acknowledgments

MANY PEOPLE HAVE contributed to my thinking for this book, but any errors of fact or interpretation are my own. I thank those who read earlier drafts and made their very helpful comments, including the anonymous reviewers whose care and attention to detail has made a better book. Professor Joey Weiss of Wesleyan University, retired lawyer Todd Miller, University of British Columbia archaeologist colleague Professor Michael Blake, and Susan Blake, are among those with whom I discussed my ideas over a coffee or a Zoom call. Lawyers Amber Prince and Myrna McCallum are an inspiration for their thinking about trauma and their work in the human rights tribunal. Gladys Radek, the complainant in the important *Radek v Henderson Development and other* (No. 3), 2005 BCHRT 302 case before the British Columbia Human Rights Tribunal, and the complainant (whose name I have rendered Clara Menzies) provided their important perspectives both to the tribunal and in conversations with me. My thanks and best wishes to them both.

I also thank the lawyers with whom I have worked over many years, particularly David Hawkins, Harry Chesnin, and Sarah Rauch. Al Grove, a thoughtful legal historian, has prompted new ideas concerning legal processes.

UBC Professor Julie Cruikshank helped me form ideas regarding oral history evidence. Several Brazilian colleagues engaged in conversations over the decades regarding the problems facing Indigenous peoples (see Younging, 65) in legal systems, particularly Professor Stephen Baines of the University of Brasilia, Dr. Gustavo Menezes, of FUNAI (the Brazilian Federal Indian Agency), and Professor Cristhian da Silva, also of the University of Brasilia. The University of Brasilia kindly twice hosted me as a researcher, which gave me the opportunity to talk to government officials at FUNAI and at the *Ministério Público,* and to public prosecutors. The late Dr. Daniel Brasil, my Brazilian PhD student and member of the Brazilian diplomatic service, provided wonderful insights, along with Cuban rum, on my back deck in Vancouver, in Cuba, and at his house in Brasilia.

Students in my Anthropology of Law seminar at UBC over several years provided a great deal of stimulation and original research, and the work of students from the class is contained within the book. Riley Bertoncini gave tremendous energy and insight into his reading and analysis of more than 100 decisions in the BC Human Rights Tribunal, and Maeve McAllister read and commented on all the decisions involving Indigenous people between 2015 and 2020. Thanks to you both and also Yuval Kehila. Graduate students under my supervision past and present brought their own distinct insights, among them Professor Jane McMillan, former Canada Research Chair at St. Francis Xavier University, Professor David Milward of the University of Victoria, Celeste Haldane, the Chief Commissioner of the BC Treaty Commission, Fumiya Nagai, of Japan, a scholar of international human rights, Molly Malone, Brian Thom, a faculty member at the University of Victoria, Thomas McIlwraith, at the University of Guelph, Tal Nitsan, Professor Kate Hennessey, Sharon Fortney, Ingrid Johnson, Jennifer Hamilton, Professor Keith Carlson, Linda Nading, Cindy McMullan, Patty Ginn, Professor Kisha Supernant, Chris Smith, Emma Feltes, Chris Arnett, Erin Hansen, Peter Merchant, Jordan Wilson, Jeff Schiffer, Brenda Fitzpatrick, and Rodrigo Ferrari-Nunes. Thanks to you all.

Morgan Ritchie, Bill Angelbeck of Douglas College, and Métis scholar Rick Ouellet are among my regular friendly and insightful confidants. Professor Daniel Boxberger of Western Washington University has been an inspiration as has Professor Gordon Christie of UBC law and Professor Pierre Morenon of Rhode Island College. Dr. Amelia Radke of Australia has contributed a wealth of ideas regarding issues facing Indigenous people in court. Colleagues in the Department of Anthropology, UBC, have been helpful for years, particularly Bill McKellin, Carole Blackburn, and Charles Menzies. Professor John Barker arranged an evocative trip to the Maisin people of Papua New Guinea, where I was able to get a sense of their responses to the legal dilemmas they face.

Special thanks go to Doreen Maloney and Scott Schuyler of the Upper Skagit tribe for the many years of conversation and their kind sharing of their knowledge. Thanks to the late Grand Chief Frank Malloway and Sonny McHalsie of the Stó:lō Nation for their many insights. The late Rocky Wilson, Lindsay Wilson, and Jim Hornbrook, all of the Hwlitsum First Nation, and Shauntelle Nichols and her family of the Pender Harbour First Nation have kindly contributed their insights, as has Willie Charlie, a remarkable Sts'ailes First Nation leader.

The outstanding UBC Press editor, Darcy Cullen, and the press director, Melissa Pitts, will always have my gratitude for their help in nurturing my book ideas. Many thanks to Lesley Erickson and Michelle van der Merwe for their hard work on the manuscript. My thanks and appreciation to Ace Forsythe, a lawyer and wise friend. Sociologists Roy and Frankie Todd, my thanks to you for your insights, friendship, and kindness.

My family is a source of continual inspiration, information, and assistance. Thank you! to my wife and savvy reader of drafts, Laraine Michalson, my son Cameron Miller and his spouse, Métis journalist Cara McKenna, and my other son Alastair Miller and his spouse, Siobhan Sabourin. I follow in the footsteps of my grandparents, Rev. John Granville Law and Myrtle Rose Law, and their daughter, Rose Law Miller. I hope I reflect their influences.

Witness to the Human Rights Tribunals

Introduction

BC Human Rights Tribunal, Downtown Vancouver, September 2019.
A police officer who had been involved in an episode of mistreatment of an Indigenous woman testifies under cross-examination.

"Can I ask a question? I don't understand why I'm explaining policing matters to the Human Rights Tribunal." The officer gets testy and gives a long discussion of police processes and practices.

"Thank you for the lesson in criminal law." The lawyer for Clara Menzies, an Indigenous woman and the complainant, says.

Later that afternoon, the tribunal jurist holds a feather and the giving of true testimony at the hearing continues. Menzies (a pseudonym for the complainant) is agitated and speaks of the colonial system to which she hasn't given consent. "How can genocide be reconciled? Why should I have to keep explaining?" She dislikes the repetition of questions from the lawyers seeking to get clear answers.

The tribunal jurist is unperturbed. "Just answer the questions one at a time."

Menzies appears to be triggered by these events. Later, she asks why she has to keep answering the same questions.

"This is how the process works – some questions will overlap. Keep answering the questions."

✳ ✳ ✳

WHAT HAPPENS WHEN Indigenous people enter the legal systems of Canada and the United States? There are countless ways to approach this question, but I come at it from the perspective of my own work as an anthropologist who has served as an expert witness in legal venues in Canada and the United States and, more specifically, before the BC Human Rights Tribunal.

Human rights abuses generally concern discrimination against the cultural and economic rights of individuals and collectives, including Indigenous nations. Institutions, including tribunals, have been established at the international, national, and regional levels to address these forms of discrimination. The BC Human Rights Tribunal, located in Vancouver, British Columbia, Canada, is an example of a regional (provincial) tribunal directed primarily at individual rights, although class action suits have occurred (including the *Radek* case, which I describe in this book). The province created the tribunal after the Second World War with an emphasis on establishing social, cultural, and economic rights. The *Human Rights Code* of British Columbia was enacted in 1967, establishing a full-time administration and commission. Human rights complaints could be brought to a dedicated agency. From 1983 to 1997, the *Human Rights Code* was administered by the BC Human Rights Council. Later, with the closure of the BC Human Rights Commission, formal complaints were filed directly with the BC Human Rights Tribunal, with the intervening investigation provided through the BC Human Rights Council and BC Human Rights Commission (Froome 2007, 6–7; CAUT 2002). The commission has since been reestablished.

In the English common-law tradition, the people called to testify in court belong to two groups: (1) lay complainants and witnesses, who testify only about what they have personally seen or heard and (2) expert witnesses, who can give opinions about events and processes beyond their own direct experience and who can make inferences relative to the issues at hand in court.

Complainants before tribunals, such as Clara Menzies, have experienced discrimination with a demonstrable impact on their lives. The *Human Rights Code* allows only specific instances of discrimination to be brought to the tribunal by particular categories of people. The forms of discrimination include race, place of birth, colour, ancestry, and religion as experienced in employment, services, accommodation, and more. In the case of the BC Human Rights Tribunal, complainants bring their issues to the direct-access tribunal. Despite the large number of inquiries, most of the cases are either not accepted, are handled through mediation, or are simply abandoned. Cases that are accepted but not successfully mediated are generally heard in an office tower in downtown Vancouver. There, tribunal members hear the cases individually and render a decision, which may be appealed to courts. There is no mechanism to enforce an order from the tribunal, and a successful complainant might have to go to court to seek enforcement. Only a minority of the cases involve Indigenous people and institutions.

I draw on my own work as an expert witness and on that of others to reveal the difficulties that legal processes – in human rights tribunals and other legal forums – impose on Indigenous people. Today, the number of countries using anthropologists as expert witnesses is increasing, as anthropologist Leila Rodriguez (2020; see Sikkink and Waling 2007) notes regarding developments in South and Central America. In British Columbia, as elsewhere, the end result of human rights tribunals is often perplexing. I found that this is because Indigenous experiences are first transformed into anthropological stories, and then they are transformed into legal stories. Throughout my career, I have been involved in cases dealing with treaties (Miller 1985, 2006, 2010), land claims (Miller 1995, 1999, 2018b), fishing rights (Miller 2012b, 2013; and see Miller and Angelbeck 2006), human rights (Miller 2003, 2006, 2008, 2010, 2018; see Sharma 2015), personal injury, family law, criminal law (Miller 2011, 2012a, 2012b, 2012c, 2012/13), an inquest (see Yukon 2020), and many other sorts of cases at various scales, from multiple tribes in federal court to single families and individuals in local courts. What these cases have in common is the diminution of Indigenous people's lives through the application of stereotypes, forms of discrimination, and the incapacity or disinclination of jurors to understand Indigenous worldviews and displacement. I detail how experts and lawyers might overcome this obstacle and produce more useful testimony in tribunals. My own successes and failures are part of the story because they have allowed me to see dimensions of the legal processes I might not otherwise have noticed.

As I show in Part 1, "Anthropology and Law," in both courts and tribunals, lawyers and judges subject the discipline of anthropology – its methods and findings – to intense scrutiny. Our ideas and disciplinary practices are not viewed as significant on their face; for this reason, anthropologists and social scientists more generally have a stake in these legal processes. In turn, the application of anthropology to legal questions, something that happens routinely, is rarely analyzed by those serving as experts, in part because anthropologist-experts do not want to leave a record of their own approaches in litigation that might later be used to their disadvantage in court. Nevertheless, the fruits of our intellectual labours as social scientists are perhaps more significant in courts of law than they are in academic journals or courts of public opinion.

For these reasons, in Chapter 1, I describe my own role in litigation involving Indigenous people and how this experience made me aware of problems inherent in the legal process, which is a form of symbolic violence that diminishes Indigenous people's voices and stories, perpetuates Indigenous people's trauma, and hampers their efforts to redress violations of their human rights. This widely critiqued concept is discussed further in Chapter 2. Anthropologist-experts are called upon to enter evidence about Indigenous people's histories and experiences in the courts, but once they enter the courts their expertise is called into question, a further act of diminishment. In Chapter 3, I outline the way anthropologists can be discredited in the courts and the practice of thinning, a term used to describe efforts by opposing counsel to limit expert testimony and the case brought forward by Indigenous litigants. Chapter 4 discusses the way the adversarial system makes the job of anthropologist-expert more difficult by often pitting anthropologists against each other, which can undermine belief in their objectivity, discourage anthropologists from publishing their research, and reduce the pool of experts willing to participate in the system. Chapter 5 examines the many problems anthropologists face while working with lawyers, including mutual misunderstanding about each other's disciplines, lack of ethical guidelines, and fundamental differences in the way anthropologists and lawyers use language and how they think. I ask what lawyers should teach anthropologists about working in court and vice versa.

In all these discussions, I include details from Canadian and US federal courts, human rights tribunals, district and state courts, and commissions and other legal venues of trials, hearings, and processes I have engaged in and for which I have acted as a consultant. These chapters, I believe, create a thick context for looking specifically at a human rights tribunal, the British Columbia tribunal (BCHRT), and for understanding the tribunal in the larger context of Indigenous litigation generally. The diminution I observed constitutes both the grounds for bringing the cases and the experiences of Indigenous people in the process of preparing for and attending legal proceedings. I encountered nothing different in the BC Human Rights Tribunal.

In Part 2, "The Tribunal," I use the anthropological tools and perspectives developed in Part 1 to explore the workings of this tribunal: the physical setting, the litigants, and the expert witnesses. Here, I shift from my role as anthropologist-expert to anthropologist-ethnographer. I rely on my own extensive field notes from several hearings. In addition, I examine all the BCHRT decisions between 1997 and 2020 to see what trends might be discernable. Chapter 6 sets the stage by taking a more intimate look at the tribunal, to explore whether the concept of human rights is a useful frame for Indigenous people and communities. I note the difficulties of filing charges, the unlikelihood of winning a case, and the alienation the process can produce, among other issues. Chapter 7 focuses on *McCue v The University of British Columbia* (No. 4), 2018 BCHRT 45, brought by an Indigenous University of British Columbia professor denied tenure, and Chapter 8 explores the *Menzies v Vancouver Police Board* (No. 4), 2019 BCHRT 275, which involved an Indigenous complainant mistreated by the Vancouver police. I use the ethnographic materials from these cases to show the way trauma experienced by the Indigenous litigants is reproduced in the tribunal process. I conclude that critique and transformation of human rights tribunals must begin by addressing the violence and trauma (in particular the sense of fear, overwhelming injustice, and rage) experienced by Indigenous people who bring complaints before tribunals.

The sense of injustice and violation expressed by Clara Menzies before the BC Human Rights Tribunal that opens this Introduction is a painful example of this trauma. Menzies was responding, in part, to a police officer, who stated out loud that he did not get why he had to bother appearing in legal proceedings brought because of charges of police misbehaviour. The circumstances of *Menzies v. Vancouver Police Board* are manifestations of a larger issue: the place of Indigenous people in contemporary society and their relation to the state. The trauma of the courtroom and tribunal hall is metonymic of the violence of colonialism more broadly (see Povinelli 2002).

But the goal here is not simply to blame judges for the difficulties that Indigenous litigants face in the legal system or experts experience in giving evidence. Nor is the goal to simply critique the legal systems of the two countries where I have worked as an anthropologist-expert. Judges, tribunal members, and other legal officials face complex and vexing questions in their work, and they work in systems they have inherited and many hope to reform.

In the spirit of reform, I draw on diverse cases to reveal the issues of expert witnesses and to propose ways the BC Human Rights Tribunal – and other tribunals – might be revised in the interests of Indigenous complainants. I suggest ways the tribunal might be transformed to better address and reduce the symbolic violence and trauma experienced by complainants and ways anthropology and social sciences generally might best contribute to providing Indigenous complainants a chance to clearly present their claims to the tribunal.

As noted by historian Arthur Ray (2011, 2016) and anthropologist Dan Boxberger (2007), new data and approaches emerge as we prepare for court; what happens in the courts has real meaning for other experts. Social workers, health professionals, and many other practitioners also come under the scrutiny of judges and lawyers and have a stake in ensuring that their perspectives and insights are heard and considered. They, too, wish to make clear the sometimes-harsh circumstances facing Indigenous people in hospitals and other public services, and they, too, are grappling with understanding the role trauma plays in the lives of Indigenous people.

A Note on Sources and Terminology

There are features of legal processes that are best understood from the inside, as an actor in the formal and informal proceedings. Being inside gives more access to documents and to the action, the conversations, decisions, and relationships that develop before a case enters the courtroom. For this reason, much of my data comes from cases for which I have been retained as an expert and have submitted an expert report and/or testified to the tribunal. Paul Burke, in *Law's Anthropology* (2011), mentions the difficulty of obtaining critical anthropological reports used in litigation, a problem I overcome by using my own reports, in some cases verbatim portions to probe inside the processes anthropologists undertake in entering into the legal system. In some instances, I include them to show what content has been barred from entry into proceedings by legal arguments, that is, thinning, and the restraints this poses on producing a more effective anthropological testimony.

The terms used to identify Indigenous people are changeable, sometimes quickly becoming disfavoured. Just a few years ago, the cover term for various peoples was "Aboriginal" (See Miller 2004, for a discussion of the various definitions of Indigenous people that have been created by states and international organizations). Currently, in Canada, the terms Indigenous and Aboriginal (in law) encompass First Nations, Métis, and Inuit groups. The groups with political recognition by the state, Canada, are commonly referred to as bands or, when grouped together, tribal councils.

Their lands are termed reserves, but there are exceptions, including for those groups that have got out from under the *Indian Act* and now own their own territories under other legal arrangements. In the United States, Indigenous refers to American Indian tribes, whose lands are termed reservations. In both countries, many people object to cover terms and prefer the specific names of their groups. Sometimes, collections of groups that share common histories, languages, and cultures are referred to as nations, but this term is also used for individual tribes/bands. In addition, because the term "Status Indian" is commonly used, as in Canadian legislation, I retain its use.

I use the term "state" to refer to the instruments of governance and the governments themselves. In particular, that includes the United States of America, Canada, the state of Washington, the province of British Columbia, and also the Canadian Department of Justice, which acts for Canada; in this case, I use the term "Crown." I have pointed out in *Invisible Indigenes* (2004, 46) that the state administratively reduces the number of Indigenous people through the act of non-recognition. Further, the state is not a "rational actor mediating between interested parties"; instead, the state is "made up of political actors and irrational, in that policies and practices are themselves frequently at odds" (Miller 2004, 46). Courtrooms and tribunal halls represent the state's sovereignty through judicial power (Bourdieu 1987, 838).

Part 1

Anthropology and Law

1

My Life in Anthropology and Law

I HAVE OFTEN WONDERED why I have spent so much time, such a great percentage of my adult life, preparing for and in litigation at the request of Indigenous communities and their lawyers, tasks I do not seek out. In part, this reflects the circumstances that Indigenous communities – American Indian tribes and First Nations, Inuit, and Métis bands in Canada – find themselves in. The current legal nightmare they inhabit has roots deep in the past.

A Brief History of Law and Colonialism in Canada and the United States

Canadian law has long distinguished "Indians" as a legal category. Initially, before the creation of the Canadian state, Indigenous nations were treated by Europeans as distinct peoples with their own systems of law. Over time, they became subsumed into the Canadian legal system, and their own law and legal practices were regarded as relics, although they were not erased by the common law. The lands that now compose Canada were thought to be good for colonization by the French, English, and other Europeans, the earliest of whom arrived starting in the beginning of the sixteenth century. These Europeans and European Canadians eventually practised direct rule of colonies rather than the systems of indirect rule that characterized some other British colonies, such as India, for example. There was no compelling reason to closely study Indigenous legal practices; rather, these were to be replaced as quickly as possible. The Royal Proclamation of 1763 set the terms for the negotiation of treaties with Indigenous nations.

Historians tend to see the period of the American Revolution and the War of 1812 as the dividing line between the period in which European-descended populations treated Indigenous people as Nations with the potential to be military and political allies and the subsequent period when this was not necessary and Status Indians became, gradually, wards of the state. Prior to this the French, British, and, later, Canada entered into a variety of treaties with Indigenous Nations: Treaties of Peace and Neutrality (1701–60), Peace and Friendship Treaties (1725–79), Upper Canada Land Surrenders and the Williams Treaties (1764–1862/1923), Robinson Treaties and Douglas Treaties (1850–54), and The Numbered Treaties (1871–1921).

The Dominion of Canada was created in 1867, and, subsequently, the underlying concept of Canadian policy has been to assimilate Indigenous Peoples and communities economically, to acculturate them, and to amalgamate the remaining populations biologically through intermarriage. All of this was encapsulated in the *Indian Act* of 1876.

More recently, spurred by the Indigenous rights movement and awareness of the legacy of colonialism, Canada has entered into a variety of modern treaties and agreements with Indigenous Peoples. Established in 1974, the Office of Native Claims defined two types of modern land claims: specific and comprehensive, to address the failure to adhere to the terms of promises under the Indian Act and clarify issues of title. The Specific Claims Tribunal (2008) has since supplanted the Office of Native Claims and is the federal body that continues to hear specific and modern land claims.

A major shift came with the *Constitution Act, 1982*, section 35, which recognizes and affirms Aboriginal rights. Treaty negotiations have been underway in British Columbia since 1991, with a small number of treaties concluded. Recent legal decisions have concerned the federal government's duty to consult with Indigenous groups and the recognition of the Métis as Indigenous Peoples along with the First Nations and Inuit.

The history of Indigenous Peoples and the law followed a similar but slightly different trajectory in the United States. Contemporary American Indians, also called Native Americans, are the descendants of the original inhabitants of the territory now encompassed by the United States. They are members of 561 tribes recognized by the federal government or state government and are regarded in law as "domestic, dependent nations." They retain specific economic, political, social, and cultural rights. State, federal, and tribal laws govern these communities, called nations or peoples by their members. Unlike in Canada, Indigenous people have only one legal category of membership.

Europeans, French, British, Dutch, and others entered North America from the east coast in the early seventeenth century; the Spanish entered from the southwest a century earlier. The defeat of the French and the Royal Proclamation of 1763 established the conditions for the negotiation of treaties with Indigenous nations and legally defined the North American interior west of the Appalachian Mountains as Indigenous lands. This proclamation continues to be part of Canadian law, as well. But the expansion westward in the United States in the nineteenth century gradually forced large numbers of Indigenous people to move further west. *Johnson v. M'Intosh,* 1823, the first of the "Marshall Trilogy," three court cases heard by the US Supreme Court, became the foundation on which American Indian law is decided and holds that the tribes have only the right of occupancy to their own lands.

The federal *Indian Removal Act of 1830* authorized the president to conduct treaties to exchange Native American land east of the Mississippi River for lands west of the river. Thousands of Indigenous people died during the enforced movement out of their lands in the southeast, in what has been called the Trail of Tears. The brutal removal led to conflicts between Indian nations and US troops as a result of the Indian removal policy, and in 1876, the United States government ordered all remaining Indigenous people to move onto reservations and stopped negotiating treaties. Later, the *Indian General Allotment Act, 1887,* known as the Dawes Act, authorized the division of Indian tribal land into allotments, replacing the tribal system of common property. The Dawes Act had disastrous effects on Indian tribal identity and culture, and Native Americans lost some two-thirds of their land to non-members living in tribal areas.

US policy towards Indigenous people and nations has fluctuated between efforts at termination of federal recognition and recognition of autonomy. The *Indian Reorganization Act,* of 1934, also known as the Wheeler-Howard Act, reversed the Dawes Act's privatization of common holdings and supported tribal self-government. The act also restored to Native Americans the management of their land and attempted to provide economic benefits for American Indians. But termination and assimilation, which affected more than one hundred tribes, became the policy from the 1940s to the 1960s. The *Indian Relocation Act,* of 1956 led to the relocation of thousands of people to cities. The policy switched back to recognition of sovereignty and self-governance. Federal statutes, such as the *Indian Civil Rights Act of 1968* (also known as the Indian Bill of Rights) and the *Indian Self-Determination and Education Assistance Act of 1975,* deal with Indian rights and governance. Many tribes have created their own courts, with considerable civil and criminal jurisdiction.

So, in theory, the effort to assimilate is no longer Canadian or US policy. But in my own experience as an expert witness in civil and criminal cases and human rights tribunals, I have found, as has my colleague Gustavo Menezes in Brazil (Miller and Menezes 2015), that the commonly held wisdom is that Indigenous people either once existed but no longer do or are assimilated (see also Weiss 2018). These beliefs sometimes create an obstacle to providing clarity or context on the legal issues at hand.

The Legal Context Today and My Role in It

It is certainly true that Indigenous people have defended themselves, using the law in many cases, since their early contacts with Europeans. The Indigenous people of what became New England, for example, early on attempted to use colonial courts to defend their land and their persons in the seventeenth century (Philbrick 2006). This is not the place to describe this long history. Yet, there is something distinctive about recent decades, a period in which Indigenous people of North America have created the capacity to bring important cases and to enter into courtrooms with their own lawyers and their own tribal governments backing the effort.

The new capacity and energy to regain control over their lives has been recently described as a resurgence (Asch, Borrows, and Tully 2018) and, relatedly, a refusal (Simpson 2007, 2014; McGranahan 2016), processes that reject non-Indigenous perspectives and practices, including courts. It is easy to overstate the new, improved circumstances of North American Indigenous communities, however, and many remain trapped in lengthy litigation, sometimes lasting decades, to protect themselves and to rearrange their relations with the state. For this reason, anthropological experts continue to be engaged to provide evidence for Indigenous litigation. For at least some anthropologists of my generation, an overriding issue, perhaps the primary focus of research and writing, has been to understand and aid the movement towards Indigenous sovereignty and autonomy. This has led us into courtrooms and law offices.

My time as an anthropologist from the 1970s to the present has been characterized by repeated efforts of Indigenous groups to defend their lands and waters, to gain access to hunting, fishing and other animal relatives, and to assert their human rights as they have come to be encoded in law. And since I have been engaged in litigation as an expert anthropologist, I wish to understand what these various sorts of legal defence have in common. Why these sorts of legal entanglements at the same time? How are these legal forays related? And what do anthropology and the social sciences have to offer these legal processes?

Because my own work in litigation gives a distinctive view of our legal institutions, I have come to realize that I am in a position to make an assessment, from my own perspective, of these institutions and their efficacy for Indigenous people and groups who enter into them. I do this by working at the interstices, the critical points of contact, between the mainstream society and Indigenous society. This is not solely about cases won or lost by Indigenous people. There are other issues at stake, as I will show, and cases won are sometimes lost as well. And other members of other disciplines and in different social positions provide their own perspectives on legal processes. I do not write as a police officer, legal practitioner, professor of law, historian, tribal member or leader, museum curator, judge, tribunal member, or some other anthropologist. These people have their own stories to tell. I am a white, late-middle-aged anthropologist in Western Canada. This is my story.

My story derives from the sort of engagements I have been asked to undertake and have carried out. I think of this as beyond participant observation, in that I am not limited to participation in the daily lives of Indigenous communities, although I have done that. In the 1990s, I directed an ethnographic field school based in the Stó:lō Nation. In addition, I have learned from eight summers spent in residence in his longhouse with the late Grand Chief Frank Malloway (Siyémches), of the Yeqwyeqwí:ws First Nation, on the Fraser River, in British Columbia. I have spent forty-five years with other Coast Salish peoples, documenting fishing, hunting, and gathering practices and engaging in ritual events, and with many others in Indigenous North America, Brazil, Papua New Guinea, and Taiwan, hearing about their legal, cultural, and other issues.

But I am not solely an observer. I have spent nearly forty years working regularly in long-term collaboration with the council and members of the Upper Skagit tribe, located on the Skagit River, Washington, and for whom

I have edited an historical atlas (2021). I have participated in several bouts of their treaty litigation and in tribally sponsored studies of their historic culture, place names, and vision questing locations. On occasion I have had to write detailed accounts of the lives of communities and of the ancestors of the present-day members. Sometimes I have been asked by communities to write documents for court that define them as a people, and to define their culture, residences, economy, political organization, history, and other intimate features of their lives and those of their ancestors. These requests emerged from legal requirements Indigenous communities face, for example, in trying to gain official recognition by the state.

It is always troubling as an outsider to be placed in such a position and to write in ways that could define and limit their futures in unexpected ways. But our legal systems continue to require that this work be done, and it is my job to be sure that the work I do is recognizable by both the community members and the court, even though it is, in part, in anthropological language that community members may not ordinarily use. In addition, in some cases after years of work with a community, I am in a distinct position to understand their history and to know the anthropology related to them. There is often no one else in this position and then, when asked by communities to assist the court to understand, it is hard to refuse after the hospitality extended by these individuals and communities to me. My work has also made me an observer of the ways the system fails Indigenous people, both in regular litigation and in human rights tribunals.

Litigation Work

I have been asked to participate in cases that fall into several categories. These cases provide evidence that refines, illustrates, and supports my claims about the often-adverse relationship between legal systems and Indigenous people, and the relationship between the law and anthropology. Each case adds something distinct about one or more of these topics, and the diversity of these cases reveals something of the variety of cases Indigenous people are drawn into and the presence of the legal regime in the everyday lives of people.

I provided evidence in the United States in criminal and family law cases but primarily in federal treaty cases – including rights to fishing, shellfishing, and hunting. These cases originally were brought against state governments but later broke out into conflict between tribes. Typically, my work in the cases involved reconstructing the Indigenous world in an earlier period, often the time in which the treaty was signed or the time of first contact. As with the human rights cases, the problem was understanding how colonial processes disrupted Indigenous lives and the ways in which Indigenous people have set about carrying on their cultures and social lives in the face of disastrous imposed changes.

After some years doing episodic treaty work, I was drawn into examine the role of oral history evidence in litigation. In particular, this work derived from a decision in the Canadian Supreme Court, *Delgamuukw,* 1997, in which paragraph 88 of the decision states, "[justices] order that this type of evidence [oral history] can be accommodated and placed on an equal footing with the types of historical evidence that courts are familiar with, which largely consists of historical documents." Following that, a debate arose about what this meant and how this accommodation might be done. Oral history (or oral tradition) evidence clearly violated the canon of the common law that those providing evidence be available for questioning by the opposing counsel. But Indigenous oral historians are inherently unable to fulfill that requirement – they talk about things they have not seen or heard for themselves. The Department of Justice in defending Canada in litigation brought by Indigenous groups sought a way to respond by searching for grounds on which the evidence and the oral historians could be disqualified on technical grounds.

I was initially asked to see if these technical grounds met the standards of good anthropology. They did not meet the standards, in my view. Nevertheless, this approach had a long run and was successful in a few dozen cases across Canada. I later gave testimony in federal court about Indigenous oral materials. *Oral History on Trial* (2011a), in which I examine the role of anthropology in presenting and critiquing Indigenous oral history evidence in court, emerged from several talks at conferences and publications on this topic. I provided my own thoughts on remedies to make this project more successful and acceptable to the Indigenous people giving the evidence. Prior to this, I edited a volume of commentaries on the original *Delgamuukw* case (Miller 1992a).

My time living in the state of Washington and later in the province of British Columbia has placed me near an international border that split the Coast Salish culture group into roughly halves. The lives of Coast Salish people require them to regularly cross this border for Indigenous ritual purposes, to visit family, and for a great variety of other purposes, including attending church and fishing. What had once been perhaps more of an inconvenience became considerably more complicated following the disaster of 9/11 and the hardening of the border (Miller 2016a). I was asked to participate in two cases involving Salish people, one regarding crossing from the United States into Canada for ritual purposes and the other from Canada to the United States to fish. This latter case was a criminal matter involving a Canadian First Nations man arrested for fishing in US waters. The issue was that the fisherman regarded the waters as historically belonging to his tribe and his family (Miller 2014, 2016a). These cases reveal tactics used by opposing counsel to disrupt anthropological evidence.

I attended another trial in a court colloquially called "Port Court," then situated directly over the border guard stations, in which US officials denied the identity of an Indigenous man, Dr. Roberts, attempting to enter the United States from Canada. This was despite his possession of the appropriate documents. He was told by the presiding judge, in my presence, that he did not look like an Indian and that they would find something to charge him with. Dr. Roberts gave up his effort to enter the US using his authorized band card. My examination drew me into a wider consideration of the problems, including discrimination faced by members of the Nooksack, an American tribe, that arose for a fractured community whose ancestors had lived on what became the Canadian side of the border. A family from this Washington state tribe was cut from tribal membership and disenrolled, and family representatives asked me to explain to their own tribal court why they rightfully belonged. The ethnohistorical and genealogical records show the family do belong; nevertheless, they were not re-enrolled. Part of this problem arose from disputes between families, and disenrollment of tribal members is today a common occurrence across North America. Here I draw on the sometimes-arbitrary nature of legal processes and the way they may unfairly attack the identity of an Indigenous person, an issue which arose in *McCue*.

In the 1970s, I became aware of a problem largely hidden from public view: a number of American tribes and Canadian bands have no formal recognition by the state and, therefore, cannot share in many of the rights reserved or benefits derived from treaties that their ancestors signed or share in most of the arrangements worked out between the state and Indigenous communities. I first learned this when encountering the Steilacoom of central Puget Sound, Washington, and the Duwamish who live in the area that is now Seattle. Later, I worked with the Samish of Anacortes, Puget Sound, helping to prepare their ultimately successful petition for recognition; the Snohomish in their unsuccessful bid; and, more recently the Hwlitsum, located at the mouth of the south fork of the Fraser River just south of Vancouver; and the Pender Harbour First Nation, north of Vancouver. I spoke with members of the Mashpee Wampanoag, of Cape Cod, Massachusetts, a tribe that has struggled for recognition and for lands of their own, and whose members I first encountered as a five-year-old. One of my books, *Invisible Indigenes* (2004), featured the role of anthropologists in the federal recognition processes in the United States and Canada of non-recognized tribes/bands.

My involvement with these various groups included writing portions of petitions to federal agencies, attending numerous meetings with federal fisheries officials, port authorities, and others, and simply giving my opinion about the processes to recognition and about rights to resources. In the case of the Hwlitsum, I undertook with colleagues detailed ethnohistorical and ethnographic accounts of Hwlitsum ancestors and the contemporary community. For the Samish, after they won re-recognition, I spoke with the tribal council about their creation of a tribal court. I published a chapter examining treaty law from an anthropological perspective (Miller 2016b). Other of my papers look at law and the anthropology of borderlands (Miller 2016a), and the politics of apology (Miller 2006b).

The Samish case provided me a stunning introduction to the intrusion of politics into the legal processes of the United States as it relates to Indigenous people. Initially rejected for federal recognition as a tribe, the Samish used the Freedom of Information act to find that the federal Department of the Interior had colluded against the Samish to deny their status. The process was ordered reopened, and, incredibly, the same thing happened again, and the Samish were again able to prove this. A court ordered the tribe to be recognized, bypassing the responsible federal agency. Initially denying recognition to the Samish, the agency had claimed in its report of refusal that the random selection of tribal members whom I had interviewed in order to study their social networks was not random. This claim was made up out of thin air.

I have undertaken a number of other tasks. In one instance, I was asked by legal counsel to help the court understand the contributions of a Coast

Salish ritual leader to his family and community so that they could be compensated for his wrongful death in an auto accident. I did this by interviewing his parents, and I learned that he took on the roles of transporting people to ritual events and carrying out the extensive work required to host such events. In addition, although the deceased had no wage income, which commonly serves as the basis for calculating settlement payments, he hunted and fished for the family. I consulted First Nations friends from the area and calculated the number of deer and fish he would have taken and their value in dollars in order that the parents receive a financial settlement. In this instance, the invisibility of Indigenous lives became a legal issue.

In another task, I attempted to explain to a commission the spiritual properties of a large rock, three hundred metres long, and ninety metres high, which was scheduled to be demolished and rendered into saleable rock, in order that it might be protected. It was not. I was asked to explain to a court why a young man might not give full information about his culture to an arresting police officer as part of the Innocence Project; and I was asked to explain to a district court why a young girl should live with her grandmother to learn the spiritual practices of her culture, and not with her father and stepmother. In Coast Salish societies it is a common practice for children to be placed with family members, but in this case the stepmother objected to support payments for the little girl being made to the grandmother.

Finally, another area concerned why Indigenous women have gone missing and are presumed or found to be dead, an issue that became publicly visible in the 2010s. I attended a conference, "Missing Women Commission of Inquiry: Unpacked and Revisited" in 2013 and spoke with several of the family members of the missing women (Miller 2011b, 2013). Although I did not give testimony, I was struck by the difficulty posed for Indigenous women giving testimony before the commission on behalf of missing family members – they had to walk the length of the hall, past all the police gathered there with their lawyers, and stand and speak and answer questions in front of a hostile audience. There are lessons here from this commission about power and legal processes and expert involvement. The trauma brought on by the process itself, the pain, fear, and disillusionment, were clearly and explicitly articulated by the family members in the conferences.

Human Rights Tribunals

It is no accident that it was the experience of Indigenous women that drove home the issue of trauma and the problem of the law's diminution of Indigenous people. One feature of my study of the BC Human Rights Tribunal has been that most, but not all, of the people involved were women, including the four complainants whose cases I detail in this book (Gladys Radek, June McCue, Clara Menzies, and Ms. Blackjack), the lawyers in the *Menzies* case, and the lawyers in some of the other cases I address. Anthropologist Sally Engle Merry (1990, 4), in her study of the legal consciousness of working-class Americans, finds that women bring suits because, rather than in spite of, the fact that they are relatively powerless.

In a world that values or even privileges strength, the willingness to use violence, and the possession of economic resources, women have less power. They appeal to courts because they are vulnerable and hope to find an ally. In the BC Human Rights Tribunal, over 60 percent of suits were brought by Indigenous women. The opposite can be true as well, as anthropologists Patricia Ewick and Susan Silbey (1998) found in their own study of the legal consciousness of American men and women. Some women, and some people generally, regard the law as outside of their experience and not a part of their lives. Radek, McCue, and Menzies, in my conversations with them, saw the law not so much as their great hope, but as a possibility and perhaps something that, at its best, could and should be of assistance to them in making public and righting the wrong they experienced.

These women held the widely shared Indigenous cultural notion of women as protectors of their family and by extension, of their communities, however defined. Gladys Radek was an Indigenous woman in her middle years who watched the abuse of Indigenous people by security guards in a Vancouver mall from across the street in her apartment in Native Housing. She decided to take it upon herself to act on this discrimination and had the grounds to do so once confronted herself in the mall. Clara Menzies, too, stated that she took on her human rights complaint as an Indigenous mother for her son, but also for others. Taking on social conflicts in defense of their community is often a gendered role for middle-aged (but sometimes younger or older) Indigenous women (see Schweitzer 1999, for an example of those making this argument, and, further, this point is often made by speakers in Indigenous events in Coast Salish longhouses or in public gatherings).

But there is another important way in which law is gendered for Indigenous people, namely the ways legal systems act on, ignore, and expose women to harm. Professor of American Indian Studies Dian Million (2013, 7), for example, writes that the pervasive gendered violence is a feature of colonial power relations. Canadian Indigenous leaders Beverley Jacobs, Yvonne Johnson, and Joey Twins (2021, 252) point to a significant issue regarding women and the issue of trauma beyond the three cases I present here (and largely beyond the scope of this book):

> We were also very well aware of the intergenerational traumas and the circumstances that Indigenous women faced prior to them entering the criminal legal system. NWAC and Justice for Girls found: 'The state has effectively trained many aboriginal women to believe they are on their own in circumstances where they face violence ... when women are forced to meet violence with violence, the travesty is they are then susceptible to facing criminal charges.'
>
> We continued to be disappointed that the system and the state continued to abuse and violate the women. A large number of Indigenous women and girls are criminalized because of the intergenerational traumas, historical traumas and current traumas that they have lived and survived.

My experience confirmed these observations. In each case, something new was revealed about the tribunal and how it operates and how individuals experience it.

Radek, as I have mentioned, concerned a First Nations woman who was mistreated by security guards in a large mall in downtown Vancouver. This case was heard by the British Columbia Human Rights Tribunal (2005) and has turned out to be significant. A second case, the Knucwentwecw Society Human Rights Complaint before the BCHRT in 2006, for which I was retained, was never heard; the issue was resolved shortly after I submitted my expert report to the BCHRT but provides an insight into tribunal processes (Miller 2006b). This case arose after an inter-tribal group in a rural area in British Columbia attempted to create a small residential centre for youth at risk and was opposed by several townsfolk who placed egregious ads in newspapers and signs on streets associating Indigenous youth with violence and rape. In this instance, the complainants' lawyer took actions including filing my expert report with the tribunal, and eventually the respondents gave up and agreed to remove the signs and to submit no more ads.

A third case is an outlier as it was with the Yukon Human Rights Tribunal (Miller 2014), for which I wrote an expert report and gave live testimony in the form of remote direct examination and cross-examination. This case was about discrimination in hiring practices. The particular feature was that the tribunal found in favour of my opinion that discrimination against an Indigenous man in hiring had occurred but found this did not affect the hiring process, and the decision gave him no remediation. The lawyer acting for the complainant found this puzzling and I do, too, and I wonder what the client made of this. Perhaps he felt his time and effort had been wasted.

A fourth case involved rough police behaviour towards an Indigenous woman, Clara Menzies, living in Vancouver. In this case, too, I was commissioned to write an expert report and give testimony about the incident and how it may have affected an Indigenous woman.

In addition to these cases, I also attended cases as a witness. The most significant of these was *McCue v. UBC,* heard in 2016. In this instance, I attended the three weeks of hearings and read the decisions, both preliminary and final. But I also spent time with June McCue helping her carry the several large suitcases of documents she brought from her home to the tribunal and hauled back each evening. We talked at the breaks and on the rides after the conclusion of the day at the tribunal as she dropped me off at my home. I had no formal part in this case, although I sometimes provided my opinions about what the counsel for UBC was arguing and how the hearing was going. I had informal conversations with professorial colleagues at UBC about the implications of the case. My concern was with the case as heard and performed in the tribunal hearing, which gave me a powerful glimpse into the efficacy of the tribunal and its human costs. This hearing, for all its legal trappings, registered on the human scale as profoundly disturbing. In that McCue acted as her own counsel and without legal assistance at the tribunal hearings, the case was also disturbing in a legal sense.

In these cases, I attempted to explain to the tribunal members my understanding of how and why Indigenous people face discrimination in their access to public settings, in hiring, and in treatment by police, security guards, and others. My task was to describe the nature and historical trajectory of discrimination, stereotyping, and popular culture in North America and how these act to systematically disadvantage Indigenous people. Watching these cases play out, I noticed the significant obstacles that the complainants faced in bringing and conducting their cases, and I watched with dismay the feelings and emotions of these litigants. I wonder what a human rights tribunal might look like to better serve these participants. It is a concern I share with Indigenous and non-Indigenous scholars and expert witnesses around the world.

2

Symbolic Violence, Trauma, and Human Rights

WHAT I OBSERVED IN my work is that diminution constitutes both the grounds for bringing cases and the experience of Indigenous people preparing for and attending legal proceedings. All the types of cases I have participated in undermined the credibility of Indigenous people in public settings by opposing counsel and the legal processes and by the insistence of the mainstream society and the state that Indigenous people accept and internalize their position in society based on this diminution. Diminution occurs in terms of the laws they are challenging, which embed in them antiquated notions of wardship and assimilation, failed treaties, dated neo-evolutionary anthropological models by the state, and forms of defense tactics and language. The diminution also results from the long and dreadful legal processes themselves, which drag on for years in many cases (over three years in the *Menzies* case and much longer, even decades, in many others) and in some instances ought not to have been defended by the state. Diminution involves the transgressions experienced by elders giving testimony and the violations of Indigenous protocols of deference to knowledge holders and spiritual practitioners. Communities are sometimes set against each other.

This diminution is especially significant in an era when Indigenous people are trying mightily to re-establish and restore historical practices, ways of living in the world, and epistemologies of their ancestors. This is their right under the terms of the United Nations Declaration of the Rights of Indigenous Peoples, which guarantees their rights to enjoy and practice their cultures and customs, their religions, and their languages, and to develop and strengthen their economies and their social and political institutions. Many wish to escape the neoliberal world by reviving their cultures and languages.

Indigenous Voices Regarding Law

I reference Indigenous voices in a variety of ways, and I want to be clear about the presence of their voices. Some are Indigenous legal experts and include Justice Harry Laforme (Mississaugas of the New Credit First Nation), James (Sákéj) Youngblood Henderson (Chickasaw Nation), and Aaron Mills (Anishinaabe), John Borrows (Chippewa of the Nawash First Nation), David Milward (Beardy's and Okemasis First Nation), Patricia Monture-Angus (Mohawk Nation), Jean Teillet (Métis), Val Napoleon (Saulteau First Nation), Darlene Johnston (Chippewa of the Nawash First Nation), Dian Million (Tanana Athabascan), Beverley Jacobs (Bear Clan, Mohawk Nation of the Haudenosaunee Confederacy, and member of the Order of Canada), and Justice Ardith Walkem Walpetko We'dalx (Nlaka'pamux Nation). Other Indigenous lawyers include Amber Prince (Sucker Creek First Nation), June McCue (Ned'u'ten from Lake Babine, a complainant, lawyer, and legal scholar), and Myrna McCallum (Métis-Cree), a proponent of "trauma-informed lawyering" (McCallum 2020). Some voices are Indigenous scholars in anthropology, including Audra Simpson (Kahnawake Mohawk) and Riley Bertoncini (Métis). Shawn Atleo (Ahousaht First Nation) is a political leader, as is Chief Roger William (Xeni Gwet'in). Still other voices are women writing collectively for the Native Women's Association of Canada, the Swinomish tribal women authors of *A Gathering of Wisdoms* (Clarke 1991), and those in the publication *Red Women Rising* (Martin and Walia 2019). One voice is an Indigenous police liaison officer (name withheld). Others are the researchers and authors (not all of whom are Indigenous) of the Royal Commission on Aboriginal Peoples (1991) report, *Looking Forward, Looking Back*. Several voices enter into the story through interviews with me, including Alice Williams, of the Upper Skagit tribe, family members disenrolled from the Nooksack tribe (names withheld), Gladys Radek (from Gitxsan Wet'suwet'en territory), and Clara Menzies (Indigenous Nation affiliation unknown to me). Some, like Tanya Silverfox, are community members. Some voices are shown through their work, including Musqueam elder Roberta Price, who opened a hearing of the BC Human Rights Tribunal with a prayer, and June McCue, who lends her voice during her cross-examinations of witnesses in her own proceedings at the tribunal.

In other words, in my work I present a broad range of Indigenous perspectives. To start with the academic voices, a number of Indigenous legal scholars have advanced similar or related views to my own about Canadian law and diminution. James (Sákéj) Youngblood Henderson (2002, 2), for example, takes note of the need to "decolonize judicial precedents," and of the "existing colonial ideology of contrived superiority of European law and humanity and the psychology of cultural and racial inferiority of Aboriginal peoples." Justice Harry Laforme (2005, 15) notes: "Indeed, over the past 20 years, various commissions of inquiry have confirmed the existence of systemic racism against Aboriginal people at all stages of Canada's criminal justice system." He points to "a foreign justice system that appears to consistently put Aboriginal people at a disadvantage ..." (17). Aaron Mills (2010) writes that Canadian law retains its colonial identity and the legal framework practices colonialism. Sharon Venne (Notokwew Muskwa Manitokan) (1998), a lawyer and expert in international law and a fierce critic of Canadian law and political practices, writes of the colonial genocide of Indigenous people and the importance of Elder knowledge about their rights.

John Borrows (2002), in advancing the case for the resurgence of Indigenous Law, details the failures of the Canadian legal system in regard to Indigenous Peoples and questions the law underpinning Canadian title to land and resources. Borrows and others, particularly Val Napoleon (2019), in her many publications, including a graphic novel (2013), are working on revitalizing Indigenous Law in an effort to replace or parallel Canadian law. David Milward (2012) is among the other Indigenous scholars envisioning free-standing Indigenous legal practice.

My perspective has also been shaped by two events. In March 2010, I had the chance to listen to and speak at the Indigenous Bar Association Elders' Gathering on Oral History Evidence, at Turtle Lodge, Manitoba (Miller 2010). The event gave me an opportunity to describe my own research on oral histories as evidence and to see a group in action that has been engaged in working with the Canadian legal system to create space for Indigenous people. A year later, when my book *Oral History on Trial* (2011a) and Sophie McCall's book, *First Person Plural: Aboriginal Storytelling and the Ethics of Collaborative Authorship* (2011), were the topics of a panel discussion sponsored by UBC Press, Indigenous legal scholar Darlene Johnston (2012), of the University of British Columbia law faculty, noted that the Canadian Supreme Court building in Ottawa was on unceded land of her own nation and questioned why the court would be trusted (the event was *Aboriginal Oral Histories in the Courtroom: More Than a Matter of Evidence,* a UBC Press forum at the Liu Institute for Global Issues on February 8, 2012).

By listening to Indigenous voices, I have come to hold a perspective similar to that of John Reilly, a non-Indigenous retired Canadian judge of the Provincial Court of Alberta. In his provocative book *Bad Law: Rethinking Justice for a Postcolonial Canada* (2019, 18), he makes the argument that he "came to see our system as an instrument of their [Indigenous] oppression" and that rather than seeing a separate system for Indigenous people, he would rather see a single system for all built on Indigenous justice concepts (15).

Symbolic Violence and Trauma in Law

Anthropology professor Eve Darien-Smith (1999, 20; see 2007) notes that the law has a double aspect – it regulates by marking the social boundaries of particular categories of people and by working at deeper levels of personal meaning and concepts of self and society. This is the "inside/outside" feature of law. One inside feature that is related to diminution (an outside feature) is the trauma experienced by Indigenous people who directly engage with the symbolic violence of legal processes. Symbolic violence refers here to a non-physical violence rooted in power differentials and the imposition of the norms of the dominant society (see Das 2008 and Kleinman et al. 1998).

I learned firsthand that it can be hard for Indigenous people to talk about the discrimination they face, which is often at the heart of cases they bring to court and tribunal. There are few topics so personal and linked to the core of one's identity as discrimination, an act built on denying and denigrating an individual or group's identity. Ralph (2020) gets at this point with his idea of "double trauma," the trauma of having something happen and then being told by authorities that it did not happen.

Indigenous lawyers Amber Prince and Myrna McCallum develop this theme in McCallum's podcast series on trauma-informed lawyering, in which they note the importance of lawyers giving their Indigenous clients time to talk about what is important to them because encounters with police have both set off existing traumas and created new ones. It is traumatic, they say, for Indigenous people to relive how they were treated under a colonial setting (McCallum 2020). McCallum and Prince observe that non-Indigenous lawyers often fail to see the discrimination which their clients faced and that these lawyers believed that the cases brought to them had no merit. Indigenous people entering the legal system, McCallum and Prince conclude, are "up against a [legal] system not built for Indigenous people." For these lawyers, the problems and traumatic triggers for Indigenous people arise in multiple ways: in adverse interactions with police and other officials, with lawyers they do not trust and who demand they sign complex agreements and pay large retainers before providing legal services, in encountering lawyers who cannot comprehend the discrimination the clients have faced, and in viewing the sometimes arrogant testimony of police and others in courts and tribunals who express their racial and institutional privilege (2020).

These acts of discrimination and their aftermath are both historical and contemporary everyday experiences. The Swinomish, Washington state, tribal mental health team publication *A Gathering of Wisdoms* (Clarke 1991), researched and written by tribal members and to which I contributed as a researcher, aptly describes the background of trauma of the historical circumstances facing their community, the stress syndrome, the sense of alienation even from their own community, and the fatalism experienced by their youth in the contemporary world.

The Canadian Royal Commission on Aboriginal Peoples (1991, 579) makes clear the issue of trauma – mistrust, outrage, shame – in Indigenous lives to the present day. Consider this powerful statement about Canadian law and its impact on an Indigenous person by Patricia Monture-Angus ([1998] 2015, paragraph 35):

When I finished law school, I quite often described the feeling at graduation as the same feeling of relief combined with fear I had after leaving an abusive man. It felt like I had been just so battered for so long. Finishing law school is an accomplishment. Yet, I did not feel proud of myself. I just felt empty. This feeling forced me to begin considering why I felt the way I did. It was through this process that the ways in which law is fully oppressive to Aboriginal people began to be revealed. It is important to understand this process of self-reflection as an obligation that I have as a First Nations person trying to live according to the teachings and ways of my people. However, it is much more than a personal obligation. It is a fundamental concept essential to First Nations epistemology. It is, in fact, a methodology.

The realization that law was the problem and not a solution of transformative quality was a difficult one for me to fully accept because it made the three years I had struggled through law school seem without purpose. I did not want to believe it. Think about everything that First Nations people have survived in this country – the taking of our land, the taking of our children, residential schools, the current criminal justice system, the outlawing of potlatches, sundances, and other ceremonies, as well as the stripping of Indian women (and other Indian people) of their status. Everything that we survived as individuals or as "Indian" peoples: How was it delivered? The answer is simple, through law. Almost every single one of the oppressions I named, I can take you to the law library and I can show you where they wrote it down in the statutes and in the regulations. Sometimes the colonialism is expressed on the face of the statute books and other times it is hidden in the power of bureaucrats who take their authority from those same books. Still, so many think law is the answer.

In a similar vein, the Royal Commission on Aboriginal People (1996, 58) concluded: "It is difficult and disturbing to realize that Aboriginal people see the non Aboriginal justice system as alien and repressive, but the evidence permits no other conclusion."

I include here the perspective of Richard Daly (2005, 6–8), a white anthropologist writing from his experience as an anthropologist-expert in a significant Canadian case, *Delgamuukw,* because he astutely and evocatively captures something of the trauma and symbolic violence of the legal processes specific to Indigenous people through a lack of acknowledgement of one's personal dignity.

Let us take for a moment a hypothetical elderly woman seated in the witness box, a female chief from one of the several Houses of the four Gitksan or five Witsuwit'en clans. She has grown up on the land under dispute ... In town she looks poor and inarticulate, but she is a woman of reputation in her community. She is the matriarch of several generations; she holds one or more feast names ... The seat in the witness box is very hard and narrow and upright. It is meant for the criminals one watches ... The judge is announced and she has to stand for his entrance, despite her own status, venerability, and arthritis. He sits above her and does not acknowledge her presence. The lawyers look into her eyes – something if they were not so ignorant, they would know is insolent ...

But here on the witness bench she is not accorded the smallest scrap of respect. Any old lawyer can interrupt her words whenever he or she likes.

I do not wish to suggest that victories in litigation cannot be experienced joyfully and as a triumph of perseverance, as, for example, the public expressions of Chief Roger William (Xeni Gwet'in) following the 2014 *Tsilhqot'in Nation v. British Columbia* Supreme Court of Canada decision concerning title to a large swath of territory in British Columbia, after twenty-five years of struggle in various courts. Yet, this was a drawn-out and arduous experience for the communities involved.

Nor am I suggesting that Indigenous communities and individuals must be described in traumatic terms. There is a critique of the evocation of trauma. Dian Million (2013, 1–4; and see Waldram 2004) describes trauma as a portmanteau of various psychic and physical events with little in common. Trauma, she writes, is the ethos of the times and a major signifier and political narrative in an era of global neoliberalism: "Canadian Aboriginal peoples, subjects of a history of colonial violence, are thickly ensconced in the intensities, logics, and languages of trauma, particularly now as they are called on to speak as subjects of 'truth and reconciliation'" (3). The violence producing this trauma is constitutive of capitalist development rather than a by-product. The colonized subject, in our period, Million argues, becomes a trauma victim, and trauma is linked to "state-determined biopolitical programs for emotional and psychological self-care" (6). Trauma narratives, she writes, are often linked to healing discourses and healing to human rights (8).

My aim is not to introduce healing as a concept. My focus, rather, is on the legal settings and the trauma and traumatic processes I have witnessed. In the instance of the BC Human Rights Tribunal, a significant issue is how to turn experiences of racial discrimination into evidence, which can be a strange, confusing, and hurtful experience. I have also learned that those Indigenous people who prepare their own application to the tribunal sometimes struggle with their emotions and often make emotionally driven applications, which are easy to undermine by the respondent's lawyers. The fear of giving testimony in courts and tribunals can trigger significant, overwhelming stress, an issue that almost led one complainant, in a case in which I served as expert, to drop her case after her hearing was scheduled. Other complainants I have worked with have experienced ill health from the legal processes they have entered, and still others have stated that for an entire generation the focus and energy of their community has gone into legal processes rather than into looking after their own elders and reviving their cultural practices. And, because part of the process of human rights tribunals is aimed at undermining the credibility of an Indigenous person or persons who has brought an action, the process can drain and demoralize a complainant and erode their well-being.

In her case study of the Inter-American Court of Human Rights, Danish anthropologist Kirsten Hastrup (2003, 309) argues that rights-based conceptions of justice can distort understandings of suffering: "Legal language instrumentalizes, cutting out the symbolic and expressive dimensions of violence." All too often, "the *rights* part tends to dominate at the expense of the *humanity* part" (317; emphasis added). I wish to bring these symbolic and expressive understandings to the surface. Anthropologist Lori Allen (2009, 2013; see Mendeloff 2009) considered the experience of suffering that human rights activism has brought in the occupied Palestinian territories. Human rights discourse, she writes, creates a "shared charade" played out in the performance of roles, becoming a spectacle that obscures the trauma of occupation. Janzen (2016, 75; and see Elringham 2013) advocated that anthropologists read the "emotional register of narratives – an indicator of trauma" of those we work with in intense settings.

The Anthropologist as Expert Witness

To do this, it is necessary to scrutinize my own role as expert witness in the legal process. My discipline, anthropology, has been implicated in the colonization and dispossession of Indigenous people. The phrase "handmaiden of colonialism," attributed nonspecifically to Levi-Strauss and popularized by Talal Asad, captures something of the relationship of the discipline to colonial authority, but another part of the story is the role anthropologists have played as social analysts and experts in court since the 1940s.

Debate about the role of anthropologists in expert testimony regarding Indigenous people began in the United States following the creation of the Indian Claims Commission, which was designed to eliminate the backlog of Indian claims. The commission was established in 1946 and lasted until 1978, and its creation led to the establishment of a new discipline, ethnohistory, which provides new sorts of evidence for litigation, and to the creation of the American Society for Ethnohistory (see Stewart 1973, 1979; Rosen 1977, 1979; Asch 1992; J. Steward 1955; Wiget 1982, 1995, 1996; Lurie

1955, 1956). There were some points of confusion as this work got underway; Nancy Lurie, for example, observed that anthropologists in the Indian Claims Commission hearings in the 1960s were treated as surrogate Indians (Ray 2011, 34).

My Brazilian colleague and coauthor Gustavo Menezes (Miller and Menezes 2015) has written that the legal system in his country retains some suspicion of people who work directly with litigants, the Indigenous people, and are therefore suspected of bias. The same is true in Canada. Anthropological fieldwork methods, which foreground participant observation, are thought to be inherently suspect in some cases or are treated as producing trivial understandings of "Indian lore." A particular problem for anthropologists giving expert testimony is the notion that they are too close to the claimants who have hired them. This is a dilemma because fieldwork requires that anthropologists get to know the communities, the people, and the culture.

The *Delgamuukw* case in the 1990s brought these issues to the fore in Canada, provoking a painful debate among Canadian anthropologists about their role in Indigenous litigation (see Paine 1996; Boxberger 2004, Palmer 2000; Miller 1992a, 1992b; Ridington 1992; Culhane 1992, 1998). *Delgamuukw* concerned a land claim brought against British Columbia by house chiefs of the Gitxsan and Wet'suwet'en peoples and is significant for the treatment of Aboriginal title and oral history evidence. The plaintiffs lost the case at trial, but an appeal to the Supreme Court of Canada sent the case back to a lower court and led to the 1997 decision and the ruling that the province had no right to extinguish Indigenous rights to ancestral lands. Further, the decision clarified Aboriginal title and affirmed that Aboriginal title is an Aboriginal right under section 35 of the *Constitution Act, 1982*. The decision had an impact on later title cases, in particular the Supreme Court 2014 decision in *Tsilhqot'in Nation v. British Columbia,* which held that "Aboriginal title over the area requested should be granted."

Canadian anthropologist Antonia Mills (1994, 1996, 2005) produced some of the earliest efforts to explain what working within the legal domain meant in her research and testimony in the *Delgamuukw* case. She emphasized the problems of establishing anthropological authority in testifying, the clash of worldviews between Indigenous witnesses and the court, and the plaintiff's sense of the court's negative evaluation of their worth.

In his discussion of the problems of being an anthropologist-expert in *Delgamuukw,* Richard Daly (2005, 3) likewise took notice of the power dimensions: "From an analytical perspective, the courtroom deliberations constituted an arena of interactions, or overlapping fields of interest, played out upon a sloping plane of power and powerlessness. Having experienced this courtroom situation from the inside, I have gained an existential appreciation of French sociologist Pierre Bourdieu's field, habitus, and symbolic capital. The courtroom in which an Aboriginal rights case is tried is a social situation marked by a definite field of power – even spatially." This courtroom, he writes, constitutes a "vertical force field" (3). Daly questioned whether the process renders anthropologists "traitors or subalterns to the relations of ruling" (8).

The Australian Paul Burke, in *Law's Anthropology* (2011, 24), draws a conclusion similar to that of Daly: "When the law interacts with anthropology ... it is not a dialogue, but an act of digestion, in which law converts anthropology into what it needs for its own functioning ... Free anthropology becomes enslaved and transformed into law's anthropology." He emphasizes the competition between judge and anthropologist over control of the anthropological archive, judicial "structural" superiority (15) and, sometimes, judicial suspicion of the intellectual, especially those (such as anthropologists working with Indigenous people) immersed in the community. Burke also notes what he terms a "general judicial anxiety" that experts tend to favour the parties who hire them, especially if these experts are engaged in new research for the purpose of litigation (20). Further, he worries about the problem of judges creating their own anthropology and interpretation outside of anthropological evidence. Finally, he points to the judicial inclination to accept the arbitrary (such as colonial domination of Indigenous people), which is already embedded in case law, as natural, a form of Bourdieuian symbolic violence that plays a role in domination.

Burke offers unusual insights into the workings of scholars in court who attempt, as Canadian historian and expert Arthur Ray (2011, 145) puts it, to educate the judge-students in a "strange classroom," the courts. Ray observes that it was his role to educate the court about Indigenous history, but there were at least two intermediaries between himself and the court – the lawyers who retained him and those who opposed him, which made his job difficult. I have had the same sense of strangeness and have felt that cross-examination, at its worst, is like teaching a class in introductory anthropology with someone (opposing counsel) yelling obscenities in the background. Further, jurists are not students but, rather, people who must decide how to answer complex legal questions and, often, assign liability.

Ray notes that some judges whom he appeared before (147) were there to be educated on issues such as Indigenous history or the nineteenth-century fur trade; others were there solely for the facts pertinent to the case.

Law professor and anthropologist Randy Kandel (personal communication, 1998) has made the argument that anthropological expertise need not be understood like engineering expertise, in which objectivity in law is linked to distance from the project. Instead, anthropology could be understood as something like the caring professions, such as medicine or nursing, in which a health professional giving testimony might have encountered the patient. Getting to know the Indigenous community to prepare an expert report, then, ought not be considered a marker of a lack of objectivity.

There are other problems in the anthropological engagement with legal affairs. A long-time Canadian trial lawyer with Indigenous clients, Peter Hutchins (2011, xxv-xxvi) observed that "lawyers and jurists have numerous flaws – among them professional arrogance ... and an instinctual conservatism parading as *stare decisis*." These characteristics may make it difficult to incorporate anthropological insights into legal proceedings. And Ray, commenting on his own experiences as an expert, described the legal system (not just the trial itself) as a sometimes hostile and suspicious place.

Métis lawyer Jean Teillet (2011, xx) finds something similar to what Menezes observed in Brazil, noting that judges sometimes think they know history, but it is a version that may reflect their prejudices and the notion of Indigenous people as assimilated. She writes that the task of the historical expert (or anthropologist) is to challenge and displace these earlier colonial ideas of "primitive savages." She observes that this is a difficult task because of the "tendency of most judges to wedge new facts into old assumptions and beliefs."

Similarly, Canadian anthropologist Julie Cruikshank (1992, 26) has commented on what she terms "the invention of anthropology" by the British Columbia Supreme Court in the *Delgamuukw* case based on nineteenth-century positivism. She further notes the trial justice's idea that expert testimony about the litigants was "exceedingly difficult to understand." Cruikshank, Canadian anthropologist Robin Ridington (1992), and other commentators have described the ways in which the justice's view of Indigenous people and, hence, the law, reflected evolutionist models of society, long obsolete. This problem has arisen in other cases, including *R. v. Van der Peet,* in which the trial justice, relying on 1960s anthropological evolutionary models of social organization, held that the sale of fish by the Stó:lō people of British Columbia was not part of their Aboriginal right, since they were not at the appropriate evolutionary scale as tribal people to have commercial enterprises (Carlson 1996).

Burke (2011, 254, 258), too, describes "Judges [acting] as amateur anthropologist[s]," drawing their own conclusions from the separate expert submissions to the court. He notes the view of his colleague "who wondered whether a judge would approach an expert physicist in the same way." He observes that "not all disciplines are equally immune from such meddling."

There is something, I believe, about a human subjects discipline that encourages other people, with their own lifetime of experience with people, to believe they have expert knowledge equal to that developed within the social sciences. Hutchins (2011, xxx, referencing Ray) observed that judges tend to value all historical experts similarly, believing that anyone can be [or perhaps is] an historian, making historians something like clerks who bring documents to court.

The forms of restraint on anthropological and historical information and bias that Ray, Teillet, Hutchins, Burke, Cruikshank, and Ridington note are all part of the situation, but as Menezes and I have pointed out (Miller and Menezes 2015), not the whole of it. Existing negative stereotypes and the notion that anthropological testimony is not definitive like "hard" sciences and is, therefore, suspect are also situations that anthropologists have encountered.

The legal system and the courts, tribunals, commissions, and inquests themselves, then, are not the natural domain of anthropology, and our disciplinary concepts and practices must find a way to fit within the legal system. There are problems in giving testimony that arise with this approach, however. In particular, both Menezes, working in a civil law system, and I, in a common law system, focus on our common problem: the difficulties in showing to the court the bias, stereotyping, and racism that Indigenous people commonly face in quite different societies and legal orders and the consequences that flow from these attitudes.

My hope is that we can have anthropological knowledge entered into court in which the anthropologists themselves are not "traitors" or "subalterns," in Daly's phrasing, and that we are not "digested" or "enslaved," as Burke suggests, and that, instead, the testimony fully serves its intended purpose – providing clarity.

The cases I have engaged in as an expert show that legal consideration of the racialization and bias faced by Indigenous people can be derailed at one of many stages of, or prior to, the legal process. It can be blocked as not fitting into the scope of expert analysis given to explain issues such as the murder of hundreds of Indigenous women and the disinclination of the police to act and seek to understand the circumstances and whereabouts of these women. This was a situation I faced in my research in British Columbia with the Missing Women Commission of Inquiry (Miller 2011b, 2013). I was asked by the legal staff of the newly created BC Commission of Inquiry to examine internal police documents to see if there were signs of systemic discrimination that might have influenced the behaviour of the police towards the women who had dropped from sight.

I prepared a report but ultimately did not give testimony because I was asked by senior members of the commission to change my report. Unlike the working legal staff, the commission itself was not interested in the issue of systemic racism. Explanations of race and racialization can be intentionally left out by inquiry commissioners and police who fail to account for the systemic racism that characterizes all institutions, including police forces (Miller 2011b). Accounts of the lives and cultural practices of Indigenous people may be regarded in court as colourful but legally meaningless folklore, a problem I have encountered several times in giving testimony. Trivialization is a problem those giving testimony might consider in organizing their testimony.

In other instances, recognition of the history of colonial distortion of Indigenous lives is stopped simply by the failure to acknowledge such a category, as in the instance of the Legal Services Society's denial of funding to a lawyer for an anthropological expert to help expand the *Gladue* decision. *Gladue* was a Supreme Court of Canada ruling in which the court took the position that lower courts should consider an Indigenous offender's background in sentencing. This effort to extend *Gladue* to include understanding the offender's background when examining the initial interaction between police and the accused was held by the funding agency to not be significant enough to fund. This problem of misidentifying colonialism shows up in the (now purportedly obsolete) "frozen rights" concept, that Indigenous people's rights to territory or resources are tied to their practices of a century or more ago. But as Menezes (Miller and Menezes 2015) shows, this approach lives on in Brazil as well as in North America.

I do not dispute Daly's and Burke's dismal analysis of vertical power relations in the courtroom. They are surely correct. But I am equally interested in viewing the process of anthropologists engaging in the law from the perspective of power deployed at the margins, often in simple interactions, and in what French philosopher and historian of ideas Michel Foucault views as the capillaries (Foucault 1979, 1980), including the interactions long before a trial or hearing commences. Although Foucault refused to analyze courtroom trials, he writes that the court was linked to carceral mechanisms that tend to exercise a power of normalization (Foucault 1979, 308; Eltringham 2012, 433). More recently, anthropologist Mark Goodale (2017, 204) observes that post-Cold War anthropologists of law "insisted on following the capillary networks of law wherever they led ... to a portal named 'human rights.'"

The Problem with Human Rights

Richard Wilson (2006, 77) has said the following of human rights, but it would be true for other forms of Indigenous legal claims: "An ethnographic approach to human rights is especially appropriate because the human rights regime includes a vast array of different kinds of moral and political projects, which are often incompatible." Human rights became a problem for ethnographic research in the 2000s (Goodale 2017, 102), but some have found the turn less than productive (Afshani 2012; Englund 2012). Stephen (2017, 100; see Carr 2010) points out that anthropological testimony implies that the "story" told by a litigant is not validated in its own terms.

She points to a problem that has long concerned me, that the anthropological report [on Indigenous concerns] reproduces a hierarchy of knowledge, with the Indigenous perspective requiring expert validation (see Stephen 2017, 100; also see Carr 2010). My own work as an expert witness lies within this system and in that sense perpetuates the hierarchy of knowledge and power imbalances based in race, gender, and so on.

However, Goodale (2017, 23) notes that an anthropological perspective is "now a common, even indispensable, presence within academic debates over human rights ... and among human rights practitioners." Goodale (97–98) casts an interesting light on the work of anthropologists: "As a ... social field that is bound up with profound questions of suffering, redemption, collective responsibility, social punishment, and justice, human rights demands introspection and even self-confrontation from the scholar or practitioner. This is particularly true for anthropologists, whose professional interest in the theory and practice of human rights is often motivated by personal experiences of activism, struggle on behalf of vulnerable populations ... and often a broader commitment to human rights as a powerful tool for opposing the pretentions of structural power."

Studies in other areas and parts of the world have likewise exposed the limitations of viewing human rights as a weapon of the weak, in political scientist and anthropologist James C. Scott's (1985) phrasing, as a way that everyday practices can be used to limit colonial domination. Professor of International Affairs David Mendeloff (2009), writing from a psychological viewpoint, questions whether war crime tribunals ease the suffering of trauma.

In his study of the role of expert witnessing at the International Criminal Tribunal, legal scholar Nigel Eltringham (2013; and see West-Newman 2005; Moore 2001), notes that the expert role required knowledge of the crimes in question and also knowledge about cultural values and the relationship between these values and the human rights violations. Merry (2006b, 2009), Nitsan (2014), and Cheng (2011), studied the processes by which international standards of human rights became localized, or "vernacularized," and how these local practices reflect and transform the discourse of human rights. Drawing on years of experience working with UN-sponsored relief and mediation efforts in Africa, John Janzen (2016, 75) advocates reading the "emotional register of narratives – an indicator of trauma" of those we work with in intense settings. He later deployed this approach in his work as an anthropologist-expert in the courts.

What I and these scholars and many others are doing is adopting a relational rather than rules-based view of the law, a significant concept in legal anthropology (Conley and O'Barr 1990; Ewick and Silbey 1998 provide examples of those who hold versions of these positions). Briefly, a rules-based approach is related to legal positivism, which assumes, in part, a logical system in which rulings reflect laws without consideration of social relations; the relational-based view is that law is responsive to the ways in which individuals and social groups interact and even the emotional state of litigants.

The critique of human rights from a twenty-first century anthropological perspective is well underway. As an example, at the 2019 American Anthropological Association annual meetings held in Vancouver, a full day of papers were delivered under the heading "When Human Rights Fail: Human Rights on the Ground." The speakers deployed an ethnographic lens to study on the ground, rather than theoretically, the failure of the human rights concept, the paradoxes it creates, and how human rights might be reconceptualized. The session abstract reads, in part, "The human rights system's conceptualizations of humanness, has also meant that race, gender, socioeconomic class, and sexual orientation (among many other categories) may be used to deny certain groups human rights because they are not human enough to claim such rights ... Human rights discourses may be mobilized to hurt the very people they claim to protect ..." (Madron and Estrelle 2019).

The legal process of human rights tribunals can also be manipulated to thin the evidence presented by complainants.

3

Thinning the Evidence, Discrediting the Expert Witness

UNDERSTANDING WHAT HAPPENS in Indigenous litigation, and hence to Indigenous litigants, requires a deeper plunge into the role of the expert witness. The role of an expert witness is to provide assistance to the court in areas in which the judge might benefit from expert knowledge. There is no room for partisanship. Joan Metge (1998, 57), an anthropologist, observes that she did not know the rules concerning experts when engaged to provide an expert opinion and could have spared herself "considerable agonizing" if she had.

To give an example: the Saskatchewan provincial court makes their rules clear by obligating prospective experts to sign a form that contains specific instructions regarding the role of the expert. I signed my acceptance of these rules in the "Expert Witness Retention Agreement" with the client in a case heard in federal court Regina. Here is the relevant portion of these rules (Queen's Bench Rules, n.d., 23)

7. DUTIES OF EXPERT.
The Expert acknowledges they have read the following excerpt from the Queen's Bench Rules of Court for Saskatchewan regarding expert witnesses and further agrees to comply with their duties as set out in Rules 5–37(1) and 5–43:

Duty of expert witness
5–37 (1) In giving an opinion to the Court, an expert appointed
pursuant to this Division by one or more parties or by the

43

Court has a duty to assist the Court and is not an advocate for any party.

(2) The expert's duty to assist the Court requires the expert to provide evidence in relation to the proceeding as follows:
(a) to provide opinion evidence that is objective and non-partisan;
(b) to provide opinion evidence that is related only to matters that are within the expert's area of expertise; and
(c) to provide any additional assistance that the Court may reasonably require to determine a matter in issue.

(3) If an expert is appointed pursuant to this Division by one or more parties or by the Court, the expert shall, in any report the expert prepares pursuant to this Division, certify that the expert:
(a) is aware of the duty mentioned in subrules (1) and (2);
(b) has made the report in conformity with that duty; and
(c) will, if called on to give oral or written testimony, give that testimony in conformity with that duty.

Continuing obligation on expert

5–43   If, after an expert's report has been provided by one party to another, the expert changes his or her opinion on a matter in the report, the change of opinion must be:
(a) disclosed by the expert in writing; and
(b) immediately served on each of the other parties.

Other Expert Duties.

The Expert's duties also specifically include:

To truthfully represent their credentials

To formulate with honesty and due care and truthfully express the Expert's opinions in these areas where the Expert feels qualified to render an opinion and where the Client has requested an opinion.

To prepare a Written Report

To meet all reasonable deadlines requested by the Client

To retain and preserve all evidence provided to the Expert from the underlying legal matter unless the Client gives written permission.

To be available on reasonable notice to testify

To be available on reasonable notice to consult with the Client.

But agreeing to be helpful to the court, objective, truthful, and prepared hardly covers the issues that arise regarding qualification of experts in court.

Here, I wish to consider my own struggles to present my credentials and training in a manner which the court could accept and would stop the thinning or exclusion of evidence and the use of *voir dire,* a separate preliminary hearing in which the trier of law determines whether evidence is admissible and can be entered into evidence in the hearing or trial. (See gender, sexuality, and women's studies scholar Narida Bullock 2021 for her view of the *voir dire* problem). More specifically, I wanted to head off misrepresentations of my credentials. An expert's qualifications have to be relevant to the case at hand. And by submitting an expert report (if that is the case; this does not always happen), ordinarily in most jurisdictions an expert would provide a summary of qualifications and a curriculum vitae.

Here is what Canada expects in an expert report to the federal court:

EXPERTS' REPORTS AND TESTIMONY

3 An expert's report submitted as an affidavit or statement referred to in rule 52.2 of the *Federal Courts Rules* shall include

(a) a statement of the issues addressed in the report;

(b) a description of the qualifications of the expert on the issues addressed in the report;

(c) the expert's current curriculum vitae attached to the report as a schedule;

(d) the facts and assumptions on which the opinions in the report are based; in that regard, a letter of instructions, if any, may be attached to the report as a schedule;

(e) a summary of the opinions expressed;

(f) in the case of a report that is provided in response to another expert's report, an indication of the points of agreement and of disagreement with the other expert's opinions;

(g) the reasons for each opinion expressed;

(h) any literature or other materials specifically relied on in support of the opinions;

(i) a summary of the methodology used, including any examinations, tests or other investigations on which the expert has relied, including details of the qualifications of the person who carried them out, and whether a representative of any other party was present;

(j) any caveats or qualifications necessary to render the report complete and accurate, including those relating to any insufficiency of data or research and an indication of any matters that fall outside the expert's field of expertise; and

(k) particulars of any aspect of the expert's relationship with a party to the proceeding or the subject matter of his or her proposed evidence that might affect his or her duty to the Court.

(Canada, 1998, 98–106)

In my experience, there is the potential for qualifications to be misunderstood and misrepresented by opposing counsel or by the bench. The resolution is not a simple matter of presenting more materials. As I have noted, counsel for the opposition may wish to create confusion about areas of expertise, to thin them. In addition, social science language and legal terminology are often in conflict, using the same words or phrases to mean different things (Kandel 1992a, 1992b; Rigby and Severeid 1992). It may be unclear to non-academics how academic subfields link and engage each other.

In the process of being qualified as an expert by the court or tribunal, the attorney who contracts my services generally puts specific questions to me to answer in my report, walks me through my c.v., and ascertains where my degrees are from, in what areas, and related issues I specialize in. This should be straightforward. The opposing counsel may also examine me. Sometimes this can be harsh.

In the *Radek* case to the human rights tribunal, counsels for the respondent, I believe, must have thought it necessary to eliminate my testimony entirely through this process and disqualify me as an expert, because the report I filed would significantly support Ms. Radek's case. In my experience in other cases, this process of qualification can be brief, lasting just a few minutes. Having been once accepted by a court increases the likelihood of being accepted in future, at least for cases in that scholarly area.

Thinning

A common legal strategy deployed by the lawyers for the respondents in human rights cases, and also by lawyers working in treaty and resource cases, is thinning. Thinning is a process of limiting the grounds of testimony by the expert for the complainant and thereby limiting the claims or support and evidence for the claims made by the Indigenous litigant. In my experience, these efforts have focused on keeping me and others from commenting directly on the grounds of the complaint, limiting me to making narrowly focused theoretical contributions to the case. In two instances, this meant that even if the tribunal accepted my evidence regarding the nature of systemic discrimination in Canada, I could not offer an opinion regarding the facts of the case and no *prima facie* case could be made. I should add that in some instances, this was not regarded as necessary. I am not speaking here of addressing the primary legal question at stake in a case; this is reserved for the judiciary.

There are other issues associated with the process of thinning. Historian Arthur Ray, in his book, *Telling It to the Judge* (2011, 31–32), describes his experience of the process of being accepted as an expert and the efforts to limit his testimony in Canada. Opposing counsel contended that Ray's academic field, "Historical geography, or history, is not a science at all, it's not a subject at all, it's not a subject of expert opinion, it is not verifiable." Anthropologist-lawyer Paul Burke, in his monograph *Law's Anthropology* (2011, 248), writes about the curious case in Australia in which an anthropologist was accepted as an expert anthropologist but not in the subject area in which he carried out his research.

Burke (2011, 74) gives an example of thinning during the process of examination-in-chief in a famous Australian Indigenous land claim case, quoting from the court record, "HIS HONOUR: [y]ou are not leading it as anthropological evidence. You are leading it as evidence probative of the fact that Eddie Mabo was adopted; that's got nothing to do with anthropology." Burke concludes that the exchange reveals the judge's "conceptualization of anthropology ... [and] expressing a preference for the anthropology of high-level, encapsulating generalisation, rather than the anthropology of intimate description or exemplary case study." Burke's analysis fits well with my own observation of judges who appeared to enjoy what they may find to be exotic ethnographic details, what Burke calls "intimate description" but did not find to be more than irrelevant folklore.

Here is another simple, but telling, example of thinning: a state prosecutor in the state of Washington made an effort to exclude me as a witness in a criminal case concerning cross-border fishing by a Canadian First Nations man because, as a nonlawyer I was said not to be able to consider the terms of the Jay Treaty of 1794, which stipulated the rights of Indians to pass over the international border, the topic of some years of my previous research and peer-reviewed academic publications. Still, I was not a lawyer. This effort by the prosecutor to thin my testimony failed, however, in this instance.

Ray (2011, 35) writes with evident frustration of his own experience of being excluded from a discussion of what the nature of history was. "I was forced to sit mute while three teams of lawyers and the chief justice discussed the nature of historical evidence and attempted to define the fields of anthropology, archaeology, and historical geography, subjects about which they knew little. I was barred from contributing to their deliberations because I had not yet been accepted as an expert by the court."

Thinning in Action: British Columbia

In the *Radek* case, I attempted to analyze and describe the neighbourhood in which the International Village Mall, a.k.a. Tinseltown, is situated in an effort to focus clearly on issues facing Indigenous people in an area that has been described as "Indian country," and which historically has been the location where Indigenous people coming to Vancouver have stayed. This issue is a deep one, and in the nineteenth century, Indigenous people were limited in where they could go in Vancouver as part of a larger program of assimilation and restriction of movements. Some Indigenous people regarded the development of the mall as an intrusion into native space. For these reasons, it mattered where Gladys Radek was obstructed in particular. I summarized it this way in my expert report in *Radek*.

> To summarize to this point; the demographic data show a large Aboriginal population concentrated in the [Downtown East Side of Vancouver (DTES)]. This group is largely single, relatively older, and living in rental units at the bottom of the housing market. While the DTES Aboriginal population exhibits some cohesion as a community, the demographic picture indicates that the population might be particularly subject to stereotypes held by the non-Aboriginal community. First, they are not likely to be travelling about as family units, with relatively few children and spouses present, and they are older, and thereby likely appear more "suspicious" and threatening. Second, because of their mobility and places of residence, they are likely not to have easy access to laundry facilities, and are more likely to appear unkempt to non-Aboriginals. The demographic materials regarding health and disabilities supports this picture.

I relied primarily on the 2002 city of Vancouver publication *Downtown Eastside Community Monitoring Report,* 7th edition, which provides a view of the Indigenous population of the Downtown Eastside based on data from the 1996 federal census. In cross-examination in the hearing phase regarding my credentials, an objection was made to my using these materials because I was not attempting to qualify as a demographer. The materials in question are simple descriptive statistics, easily understandable to anyone with an education in social sciences. Indeed, that is the point of the City of Vancouver publication – to help people generally to understand their city. In the end, I was not prevented from presenting the demographic evidence and the understanding of Radek's circumstances that day at the Tinseltown mall.

But a problem with this line of discussion was that, in fact, I was familiar with statistics, had taken graduate coursework in statistics, and had used statistics in publications in peer-reviewed academic journals. In addition, I had taken coursework related to demographic issues in anthropology in particular. There was no opportunity to present these facts, and the tribunal member had to make her determination regarding my testimony without that knowledge.

That is one example. In the *Menzies* case there was a discussion of whether I was qualified to comment on the behaviour of police in a specific incident. This was a complicated issue, which turned on the fact that the complainant did not want police to access my notes, but the lawyers told me that there was an effort to separate scholarship on police from studies of systemic racism and discrimination that I had presented previously in legal settings.

I say "told me" because I was not entitled to participate in the *voir dire* hearing prior to the hearing itself in which my qualifications were debated. The outcome in this example was that I could not present evidence about the incident in which Ms. Menzies brought her complaint to the BCHRT. From my perspective, this was unfortunate, because I believed that I could tie what happened there to a larger understanding of policing in relation to Indigenous women and to stereotyping and discriminatory behaviour, sometimes termed "racialized policing."

Here I reproduce portions of my expert report, my analysis, which I submitted to the tribunal but was not included in the case, starting with the questions posed to me by counsel. I concluded that "Ms. Menzies' perspectives resonate with the literature on mainstream perspectives regarding Indigenous people in general and women in particular."

These are the questions posed to me by counsel for Ms. Menzies and portions of my response:

> 3. Did over-policing, racial profiling or any other form of racism play a role in how the Vancouver Police Department or individual officers (the "VPD") interacted with Ms. Menzies in this matter?

> 4. If Ms. Menzies was subject to over-policing, racial profiling or other form of racism by the VPD, what is the impact or effect on her?

Here for the sake of simplicity I combine my responses to questions 3 and 4. My comments here are based on a three-hour interview with Ms. Menzies, her complaint and the amended complaint to the BC Human Rights Tribunal and on heavily redacted Vancouver Police Department general occurrence notes from the events of July 15, 2016. Ms. Menzies's comments provide evidence of what might [be] helpful in determining the practice of racialized policing on the part of at least some VPD officers.

Ms. Menzies notes in her complaint that,

> "The first male officer told the other officers to 'get me out of there.' I said 'I am not leaving.' I repeated I wanted to witness what was happening with my son. Two officers, a male and female officer from the second police car, grabbed me and dragged me and my chihuahua dogs about 20 feet away, without explanation. The police officers were saying 'why don't you go home?' I answered that he is my son and that I was not leaving. I also told them we were on unceded land of the Coast Salish Peoples. I had bruises on my arms from the female officer. I could see her fingerprint marks on my arms."

Further,

> "The police then began questioning and searching my son. One of the male officer's [sic] deliberately obstructed my view so that I couldn't fully hear or see what was going on. He told me that he was going to charge me with obstruction of justice. I replied that he was the one who was obstructing justice because they were preventing me from witnessing what was happening with my son."

And,

"The male police officer continued to obstruct me in an aggressive manner. I have had other interactions with the police before but have never been treated so aggressively and intensely by the police. The male officer obstructing my view appeared zealous and enthusiastic in obstructing my view."

She detailed the adverse effects on her:

"This incident made me think of what it must have been like for Indigenous peoples, treated this way, throughout the past 500+ years of colonialism. It was a lot worse because many were shot, killed or imprisoned right away. Just talking about this incident brings up feelings of injustice as an Indigenous person, with our history of colonialism, a history where Indigenous people have not been treated as human beings, with rights. There was no regard for me, or my dogs when I was dragged. I was treated like a criminal. I did nothing to provoke being treated that way."

She detailed that she believes, as amended, that her race, ancestry, and colour influenced the behavior of the police towards her. Ms. Menzies is visibly a minority person who would be perceived to be Indigenous ... Further, she writes that previous negative interactions with police were factors in how she was treated on July 15.

On page 15 of the VPD general occurrence hardcopy, Officer [name withheld] writes that he,

"Attended Fraser St between E 6th and 7th Ave as a cover officer. Verbally directed and escorted an erratic, uncooperative and verbally hostile woman btb the arrested male's mother to the end of the ½ block in which the arrest occurred. Warn the woman repeatedly to maintain her distance, stop obstructing the police investigation and stop causing a disturbance with her shouting. No notebook notes."

Officer [name withheld], page 18, wrote,

"At 2359 hours, I arrived on scene at E 6th Ave/Fraser St. Upon my arrival, I observed that PC 2397 [name withheld] had a male suspect and female suspect in handcuffs on the east sidewalk. An older female/suspect's mother was not in handcuffs and yelling at police. [Name withheld] and I instructed the mother to provide police some safe space to deal with the parties in custody, but she was uncooperative and yelled 'police brutality.'"

Officer [name withheld], page 20,

"At 2355 hours I observed a male, and two females walking northbound on Fraser Street in the 2200 block of Fraser. One of the females was older and was walking two small dog [sic] on a leash ...

"I activated the emergency lights on my marked police vehicle and stopped next to the suspect. I exited my vehicle and ordered the suspects to put their hands over their heads. I told them they were under arrest for assault with a weapon and uttering threats.

"All three parties who were identified as suspect [name withheld], and an unknown older female immediately started yelling at the top of their voice, 'Police brutality, you have no right, I'm going to sue you, Fuck the police, I didn't do anything' and other insults ...

"While I was searching that pocket, [name withheld] kept yelling, 'you have no right to touch me, I'm going to sue you, don't touch my privates ...'

"Throughout the entire time the older female with two dog [sic] who was believed to be [name withheld] mother (referred to as MOTHER from this point forward," but refused to provide her name was interfering with police actions. She was standing in close proximity to myself and two suspect [sic] who I had in custody. She was repeatedly asked to step away and watch from a distance but refused and also continued to yell profanities trying to interfere with PC 2397 while he was performing his duties. While I was dealing with all three parties I was aware that they may be armed with knives based on the information received from the victim and unknown complainant.

"With a cover unit on scene I was able [sic] direct the other members to move the MOTHER away from the suspect. With MOTHER at a safe distance I was able to explain to [name withheld] why he was placed into handcuffs and her [sic] was provided with his charter rights (emphasis mine)."

Analysis

There are several significant features to the interactions of the police and Ms. Menzies. Taking the accounts together, they show that the police expressed concern that Ms. Menzies was too close; was yelling; and may be armed. She appeared to be taken as a threat, at least by one officer. The police accounts are not fully clear about the timeline of events. Ms. Menzies, in our interview, stated that she yelled "police brutality" when she was being dragged by her arm, bruising it, some twenty to thirty feet away. Her account is that she didn't become agitated until the officer grabbed her arm and dragged her. This is not evident in the police written record, which reports her use of that expression without context. This is a quite significant difference in statement, in as much as being dragged by the arm could appear to be abusive. Further, the police accounts muddy precisely who was yelling what and when.

Further, in Ms. Menzies's memory of the evening's events, she was walking her dogs and saw her son waving at her, and telling her that a friend had been raped. The police, she observed, may have been following her son and the young woman with him. The officer told Ms. Menzies to leave, and she moved closer, trying to hear what was being said to her son. She wanted to know where they were taking him.

The police statements can be understood to support the conclusion that they did not express any consideration for Ms. Menzies and her son as Indigenous people, despite the fact that the episode occurred near housing for Indigenous people (Native Housing), a youth centre with a predominantly Indigenous clientele, and [in an area that] is a hub of Indigenous activity and life. In fact, the statements do not indicate that the mother and son are Indigenous. The documents do not suggest that any of the five officers had had any training in dealing with Indigenous people or that they took any measures to diffuse [sic] the situation other than giving commands and applying force by grabbing Ms. Menzies by the upper arm and dragging her away. There is no suggestion that the officers attempted to determine what Ms. Menzies wanted or that they understood that she was expressing a mother's concern for her son.

On the other hand, there is evidence in the document that the police explained to the son why he was charged. Ms. Menzies noted in interview that the officers told her that she was no longer her son's guardian [since he was over 19] and therefore she had no role in the arrest or the aftermath. This position overlooks a widely held Indigenous perspective that a mother's connection to children persists through her lifetime and even afterwards, as a spiritual presence. Ms. Menzies stated that this was her perspective regarding her son. Further, Ms. Menzies was not viewed as a potential source of information about her son.

One might reasonably understand the events of the evening as reflecting the idea that Ms. Menzies was seen as a threat, possibly with a knife, or merely an annoyance. Ms. Menzies's account of the evening is suggestive of a disdain for her. She notes, for example, that one officer moved back and forth, over and over, to block her view of what was being done to her handcuffed son. Ms. Menzies viewed this as an effort to provoke her so that he could charge her. The officer told her that he would charge her with obstruction of justice. This scene suggests that police wished to exclude her from information about her son's circumstance. One officer, Ms. Menzies said, exclaimed "Get her out of here."

Ms. Menzies explained her reaction to the events. She stated that she felt humiliated and that as a person of colour being addressed by police, neighbors would assume that she was guilty of an offence. Further, as I have noted earlier, she felt that the event was on "unceded territory of the Musqueam Nation" and that the police response to her reflected a colonialist attitude. She stated that her feeling was that "All I hear is that there is something wrong with me, with us." She stated further that "I wear it like a coat," which means, she explained, that it is painful to see all the suffering, the degradation, the lack of pride which she believes is a consequence of colonialism and was manifest in the events of July 15. Living in a colonial environment in which race determines the responses of many citizens to others, as in everyday racism which I explained earlier, is unacceptable to her. She said that she was thrown "like a rag-doll on the street," to her a deeply humiliating experience. She put this perspective in contemporary context, saying "It's been 'Me-Too' [for Indigenous people] for five-hundred years." (This references the current climate of women coming forward with statements regarding their own histories of being sexually assaulted.)

Ms. Menzies expressed her view that lateral violence has arisen amongst Indigenous people resulting from the history of British Columbia, some of which I have explained earlier. She expressed her understanding of the view held by many non-Indigenous people of

Indigenous people as "We conquered all of these people, so what do they want now? Why don't they shut up?" In this case, the officer who shouted to "Get her out of here" represented such an attitude. She also expressed her fear that her previous experiences with the police contributed to her poor treatment on July 15. Further, her own circumstances as a poor person contributes to the popular idea, she noted, that "We're disposable; as Indigenous women, that's how we're treated by cops."

Ms. Menzies' perspectives resonate with the literature on mainstream perspectives regarding Indigenous people in general and women in particular. Furniss (1999) and others have written about common-sense racism, in which Indigenous people are regarded in a negative light, which itself creates a frame, or schema, from which one understands and acts negatively towards Indigenous people. There is nothing in the police evidence to suggest that any of them stood outside these common-sense understandings of Indigenous people. Much of what the police recorded has been redacted, so more information is unavailable. It is significant that racism can be unexamined and people engaging in behavior which undermines members of a racialized group may be unaware of it and even espouse multicultural values. Rough behavior towards Indigenous people is associated with the stereotypes I have discussed here. Comack (2012) carefully describes the rough, sometimes violent behavior consistent with racialized policing.

Ms. Menzies explicitly contrasts the police behavior towards her and towards two white onlookers. It is clear that these people stood in a different relation to the police; they were not attempting to hear the conversation regarding Ms. Menzies's son. One was, however, recording the incident, which in some settings is regarded as provocative by police, but there is no evidence that it was so regarded in this case. The white onlookers were not recorded in the police documents and there is nothing to suggest that the police paid them much attention, even though Ms. Menzies states that one of the observers was questioning why Ms. Menzies and her son were treated in the manner they were. Ms. Menzies notes that the white woman was not told to leave or threatened or dragged from the scene, as she was.

These portions of my expert report in *Menzies* concerning police behaviour and its impact on Menzies herself were dismissed in a *voir dire* process without an allowance for my opinion of the grounds on which I might appropriately provide this testimony. My testimony was thinned, to the detriment of the complainant.

Prior to interviewing Menzies, I was given a copy of the police report, but it was heavily redacted and did not give a good sense of what happened that day. I asked counsel if I might speak with the client, Ms. Menzies, and did so in the law office. I took notes as seemed appropriate to record details of a complex issue. I learned a great deal more from this interview than I did from the police report, and the interview enabled me to answer questions 3 and 4 concerning how the police department treated Menzies and whether it was connected to racism, profiling, or over-policing. These were among the questions put to me by counsel and, in retrospect, I could not have given an informed answer without the interview.

But as it turned out, I was in a no-win situation. I could not give an answer to these questions at all because I was excluded. I was careful in my written response to questions 3 and 4 not to answer the legal question of whether Ms. Menzies was the object of mistreatment by the police, and instead I pointed out that the treatment was consistent with social science understandings of mistreatment. This situation arose in part because of Ms. Menzies' fear of police learning anything about her, and this is a paradox regarding the tribunal process. The circumstances that brought her to the tribunal were the same ones that limited my participation. It points to the importance of accounting for fear in legal processes.

Thinning in Action: Yukon

There was a similar experience with thinning in the *Blackjack* inquest, heard by the Supreme Court of Yukon. In this case, too, the justice determined that my evidence regarding what had happened to Ms. Blackjack could not be entered as evidence, and this, too, was determined in a *voir dire* in which I could not participate. Ms. Blackjack was an Indigenous woman in her twenties who died while being medevaced from her community to a hospital in Whitehorse. Leaders and members of her community, Little Salmon Carmacks First Nation, were outraged at what they perceived to be negligence and a manifestation of systemic racism, and they demanded an inquest. This was refused.

At the request of the band council's legal representative, I examined hundreds of pages of documents linked to the case. These included letters from the Yukon coroner to the band; nursing documents, including the reports of care given Ms. Blackjack and standards of practice; letters from Yukon politicians; and others. Here, too, without my participation, my credentials were examined to determine if I was qualified to assist the court in understanding the facts of the case. In addition, legal counsel asked me to answer specific questions that got at how the facts of the case might be understood. These questions were as follows:

1. Definition of racism, racial profiling and racial prejudices.
2. Amplifying effect of disabilities, especially addictions.
3. The impact of 1 and 2 on Indigenous health and access to health care.
4. Application in the Blackjack matter (Roothman letter to Miller, July 10, 2019).

In this instance, I wrote a paper titled "Racism, Racialization, Prejudicial Attitudes and Stereotypes Commonly Held Regarding Indigenous People," and how these concepts helped understand what happened to Ms. Blackjack. I included a section on the nursing literature regarding these topics, and other sections on the experiences of Indigenous women in care, and the perspectives of mainstream health professionals. I detailed the problems for Indigenous people resulting from what has been called the "dominant health care culture" (Browne and Varcoe 2019, 29).

I wrote, in response to question #4, a section which was excluded:

Application in the Blackjack matter.
Findings Regarding the Case of Cynthia Blackjack

Overview
I must note that I do not have access to either the routine conversations between the First Nations people and health care providers who are involved in the Blackjack case, nor the particular conversations from the case itself. These conversations might contain the sorts of common-sense racism and stereotypes that I have described. Instead, I have accounts of these interactions written by health care authorities of various sorts, including paramedics, nurses, doctors, coroners and consultants. The documents of health care providers are meant to conform to particular formats and language. In addition, I have letters from family members, council members and a citizen of Carmacks, to help

me understand the Indigenous people's experiences with health care. These circumstances mean that the family, council and community letters bear particular weight because the authors have been able to reflect in their own language on problems they encounter.

In this section, I apply the concepts developed here in order to shed light on the death of Cynthia Blackjack based on the documents I have been provided. The materials are consistent with a pattern of racialization and systemic discrimination based on stereotypes of Indigenous people and the failure to adequately understand and respond to Indigenous peoples within their adverse colonial history. For example, there are points at which the patient is depicted as non-compliant and in which she appears to have been judged negatively for behaviors that medical professionals may find problematic; in particular, obesity, overuse of health services, and the consumption of alcohol. The attention to these issues may have allowed underlying health problems to go minimized or unaddressed.

Importantly, the set of recommendations provided by the Chief Coroner to the Government of Yukon, Department of Health and Social Services fail to consider the systemic problems in the provision of health care to the members of the Little Salmon Carmacks First Nation, beyond a slight nod in that direction. These recommendations address only technical issues, such as the need for blood testing at the point of care, the need for functional suctioning devices, the need for awareness by the medical and nursing staff of toxicity issues, and a review of policies and procedures for patient transfers. In the next section, her recommendations to the Government of Yukon, Department of Community Services, concern monitoring equipment, stocking equipment, awareness of guidelines for airway management, and in-service education. Taken together, these recommendations reveal important problems to be corrected but also, tellingly, point to an inadequate health system, one in which obvious shortcomings appear. The failure to have functional suction devices, for example, and poorly stocked supply cabinets perhaps point to inadequate funding, and is certainly striking evidence of systemic problems ...

What is missing in Ms. [name withheld] recommendations is a consideration of the role that attitudes and stereotypes health practitioners may have regarding Indigenous peoples in the provision of health care, and the apparent inadequacy of the care provided, not as a technical question but as a symptom of regarding the Indigenous clientele to be undeserving of better care. Further, the recommendations do not account for an Indigenous understanding of what transpired in the death of Cynthia Blackjack and more generally the ways in which barriers to health care itself at the Carmack facility might be determined and removed. This may be described as a problem in expert knowledge, in which the issues addressed only fall within the range of knowledge of the chief coroner, who appears unaware of or uninterested in systemic barriers to the provision of health.

One major issue is the delay of almost six hours between the decision to medevac Ms. Blackjack to medical services in Whitehorse at 11:15 and her departure at 17:11 and over seven hours since she arrived at the clinic. There are several possible explanations but these circumstances are fully consistent with problems of stereotyping and discrimination commonly faced by Indigenous people in health care settings. Health care providers may hold the perspective that Indigenous people fail to care for themselves and that chronic health problems are a manifestation of personal failure and, as a consequence, there may be a less caring approach and less effort put into providing health care. This perspective is so common that there is a derogatory term, "frequent flyer," used by Canadian health providers in reference to Indigenous people thought to fail to take responsibility for themselves and as a consequence over-rely on health services.

In this case, the attending physician initially declined to come to the clinic in Carmacks and only later changed his mind. In addition, the carelessness in selecting tubing equipment prior to departure may be associated with stereotypes of undeserving Indigenous patients. Drs [names withheld], in their report summary of the Postmortem Examination Report for the Coroner, April 5, 2014, noted, first, that Ms. Blackjack was a First Nations adult female with a past history of chronic abuse of alcohol. They wrote that the medevac arrived at 1330h and medical personnel onboard continued resuscitative measures until she was sufficiently stable for transport. In any case, the conjunction of factors – equipment that didn't work, an initial decision by the physician not to show up and attend to a patient who was regarded as sufficiently ill to require medevacing to Whitehorse, the apparently unexpected problems with intubation onboard, the long period between the decision to medevac and the actual departure, and the other problems together suggest an underlying lack of care and the systemic failure of service provision ...

Regarding systemic issues ... [adjunct professor] Michalson (personal communication, July 7, 2019), in her review of the documents notes that "The cause of death was listed as multi-organ failure, [associated with] hyperacute liver failure from unknown causes. These unknown causes might be ascribed to the problems of poverty, discrimination, and underfunding for services provided to people not considered to be important." ... Michalson asks, "Why was a 29-year old woman in that state of health? It was because she hadn't had access to proper health care her whole life. She had severe dental abscesses, so she had been treating herself with Tylenol and ibuprofen which can cause kidney and liver damage with long-term use." From this perspective, ... Michalson observes that "It was not simply a delay or the misplaced endotracheal tube or the infection she [Blackjack] had that killed, it was the systemic things that allowed her to be in that state of health. The failure of provision of appropriate health services in that community."

... Michalson observes that the documents concern the provision of health care as they relate to an individual, but an earlier case of death within the community (as noted in a letter from Ms. Roothman to Ms. [name withheld], March 2, 2015), points attention to the fact that systemic problems also operate at the level of the community.

Analysis of Documents

There are a number of documents in this proceeding and a considerable number of pages entered as evidence. Although I have read them, I will not attempt to provide a complete response to all of these materials, but rather comment on selected issues and examples. In a number of places, the language used by officials in the health care system either reveals a stereotype which is either held or supports stereotyping of Indigenous people. The following are examples: In Appeals Book I, page 160, a document "Transfer Notes" concerning the transfer by medevac to Whitehorse, of Ms. Blackjack, signed by Dr. [name withheld], begins by "Thank you for accepting this pt in transfer." The third paragraph reports "On past history she has a history of drinking lots of alcohol." In brief, this is one of the primary things Dr. [name withheld] wished to convey about the patient to the health practitioners in

Whitehorse prior to Ms. Blackjack's arrival. This is not precise language, and provides no details about how much or when alcohol was consumed, and if it was recent. It can be understood as callous, judgmental and supportive of stereotypes of Indigenous people.

Similarly, in Appeals Book 1, page 169, in providing a past medical history, in the November 8, 2013 Yukon Preliminary Death Report, [name withheld], the Chief Coroner writes in a single sentence, "known chronic alcohol abuse and recent binge drinking." The rest of the sentence concerned her immediate health complaints, so this stood as the sole thing noted about her health history. Ms. Blackjack did not die of alcoholism, yet Ms. [name withheld] wished to communicate this about Ms. Blackjack.

In several documents the positions taken by Ms. [name withheld], Chief Coroner for Yukon Territory, suggest a problem in communications with the First Nation. A letter from Ms. [name withheld] dated, August 6, 2014, (exhibit c), to Cynthia Blackjack, the mother of the deceased, was a total of five sentences long, plus documents attached, which included the autopsy report, the toxicology report and the judgement of the inquiry into her daughter's death. Ms. [name withheld] notes the recommendations she has made, and which I discuss above, and states "This investigation was very complicated and involved many experts who worked together tirelessly to provide your family answers to your questions. Our file is now closed. Should you have further questions, do not hesitate to contact our office."

This response is very cursory, without compassion, consideration, or detail, and is dismissive in tone. I have pointed to the problems identified in the literature regarding interactions which may be interpreted negatively by Indigenous peoples. Browne and Fiske (2001) as I noted, observed, "... clinical encounters have the potential to become culturally unsafe as seemingly innocuous behaviors are interpreted by patients as discriminatory, demeaning, or disempowering" when the sociopolitical background is bracketed out. Similarly, in the case of the letter by a coroner to Ms. Blackjack, it cannot be expected that a layperson can read the highly technical materials or that it would be of any use to Ms. Blackjack. The imagery of "tireless experts" would not be likely to [be] useful either, because it is the technical, expert material which would fail to answer Ms. Blackjack's questions. I would not categorize Ms. [name withheld] letter as innocuous, however. Instead, it seems likely to produce a demeaning effect, whether intentionally or otherwise.

A related communications issue was raised in a letter of February 2, 2015 to the Yukon Minister of Justice from a member of the LSC FN council, Tanya Silverfox. She wrote that the "... Chief Coroner did not ask for any input from Chief and Council during her inquiry and failed to consider the harsh realities our citizens often have to face when they need primary and emergency medical care." This is particularly important because Indigenous people commonly regard the welfare of an individual, in part, as a community concern and death as a community responsibility, in this case formally undertaken by Chief and Council ...

Part of the discussion regarding the admissibility of this evidence concerned whether I had any professional qualifications in medical anthropology. I do not describe myself as a medical anthropologist, but many of the areas of "med anth" can be subsumed in the study of the relations between the mainstream, the state, and Indigenous people, an area of study I do claim, and which this court and the various other courts and tribunals have accepted. These subtopics have been the subjects of my work; I worked over a two-year period with the Bellingham, Washington, paramedics school on their relations with Indigenous people, carried out an analysis of the history of disease of the Upper Skagit Tribe of Indians, taught courses on medical anthropology, was part of the supervisory committee of graduate students doing medical anthropology research with Indigenous and other communities, and reviewed manuscripts on medical anthropology for academic presses. And I have published in a journal within the domain of medical anthropology.

In a decision rendered on January 28, 2020, Coroner [name withheld] ruled on the question of the admissibility of my evidence in the inquest. A number of people had been present in the meeting prior to this ruling, including counsel for the coroner, for the band, for the Government of Yukon, and for two doctors who had been involved in the case. They had provided written submissions and made oral submissions on January 8. In paragraph three the coroner wrote, "Indeed, the majority of the report provides important context to assist the jury in assessing evidence and determining whether systemic racism played a factor in Ms. Blackjack's death." But paragraph four gets to the issue of whether my report "overstepped his expertise" and spoke to the issue the jury was to decide.

Specifically, the arguments for retaining the report in its entirety were that the proper time for deciding the question of admissibility is when "all counsel will have the opportunity to question him on his qualifications." Meanwhile, counsel for the Yukon argued that I had no qualifications in medicine or health care. The counsel for the two doctors claimed that I was not objective or reliable, that I was speculative and prejudicial. The counsel for the coroner claimed that I should not include conclusions about whether or not systemic racism played a part in the events.

I have learned over time and my involvement in a number of trials that a great deal of information is presented in reports and in testimony, and much or most of it is forgotten. So a strategy, then, for legal counsel may be to include statements premised on the idea that other statements are forgotten or that if they make their own claim, even if unmerited, it may be the view that prevails. Those involved in the discussion did not know the facts, or wrote as if they were unaware of the facts that I raised earlier about my involvement in medical anthropology. Ray (2011, 148) observes that judges are overwhelmed by evidence over long trials and that they are "buried in documents." This problem was made explicit in a Cree case in which I gave evidence in federal court in Regina, in 2019; the judge responded when counsel asked to enter my book *Oral History on Trial* (Miller 2011a) as evidence that he already had a great deal to read and denied the request. One could hardly blame the trial judge, who was indeed overwhelmed with documents.

It seems to have slipped out of mind the way the report was structured. Regarding the issue of stepping into the domain of decision making reserved for the jury, in my report I merely concluded that the facts of the *Blackjack* case could be understood in terms of theoretical literature on systemic racism. I did not conclude that it was such a case. And I carefully made no statement of claim about medicine. Health care is a different matter, and I have published in that field. In the end, the jury made recommendations that reflected the issues I raised in testimony. They did not find me unreliable, apparently.

Insults and Demeaning Language

Legal proceedings, in my experience, may involve demeaning language, disinformation, and incorrect inferences about the anthropologists. This has happened to me regularly, sometimes by lawyers attempting to subtly influence the judge or jury against my testimony by misrepresentation, which is routine, or attempting to simply give the presiding judge an explicit and incorrect version of my testimony. I present several examples here to illustrate how this disadvantages the Indigenous clients who cannot benefit fully from what I was asked to do. Please note that I am not undertaking a study of cross-examination techniques; far from it (see Freckelton and Silbey 2009 for an overview of cross-examination techniques). These examples concern cases of misrepresentations of academic work, efforts to depict me as too old because of movies I mention, that I would be fun to drink with, or I was an out-of-touch Ivory Tower academic and unaware of the current circumstances of Indigenous people in Canadian and American societies. The efforts at badgering through repetitive questions were perhaps aimed at making me look angry and unreliable.

Burke (2011, 78) describes what he calls "the predicament of the expert witness in cross-examination. Should the witness concentrate on giving an answer to the immediate question? Should the witness think ahead to the ultimate issues in the case, so that the framing of the answer is made with sufficient qualification, protecting it from abuse at a later date? Even if such complex thought processes are possible in the split second between question and answer, will too much second-guessing the ulterior purposes of questions detract from the appearance of frankness and honesty of direct answers?" Burke further notes the technique of cross-examination of leading the "witness down a corridor, closing each escape door as they go ... leading to the last and only available door that opens to a proposition that qualifies, undermines, or contradicts the witnesses' evidence-in chief. Witnesses have to spontaneously create their own escape door or agree to the proposition and hope for some redress in re-examination" (78–79). And the expert witness may simply be cut off by the judge before completing his thought (227).

In a deposition in a case concerning Indigenous treaty rights to hunting in the state of Washington, I was asked in cross-examination if I was an academic. This was obvious; my c.v. provided to the court and both sides of the case gave information regarding my academic career. I was not entirely sure what this line of inquiry was leading to, but I made clear that I taught at a university; also, since the beginning of my postgraduate academic training in the 1970s and every year since, I have been in the field, living in Indigenous communities and in a longhouse, attending ritual events, going on fishing boats, on hunting outings, and to other activities. Further, I had an active program of publishing, including many peer-reviewed papers and books. I had carried out a number of large-scale projects with several Coast Salish groups.

My opposite number, the anthropologist testifying for the state of Washington and providing evidence that would have the effect of obstructing tribal effort at clarifying and exerting treaty hunting rights, had done no fieldwork with Coast Salish people or, apparently, any Indigenous communities and had no publications concerning them. But in the summation provided the court, I was depicted as an "Ivory Tower academic," implying non-engagement with the real world, and set in opposition to the state's expert, who was described as actively engaged in researching the hunting issue in preparation for trial. So, that was it, I was an Ivory Tower academic, at least according to this lawyer.

Here is a second case: in presenting my expert report and testimony in the Yukon case involving the young woman who died while being transported to Whitehorse, the counsel for the territory suggested that I was too old (I was sixty-eight at the time), and my ideas of the way racism plays out in the present day are therefore dated and irrelevant. In cross-examination she brought up my reference to the film *Dances with Wolves,* asking me, Wasn't it dated? I had used this film to present the idea of the noble savage paired with its pejorative converse, the idea of the degraded savage, namely Indigenous people who lived as lesser people than their noble ancestors. This is a widely held image of Indigenous people in the mainstream population. I would say that the film starring Kevin Costner is regarded as a classic, although inept in its treatment of Indigenous issues and, therefore, is a good way to present the idea of contemporary ignoble Indigenous people to a jury. The Yukon lawyer described it as from the 1980s (it was released in 1990) and asked if I knew that the inquest was being held in what she termed a beautiful tribal centre with Indigenous artworks. These comments, I take it, were meant to illustrate that life is better for Indigenous people and, therefore, implied but unstated, that there was not systemic discrimination and racialization in the territory and in health care. I would not know that, she implied, because I was not present but, pointedly, I was too old and did not live there. Later, I noticed the irony; in testifying about discrimination based on race and ancestry, I faced discrimination based on age and place of residence.

Demeaning language can work in more subtle, indirect ways. *Citizens to Preserve Nookachamps Valley et al. v. Skagit County* was heard before the

Washington State Shorelines Hearings Board regarding a licence to blow up the rock called Tewalt Rock or Nookachamps Rock, reducing it to rubble for use in constructing a jetty. A local farm family owned the land on which the rock monolith was situated, and they were opposed by the American Indian tribe whose historic territory included the rock, and by a citizens group. In my research I found that the site had mythic properties and connections. I wrote (Miller 1999, 85), concerning the site:

> The recently deceased Alice Williams told me a story of Snake and Beaver who wished to marry Frog and Mouse, who refused them. Frog and Mouse, in consequence, were drowned by a flood contrived by Snake and Beaver (an outcome congruent with the long history of a rising and falling water table in the area). Oral material collected forty years earlier by an ethnographer and the material I collected on this occasion confirmed Tewalt Rock as Snakes' house (Snyder 1953). A quarter mile away is Beaver Lake, the mythological home of the beaver in the story (during our inspection we found several beaver lodges). Beaver Lake was also the site in which an ancestor of the current population was said to have obtained the *skedilich* power and the rights to employ a spiritually animated board in winter ceremonials. This is one of the most significant of Upper Skagit spirit powers and the site of acquisition is itself a place of spiritual importance.

My testimony prompted one of the judges on the panel to make a strange statement. I described it this way (Miller, 2008, 89–90):

> The imagery of exploding the sacred through literally blowing up a sacred site may well have been too powerful to be palatable for judges whose life experiences did not prepare them to contemplate Indian cosmological concepts, as was the case with the judges on the Shorelines Hearing Panel. I say this because of the nature of the decision rendered by the Panel, but also because of a question put to me by one of the judges during my testimony in this case. He noted that he is a "Catholic boy" and asked me to describe the Tewalt Rock in terms he could understand. In a response reminiscent of a debate in Australia over Ayers Rock (Whittaker 1994), I replied that the rock was something like a significant European cathedral. The Judge's counter, which

caused me to have some optimism about the outcome of the case, was to say "no, it's more like the holy grail." I didn't immediately think through to the conclusion he might have drawn, namely, that in accepting my proposition I required him to equate the religious tradition of a subordinated, obscure population with the grandest tradition of authority that he could imagine, surely an equation to be rejected by anyone not a wildly enthusiastic fan of cultural relativism. The holy grail, indeed, is a mythic, unembodied, unobtainable object in the Catholic, Christian tradition, no doubt a suitable analog to the Judge for what appeared to him to be an unembodied site, in fact, a non-site.

At this point, the judge, the "good Catholic boy," told me that I would be an interesting person to have a beer with. I later realized that he regarded my testimony as lore, as interesting stories about the distant past of Indigenous Peoples but irrelevant to the present day. His approach was a way of diminishing the significance of my testimony and overcoming hesitation regarding desecrating an area with spiritual significance. Demeaning language is a form of diminution of the Indigenous community and this comment was certainly that. It meant I did not have anything of significance to tell the panel. However, I did.

In another case the bench also found me to be an interesting person to have a beer with. This was in a district court in the state of Washington, in a custody battle over a young girl who had been determined by family elders to be the one to carry the Coast Salish spiritual traditions and, therefore, who needed to reside with and learn from her grandmother, who was the current spiritual worker. I attempted to explain something of the spiritual world of the Coast Salish peoples to the judge, and he, too, apparently found it fun lore but irrelevant to modern life. He ruled against the father's desire to have the child live with the grandmother in Vancouver, Canada. The lawyer for the father told me that the evidence was now in and they would win on appeal. They did.

A third judge also thought he should have a beer with me, in this case the head judge of a Puget Sound tribal court. He invited me to come to his house to talk and to drink a beer. To all these judges: I would be glad to have a beer with you or any other judge if you would let me explain and if you would take into account in your decision making that spiritual traditions are not gone from Coast Salish communities and that they are important in understanding treaties, child custody, sacred sites, and fishing.

Badgering by lawyers is another form of diminution. This is a common strategy; one veteran lawyer told me that the badgering I will describe occurs when the opposing lawyer has not got anything to say, has no other way of attacking the expert and the testimony. In a case heard before the Yukon Human Rights Commission in 2008 concerning discrimination in employment involving an Indigenous man (Miller 2014), I provided evidence regarding discrimination as a practice, how it manifested in employment, and related issues in my direct testimony. In cross-examination, the lawyer for the respondent asked me a few warm-up questions and then entered into a series of repeated questions getting at the fact that I had not been in the Yukon. The questions were phrased this way: Have you been in (name of town)? Have you been in (name of town)? and continued through a list of towns. Finally, I objected that I had already made clear that I had not been in Yukon territory. The tribunal member intervened to end the questioning. Was this a victory for the lawyer? Had he used this scheme to end the testimony and impeach my testimony, making it appear adverse? I am not sure.

This happened again in my testimony in a criminal trial in the state of Washington concerning a Tsawwassen First Nation fisherman who had crossed the international border in Boundary Bay while fishing (Miller 2014). The fisherman's view was that he was in family waters, where he held a right to fish. My testimony as requested by the lawyer acting for the fisherman concerned whether the fishing location was traditionally fished by this tribe. It was. Additionally, I was asked to provide an opinion about whether this tribe had connections to neighbouring US treaty-tribes. They did.

In cross-examination, the prosecutor asked me a string of questions starting with "Who signed the Jay Treaty?" (a treaty signed in 1794 between the United States and Canada concerning transit across the international border). I responded, "The British and the US" (this was before the formation of Canada). Then, "Did (such and such tribe) sign?" "No," I responded. "No tribes were signatories." "Did (such and such tribe) sign?" "No." This process was repeated until I objected that the question was answered. The judge intervened to stop those questions. Again, I wonder about the outcome of this badgering: Was he attempting to make me lose my cool? Or simply wasting time? Something else, or simply he had no real questions? I am not sure. This is behaviour one might expect in giving testimony,

Unexpected Twists and Turns

Real problems arise when cases take unexpected twists and turns. Ray (2011, 15) writes, "Once a case begins to wind its way through the legal process, it takes on a life of its own ... questions that lawyers and experts ... had not anticipated at the outset frequently arise and take centre-stage." An example of this comes from the Yukon inquest case involving the death of Ms. Blackjack. My participation in the inquest was via online viewing rather than in person. After going through the examination-in-chief and cross-examination, I found to my surprise that the coroner presiding over the case opened the proceedings to questions directly from the jury for about forty-five minutes. But this was good, and I enjoyed having the chance to speak directly to jurors and answer the specific questions they had. Their questions were sometimes unexpected. For example, one juror asked me what I thought about Alcoholics Anonymous, and I was unsure what the connection to the inquest was. My notes, taken simultaneously with the questions, say "Juror asks me about A.A. He looks Indigenous. I say if Christian, A. A. may be helpful but if not, many may not want to participate."

One juror asked my view of the notes taken by nurses at the clinic attended by Ms. Blackjack. My notes say, "Coroner says I can't answer but the question can be put more generally – about ways to help advocate. I answer about how to advocate [by nurses working at the clinic on behalf of patients/clients]. Do you know if they have housing, a way to get to the clinic – take them through the other [methods] of health care providers – who may not provide services." I was not allowed to talk about the nursing services at that clinic, but my notes indicate "I use their questions as a chance to reaffirm the significance of problems of racism in service delivery." And questioning by the jury allowed me to talk about what good health care provisioning might be like for rural clinics serving Indigenous people. An example I gave concerned a prescribed diabetic diet. An astute nurse or other health care worker might inquire if the family could afford this diet, if there was someone to cook this food, store the food, and if there was a way to access the food. Was the family head consulted and did that person agree to this?

To this example, the counsel for the Yukon objected that only First Nations people should "teach" how to understand Indigenous problems. My notes say that "I pointed out that I was working at the intersection between First Nations people and the mainstream [population]." I do not believe that this lawyer really believed her claim or had thought through the implications of barring non-Indigenous people from having opinions about topics such as service delivery. But it is an example of the unexpected. The lawyer's statement was strangely ideological and did not fit easily with the idea she had proposed earlier, that racism had dissipated in the Yukon.

During this process I was asked what my recommendations were for the health clinic servicing the reserve. I had not expected this and would have worked on recommendations in detail if I had, although I did give an answer. I gave an answer because I have thought about this question over many years, read academic papers about it, and discussed the issues with health professionals and, therefore, could answer off-the-cuff. The jury, in making their recommendations, included the request for a nurse-practitioner, an idea that came from my response to the questions put to me.

In addition, in cross-examination I was asked by the counsel for the Yukon an open-ended, abstract question. These sorts of questions are notorious for the ability of responses to be misconstrued or intentionally misrepresented. My notes recorded during the inquest regarding this question put to me by the lawyer for the Yukon state: "Individuals should be allowed to do what they want – Blackjack. I comment on the necessity of community education – and give the example of diabetes which is thought of as a life course event [in southwest US tribes], and not as a biomedical event; therefore, education about this is needed. Asks open-ended question – which allows her to conclude in her summation anything she wants about my opinion." It was a trap, a query entering into philosophic questions about human agency. One might wonder why I was allowed to answer a question dealing with philosophy. And I wish I had been informed that I might be asked something like this.

Two issues emerge here: first the unexpected happens; second, if the opportunity arose I could have explained why and how I can read nursing notes. That chance never arose and I had no reason to have included my skill in reading notes in my qualifications, particularly in regard to medical anthropology. My notes from the inquest say, "Did I fail to say regarding reviewing nurse notes that I didn't make medical opinions – instead I would be reading documents with my comments on racism and stereotypes in mind." The question about individual agency (Do people have the right to do what they want?) was intended to lead me down a corridor, but I do not think it did. I was able to point out that there are important obligations of society to individuals.

Since the issues that arise in court are unexpected, it is difficult to anticipate what to put into one's statement of qualifications. If too much information is entered, then a focus on the relevance of testimony is lost to the primary issues of the trial/hearing. If too little is recorded, then issues may arise about which I have something to say but cannot. Some lawyers seem to prefer short, tight statements of qualifications and curricula vitae. But in my experience, the lawyers provide little or no guidance on this.

Lack of information on the duties and role of the expert witness, badgering and using demeaning language to undermine expert witnesses in court, and the thinning of evidence all serve a purpose: to discredit the expert witness. More important, they undermine and diminish the cases brought by Indigenous litigants.

4

Entering Evidence in an Adversarial System

IN THE PRESENT ERA, anthropologists serving as experts are generally countered with another social scientist or an historian hired by the other side. Burke (2011) gives a sustained and engaging look at the testimony given by a variety of anthropologists on the same issue of Indigenous land claims in Australia, each presenting a different version of Aboriginal social organization. In western Canada it is a relatively new situation, and in British Columbia it is only since the 1970s that anthropologists have appeared as witnesses in Indigenous litigation. The first case was the testimony of University of British Columbia anthropologist Wilson Duff in the 1973 *Nisga'a* case. The Crown offered no anthropological expert and Duff was unopposed, a situation that would be unusual today. But anthropologists opposing each other – even though in theory they are both aiding the production of justice – is often an ugly circumstance. It can divide people who might otherwise be colleagues, or it can create the sense that one party was incorrectly supporting or undermining an Indigenous group's rights. Veteran expert Ray (2011, 10) notes that struggles between experts have intensified. I should note that in human rights cases in my experience, there has not been an expert for the respondent, although one was proposed in *McCue* and other witnesses were called.

Ray (2011) writes that pitting experts against one another can drive both parties into extreme positions, even the opposite of one another, that drift away from the murky middle ground Indigenous issues, such as the nature of ownership, often occupy. Being pitted against another can push one into an effort to disprove the opposing expert as opposed to finding defensible and meaningful anthropological conclusions.

Lawyers sometimes recruit their own expert to critique the testimony of another anthropologist and give real-time information about how to cross-examine. This is an unpleasant intrusion into disciplinary collegiality. However, I have been asked to do this and on one occasion, after having heard online during the daytime what I considered the misinformed testimony of another expert in a federal court, I awoke from sleep at 3:00 a.m. with an idea of how to clarify in a few sentences the problem with his testimony. The issue at trial was the nature of oral history (tradition) and, ultimately, whether the elders of an amalgamated Cree Indigenous community should be able to give oral historical evidence and, then, whether that evidence should bear sufficient weight in explaining how their ancestors responded to their communities being merged by Canada and to the seizure of a sizeable portion of the lands reserved under treaty. The two historic Cree communities that had been merged wished to be separated, and both wanted their lands back.

In my expert report (Miller 2018b, 6), I established that Julie Cruikshank, a member of the Order of Canada and winner of major awards for her scholarship, is a leading authority and that I relied on her definition, writing, "I employ Cruikshank's working definition, 'Broadly speaking, oral tradition (like history or anthropology) can be viewed as a coherent, open-ended system for constructing and transmitting knowledge,' and her conclusion concerning 'the evolving recognition that oral tradition anchors the present in the past'" (Cruikshank 1994, 408, 407). I set this idea that "oral tradition anchors the present in the past" with the view espoused by the expert brought by the Crown: "However, an oral tradition, by virtue of its orality, is a product of the present in which it is told, heard and recorded" (von Gernet 2018, 17). Oral history, then, is either anchored in the past or a product of the present. I emailed my idea right then, in the middle of the night, to the lawyer with whom I was working. He opened his continued cross-examination the next day with the issue I proposed.

Still, the practice of using anthropologists to critique each other on the stand is unsettling. The practice extends to critiques of each other's expert reports, but these are in the light of day. Ray (2011, 71) describes the "war of paper talk," of rebuttals and surrebuttals between experts before testimony even begins, leading to a requirement to defend original submissions, rebuttals, and surrebuttals. It is time-consuming and often seems counterproductive. It runs up the billing hours, a problem for the taxpayers.

Metge (1998, 57), an experienced anthropologist and expert witness, observed that the Waitangi Tribunal's rules frustrated her: "Tribunal procedure prevents direct exchange between witnesses in public: responses, refutations and new insights must be channelled through counsel as questions for use in the examination of witnesses or embodied in submissions filed for later presentation. As a result, some of the attractive features of open, academic debate are lost: immediacy ... I found it frustrating to sit silently while a witness misquoted my work or made sweeping or inaccurate generalizations." She found tribunal processes, on the other hand, inhibited rudeness and required criticism to be carefully worded and grounded in reputable sources. This latter part of her experience has not been mine.

The concept of an expert before the court, as I understand it from an anthropological perspective, is someone who can assist the court/tribunal/hearing board to understand issues in question. The state of Washington, where I have given evidence several times, gets at both the issue of assistance and the basis of the expert's knowledge in a single sentence.

ER 702 TESTIMONY BY EXPERTS
If scientific, technical, or other specialized knowledge will assist the trier of fact to understand the evidence or to determine a fact in issue, a witness qualified as an expert by knowledge, skill, experience, training, or education, may testify thereto in the form of an opinion or otherwise. [Adopted effective April 2, 1979.] Comment 702 [Deleted September 1, 2006.] (Washington State Administrative Office of the Courts, n.d.)

The expert, as opposed to a lay witness, can draw on materials that enable the formation of an opinion about the questions put by the counsel, which are answered in direct examination and cross-examination or in response to questions posed by the jurist. But the ability to articulate something of the lives of Indigenous litigants and the adverse circumstances which brought them to court depends on (1) establishing academic and practical credentials and (2) successfully entering evidence into legal proceedings. This seems simple in theory but is difficult in practice.

Who Is the Audience?

When an expert prepares a report, who is the audience? Academics typically write for their peers. An audience of a judge is likely different from an audience of a jury. But in either case, one cannot assume expertise in anthropology, and it is difficult to decide how scholarly to make the text. It is clear, though, that an expert report is not a regular academic publication, with a complete set of citations. It cannot treat side issues. Ray (2011, 122) indicates, however, that a literature review serves a purpose in an expert report, determining what he calls "current knowledge" in his field.

And as Burke (2011, 274) argues, the expectation is that an anthropologist will help simplify ethnographic complexity in cases like a land claim where anthropological facts and concepts are already in circulation. In another sort of case, such as a human rights tribunal, that will not be the circumstance. I have been caught by surprise in Canadian federal court by questions from the judge that made me realize his starting point of understanding my testimony was much less developed than I expected. I appreciated the questions, though, because it helped me calibrate my further oral testimony.

My answer to the problem of complexity is that plain language is generally better. Ray (2011, 78) describes a trial judge asking him while he was on the stand for repeated clarification of his expert report, "because I have a big mark here on page 70 and 71 when I read it, and I still don't – I thought I would get an explanation of what I read, but I still don't understand it. I would ask you to, please, let's go back over again ... " This strikes me as a good process of clarification. Ray (15) adds the note that material cannot be added to the record for appeals court after the trial, and judicial "invention" can best be minimized by introducing all relevant materials. It is easy to forget that people, even academics in other fields, often find anthropology mystifying and jargonistic, and judges or jurors have to understand it in a way that is meaningful to themselves.

The Pitfalls of Publishing Academic Research

There are conventions in the academic world primarily around producing research that is examined by other, generally anonymous, experts as of sufficient quality to be published. These conventions are sometimes disputed in court. I commented in a response paper to an expert report in a Canadian federal court that the author of the report had represented papers published in a journal he had created and edited as peer-reviewed publications (Miller

2018b). A criterion of an arms-length review is that anonymous reviewers can form opinions independently on the merits of a paper. That could not be the case in a journal edited by the paper's author. This anthropologist, frequently used by the Crown in cases brought against Canada by Indigenous communities, had few peer-reviewed papers, so the Crown lawyers attacked the premise of peer review and asked on cross-examination (in words to the effect) if other work could have merit and if those without peer-reviewed publications could have standing in the community of academics.

This question was a trick. Of course, work that has not been reviewed can have merit, but it remains different from peer-reviewed work. There is a lot of important "gray literature" often produced by academically trained people who work on contract rather than in universities or colleges. But this work sometimes has forms of evaluation behind it: competition for grants may be a form of peer review, or review by academics working for agencies may serve this purpose. In the case of the Crown expert, the papers may not have undergone these forms of evaluation. The line of questioning was opening me up to being represented as though implying that these authors, their papers unevaluated by peers, had the same standing as those authors whose work had been peer reviewed. I would say this situation can occur but is rarely the case.

An example of an academically trained expert who published very little yet commanded respect for the quality of her work was the late Dr. Barbara Lane, the anthropologist who did the baseline work and gave the critical testimony in the hallmark 1974 US treaty fishing case, *United States v. Washington*. In this case, the court ruled that treaty language of 1855, in which the Indigenous people of Puget Sound and the settler population had rights "in common," was taken by presiding Judge Boldt to mean each group, settlers and collectively the various local Indigenous tribes, had rights to half the salmon catch. Barbara Lane told me that she avoided publishing so that over many years she would not make public opinions that did not match those she had formed and presented in court earlier. Ray (2011, 37), who was highly successful in academic publishing, reports that he ran into this problem.

Influence of Litigation on Anthropology and the Archive

Dan Boxberger, a retired but still engaged professor from the Department of Anthropology at Western Washington University, has acted many times as an expert and written that the anthropological literature on Coast Salish peoples of the west coast has been built on research connected to litigation since the beginning (Boxberger 2007), so clearly there has been a deep engagement with legal issues by anthropologists. For example, the late Herbert Taylor, an academic who taught both Boxberger and me, published few academic articles but carried out significant research for litigation, which entered into the larger anthropological literature. In my anthropology department at UBC, several colleagues have written a number of papers for court but not appeared as a witness on the stand. Ray, in a 2004 talk, states that "much of what is taught [in history] is the product of litigation work."

Burke (2011, 277–79) observed the important relationship between the history of anthropology more generally and law, noting the circulation of ideas between the two domains, particularly concerning the study of primitive law and legal pluralism. More recent, he notes, is "the struggle between judge and anthropologist over the authoritative interpretation of the anthropological archive." In his view, judges give undue weight to anthropologists in the archive with a high public profile. Burke also reports the "heightened reflexivity" about theoretical constructs on the part of anthropologists that comes from participation in legal processes (184). Burke (2011, 86) notes the issue of reinterpretations of evidence once given, which he says is an assertion of structural superiority of the court over the expert and "carries with it a certain anti-intellectualism, or at least an aversion to explicit theorizing, which is often cast in opposition to fact-finding."

I agree with this proposition, as does my coauthor Menezes (2015). Tests of fact and theory in court are different from those faced in academic peer review but push towards a clarity that might be negatively considered as simplification or positively seen as concision. Both sorts occur. It is a good thing if one's work can be explained to a lay (or law) person.

Engagement with law stirs the anthropological pot and has done for a long time, as Boxberger notes. Particular sorts of issues become central to anthropology, to at least one group of practitioners, because they are repeatedly addressed in treaty, land, and fishing claims, and other forms of contemporary litigation. An example for Indigenous litigation from the southern northwest coast of North America is the question, What is the nature of ownership in the contact period? Did Indigenous people have the concept of ownership and title? What are the social groups in an otherwise fluid society and to whom does title reside? How do these issues map onto the state-derived current system of treaty-tribes in the US and the recognized bands and tribal councils in Canada?

In two examples, a neo-evolutionist anthropological model of forms of social organization (bands, chiefdoms, tribes, states), said to be associated with particular forms of religious organization, economy, trade, family, and political organization, was used to argue that an Indigenous group did not have trade transactions in the nineteenth century. Instead, this argument goes, they practiced barter or gift exchange and, therefore, could not have sold salmon or cigarettes or other commodities (see Ray 2011, 38, regarding the use of Julian Steward's dated cultural ecological models in the *Delgamuukw* case). This logic is circular, and the problem is that one cannot move from theoretical schemes into pronouncements about empirical questions.

Did Indigenous people at the time of contact have market forms of exchange? The issue faced in the Van der Peet case (*R. v. Van der Peet*, [1996] 2 SCR 507) is the first example. In this case, an expert for the Crown argued from a dated, neo-evolutionist perspective that there was no definitive market exchange taken by the defendant's ancestral community and therefore the defendant could not engage today in commercial sales. Experts for the Stó:lō indicated otherwise and the court ruled, "As a consequence, I conclude that the Stó:lō Band, of which the appellant is a member, possess an aboriginal right to sell, trade and barter fish for livelihood, support and sustenance purposes. Under s. 35(1) of the Constitution Act of 1982 this right is protected" (para. 221). Carlson (1996, 8) understood the decision this way: "In the court's opinion, Mrs. Van der Peet had not demonstrated that her sale of fish was consistent with a pre-existing Aboriginal right. However, they did not say that Mrs. Van der Peet, or any other Stó:lō, did not have such rights. In other words, in the absence of a competing model to that presented by Crown counsel, the court adopted an outdated anthropological model based on core culture traits to assess a First Nation's eligibility for market-style Aboriginal rights. Such a model is not only based on outdated anthropological theory ... "

The Masks Anthropologists Wear

It is curious to consider, in the sense of Goffman (1959), the masks worn by anthropologists who are willing to go to trial and the way they project their concept of self, their competence, and their trustworthiness. One Crown expert I have encountered presents himself as a scientist who is disinterested in the outcomes of the cases in which he gives testimony. He states in sworn testimony in court that he does not care about the outcome. He regularly describes himself as engaged in science and projects the sense that he is engaged in "normal science," akin to hard sciences such as physics or chemistry, in which research findings have a sort of ontological status as truth. Others, he writes at length in his reports to the court, are postmodernists with no allegiance to or belief in truth (von Gernet 2018). However, I see it differently.

In my critique of the evidence presented by the Crown, I pointed out in one trial that "sociocultural anthropology is at heart a fieldwork discipline. This is why fieldwork, and particularly long-term work, with Indigenous Peoples, in their communities, is important to understanding their oral materials and how they are generated. Indeed, the idea of culture, and cultural difference, is one of the building blocks of the discipline of anthropology" (Miller 2018b, 12–13). Burke (2011, 22–23) writes that [sociocultural] anthropology, a non-experimental discipline, cannot be modelled on the idea of scientific expertise, a source of critiques of anthropological evidence. This can be a conceptual problem for courts, which may struggle to grasp the sort of data anthropology sometimes relies on. An emphasis on fieldwork might blunt this critique and present an image of an ideal anthropology – and the intimate, extensive, empirical knowledge based on immersion in the society. Bullock (2021) describes this as the problem of qualitative data in court. Scholarship without long-term fieldwork can lead to misunderstandings or gaps in comprehension. One consultant anthropologist I have spoken with expressed the view that contemporary communities know little or nothing of the lives and views of their ancestors. In my experience, this is far from the truth (see Merchant 2020 regarding Indigenous people's awareness of their ancestor's practices and perspectives).

A practical issue regarding the entry of anthropological evidence into the law is that there is a limited pool of people testifying for the state. This circumstance has led to a small group of people doing multiple cases for the state and, therefore, generally in opposition to Indigenous interests. Another group of people have experience only with the Indigenous side. One scholar whom I respect for the quality of his work, Dan Boxberger, testified for the state in an important treaty case. (I was hired by the other side, giving testimony for an Indigenous tribe). Recall that the duty of an expert is to impartially give evidence that will help the court, without bias. Further, experts are asked to provide answers to particular questions initially posed by counsel that sought the expert. The distinction here is between the need to allow anthropologists to give properly understood expertise on "both sides" of a case and the very different ways in which anthropological expertise as such is thinned by these processes in ways that distort the possibility for any actually productive expertise in the court. The anthropologist in this case, in my view, did precisely that for his client, the state. He answered the questions posed to the best of his knowledge, and these answers did not favour the state. Despite this, he was the object of some hostility from tribal members who disliked his participation for the state. Nevertheless, he later was hired by tribes for expert work.

Part of the blame for the limited pool of state experts is the negative response of Indigenous people, who themselves are more than aware of the historical injustices their tribes and even themselves as individuals have experienced and who are leery of the court process even as they engage it. Boxberger (2004, 332) himself writes, "There has been much written in the last 50 years about the nature of anthropological testimony in Native America cases ... In general the tenor of the discussion has been that the 'good' anthropologists work for the Indians and the 'bad' anthropologists work for the other side ..." That is a problem.

Commentary in a 2004 Department of Justice session on expert witnessing, held in Vancouver on February 2, and at which I spoke, noted that in-house experts are valuable – an Aboriginal team – and that historical expertise must be available to the Crown in the years before litigation to help develop elements of the case. This makes the discipline available to lawyers. These experts would be precluded from the courtroom and would be unlike a "hired gun." Further, such a research team would create "corporate knowledge," which would benefit the lawyers who rotate in their areas of practice.

Possible Solutions

One resolution to the problem of a small pool of experts is the use of anthropologists that all sides have agreed upon to act as a Master. There are several cases of this – the late Barbara Lane served this purpose in treaty fishing litigation in Oregon and legal scholar Douglas Harris has undertaken a similar task in British Columbia. Boxberger (2004, 332) notes that Julian Steward in the 1950s called for a practice of pretrial hearings to present data in a fact-finding exercise. In the 1970s, Princeton anthropologist Lawrence Rosen (1977) called for the presentation of evidence without the question-and-answer format. UCLA professor of anthropology Ralph Beals suggested an anthropologist be appointed as "friend of the court" and present evidence, similar to the Master format.

Another approach is for an anthropologist appointed by the state and the one appointed by the Indigenous groups to work together and produce a joint ethnographic/ethnohistorical report to the court. Dr. Molly Malone, who works for the Firelight Group of consultants, has done this sort of work successfully. A panel is a third alternative, as I note below. Burke (2011, 160) describes a "hot-tubbing" process in Australian law, which is "a meeting of all experts to attempt agreement on issues in the case" that can be required under Australian Federal Court guidelines for expert witnesses. Metge (1998, 57) says simply that anthropologists should work for all parties so that court time is not wasted on poorly conceived research or badgering expert witnesses about credentials.

Under Canadian federal court rules, Canada allows for panels or conferences of experts:

EXPERT WITNESS PANEL

282.1 The Court may require that some or all of the expert witnesses testify as a panel after the completion of the testimony of the non-expert witnesses of each party or at any other time that the Court may determine.
SOR/2010–176, s. 9
Marginal note: Testimony of panel members

282.2 (1) Expert witnesses shall give their views and may be directed to comment on the views of other panel members and to make concluding statements. With leave of the Court, they may pose questions to other panel members.
Marginal note: Examination of panel members

(2) On completion of the testimony of the panel, the panel members may be cross-examined and re-examined in the sequence directed by Court.
SOR/2010–176, s. 9

(Canada, "Case Management and Dispute Resolution Services (continued)," Justice Laws Website, https://laws-lois.justice.gc.ca/eng/regulations/sor-98–106/page-22.html, accessed May 11, 2020.)

Or, an expert might be asked to confer with another, also in Canadian federal rules:

EXPERT CONFERENCES

5 An expert witness who is ordered by the Court to confer with another expert witness

(a) must exercise independent, impartial and objective judgment on the issues addressed; and

(b) must endeavour to clarify with the other expert witness the points on which they agree and the points on which their views differ.

(Canada, n.d.)

These are potential solutions but the main problem remains. The legal system in which anthropologist-experts operate makes it difficult to do their jobs – to remain impartial, independent, and objective while articulating something of the complex lives of Indigenous litigants and the adverse circumstances that brought them to court. That we are often required to work with lawyers – who, in training and experience often come from a very different place – complicates things further.

5

Anthropologists versus Lawyers

HOW ANTHROPOLOGIST-EXPERTS and lawyers work together has implications for the processes and outcomes of litigation brought by Indigenous people, and there are a number of problems with their relationship: lack of knowledge about each other and how to work together and major differences in how they compose teams, use language, and think. Kandel (1992 c, 57) points out that most lawyers do not know what anthropologists do and calls for anthropologists to "educate your counsel beforehand." She also calls for a mutual understanding between anthropologist and lawyer on the theory of the case (59). Part of the issue is that the "expertise" required to serve as expert witnesses in the law is at odds with the "studied naivete that characterizes anthropological research" (Kandel 1992c, 53). Anthropologists, asserts Kandal, associate expertise with holistic, unerring, and interpretive understanding that comes from fieldwork. "Expert" as a legal term, she notes, is a more "modest and pragmatic meaning." I disagree entirely with Kandel that fieldwork-based anthropologists feel their work is unerring. The contemporary practice of reflecting on one's work and positioning oneself rules this out. But I do agree with her other propositions.

Lawyer, Witness, and Indigenous Client Do Not Constitute a Team

In my experience, there is a range of relationships between anthropologists and lawyers representing Indigenous clients that can pose problems. Sometimes, these relationships are long-enduring and are built on trust and mutual respect. Over the twenty-five years I worked with one lawyer employed by a US tribe, I had come to think that we worked well together. He had helped me through the first trial in which I was called as a witness, letting me know what the process would be like and how it would work. Importantly, he told me I must prepare for questioning and try to anticipate what I might be asked. But more recently, we were somewhere in the middle of a particular treaty issue when, suddenly, something went wrong with his relationship with the tribe and he was gone.

In another startling episode, the lawyers I had worked with regarding a Canadian First Nation were abruptly terminated and another lawyer hired. The new lawyer was aggressive in his tactics, and at a band meeting promised members a huge financial settlement. He quickly arranged a public relations stunt to publicize the First Nation's circumstances (a chief later told me that this event and approach had damaged his community's relationship with surrounding First Nations). Meanwhile, a member of the original legal team phoned to inform me that there were ethical concerns with the new man and that he had been fired by another First Nation. In this case, too, I liked and respected the original team. In the end, I thought my relationship was with the band and, more specifically, I had an obligation to finish the work I had begun. But I had an entirely different relationship with the new person and his team, and I remained concerned about how my evidence would be used.

In a third instance, the lawyer, Amber Prince, about thirty years younger than me, told me that I was more experienced in human rights cases than she and asked my opinion about how to proceed in preparing. I was a bit surprised. In the hearing itself, she was highly competent and effective.

As with many anthropologists, legal work with Indigenous people has had a transformative effect on one's own life, an observation I have probably heard in every public talk by prominent specialist lawyers, such as Stuart Rush and Louise Mandell, who worked over long periods with Indigenous people. This transformation is also true for Prince (2020), as she noted in an unrecorded online talk to my UBC anthropology of law class, and this fact underlies the relationships between the groups.

These cases bring up the issue as to whether a witness and the legal staff are a team. They are not, even though they spend time together with the same tribal people (see Alvarez and Loucky 1992). But there are team-like qualities. One lawyer, mentioned above, let me know that the tribe for which he and I worked on a variety of projects would eventually bring a treaty rights case involving hunting. In response, a few decades before the case was initiated, I began gathering relevant anthropological and historical materials and I interviewed senior tribal elders about their own hunting and their knowledge of their predecessors' hunting. By the time the case was brought the elders I interviewed had died, and their knowledge would have disappeared had it not been recorded. Since I worked with this tribe over many years and carried out large research projects with them, I was in a position to understand their ethnography and history and, subsequently, issues of treaty and other rights that go to court. This is the case for many anthropologists in North America who work with a community over many years.

Anthropologists and lawyers are also not a team in that the experts cannot re-envision their opinions on anthropological questions to make an easier case for the lawyer. Sometimes this boundary between fact and inference is not clear, and on at least one occasion I have been asked if the evidence I had gathered might be stretched a bit further. It could not, because the evidence was not an implication arising from known information and could not be "thought of another way" and become true. And I could not have supported that opinion if questioned on it in court. Most lawyers, but not all, in my experience, emphasize the importance of supportable positions in court. But the fuzzy boundary might be reached in reorganizing a report to conform more exactly with ways in which a lawyer might wish to present the expert's case.

Burke (2011, 272–73) writes that constant pressure exists to push anthropologists into advocacy at every step of the process of preparing an expert report (regarding anthropological advocacy and courts see de la Cadena and Starn 2007; Kuper 2003; Trigger 2011; and Kandel 1992c and see 1992a). That is not my own experience in Canada and the United States. Anthropologist Joan Metge (1998, 55), writing about her experiences in New Zealand, notes an interesting turn in her own understanding. "In preparing my submissions I was upset and indignant when claimants' counsel asked me to modify the wording and occasionally aspects of my conclusions to fit the line of argument he was pursuing and to omit or under-state the qualifications and reservations with which I hedged them 'lest we weaken our case.' My immediate reaction was to resent and reject such suggestions out of hand; then I wondered if I was being unreasonable and simmered down enough to debate the issues. I soon realised that counsel (a Maori from outside Muriwhenua) had an excellent grasp both of the evidence and of tikanga Maori. Several lively discussions helped clarify the issues."

No Guidance on Working with Lawyers

The relationship between anthropologists with lawyers, from the anthropological perspective, is oddly undeveloped and seems to be overlooked. Anthropologists have their own code of ethics in North America concerning fieldwork and a range of topics. The American Anthropological Association (AAA) produced a volume on ethics (Cassell and Jacobs n.d.) and the association's *Anthropology Newsletter* runs a regular column on ethics. Jacobs (n.d.) wrote about cases of ethical dilemmas, Case 2 touching on a legal question of concern to anthropologists serving as experts:

CASE 2: WHO OWNS THE FIELD NOTES?

Jerry Vaughn contracted with a federal agency to conduct a social impact assessment of proposed topographic changes in an aboriginal habitat in a far north region of North America. The contract contained no stipulations regarding ownership of data. In order to determine the potential impacts on the culture of peoples living in that region, Vaughn engaged in participant observation (keeping a detailed field notebook of same); conducted in-depth personal interviews; and took over 1,000 photographs of people working, socializing, and enjoying other everyday and special activities. This work was carried out over a one year period. Vaughn was paid 75% of his contracted salary and other expenses before the fieldwork.

Vaughn then wrote a 150-page report detailing the areas of social life that would be adversely affected if the plans were implemented. He further noted that, if the plans were implemented as proposed, there could be no mitigations that could prevent the people's culture from being totally altered. Because of these severe conclusions, the agency director instructed Vaughn to turn over his entire research record in order that the agency could solicit another opinion on the matter. Furthermore, the director told Vaughn that unless he would turn over the record, no further payment would be made to him.

Vaughn's Dilemma: *Should he turn over the interview materials, the photographs, and his field notes, all of which contained sensitive and personal information? Should he turn over only part of his record? Or, should he refuse to turn anything over to the agency?*

VAUGHN'S DECISION

With an attorney's help, Vaughn developed a sound argument that stated that it was customary for anthropologists to keep the data they collected, that he had conducted his contracted work in good faith, that the contract contained no stipulations regarding ownership of the data, and that he was therefore due his full salary.

Vaughn later realized that, since it is possible in many instances to collect data for one's own professional use, as well as the data necessary to fulfill the terms of a contract, one needs to know in advance to whom the data for the contracted research will belong. This will permit maintenance of separate files, from the outset. He won his argument and was paid in full."

Similarly, in my own experience, a lawyer asked me to turn over to him the entirety of a fieldnote book of about seventy-five pages in order to use two pages of notes from a meeting I had attended years earlier with tribal leaders and federal Indian agency officials. I did not trust this person to treat my own notes as my property and to not use other materials in the notebook, and I did not provide the notes. Instead, I provided a handwritten copy of the section in which he claimed interest. I did not want my notes to be used harmfully, the first principle of professional responsibility.

The American Anthropology Association (n.d.) lists its principles of professional responsibility as follows:

1. Do No Harm
2. Be Open and Honest Regarding Your Work
3. Obtain Informed Consent and Necessary Permissions
4. Weigh Competing Ethical Obligations Due Collaborators and Affected Parties
5. Make Your Results Accessible
6. Protect and Preserve Your Records
7. Maintain Respectful and Ethical Professional Relationships

These principles, however, do not focus on anthropology-lawyer relations. The AAA guidelines consider several sorts of people with whom one must have an ethical relationship but does not include lawyers: "As a social enterprise, research and practice always involve others – colleagues, students, research participants, employers, clients, funders (whether institutional, community-based or individual) as well as non-human primates and other animals, among others (all usually referred to as 'research participants' in this document)" (AAA, n.d.).

Even when considering the potential impact of anthropological research, anthropologist-lawyer relations are not mentioned. The document includes the passage "They must not plagiarize, nor fabricate or falsify evidence ..." (AAA, n.d., Ethics Forum) but with reference to health research. A discussion of collaborators and partners reads, "Anthropologists must weigh competing ethical obligations to research participants, students, professional colleagues, employers and funders, among others, while recognizing that obligations to research participants are usually primary" (Ibid.). This passage, too, leaves out lawyers. Another passage concerns confidentiality of field notes: "Researchers have a responsibility to use appropriate methods to ensure the confidentiality and security of field notes, recordings, samples or other primary data and the identities of participants" (Ibid.). But this passage does not address or clarify the issues resulting from lawyers' claims on notebooks, or if and when it might be appropriate to turn over notebooks and other materials.

The Canadian Anthropology Society (n.d., Position Statements) has created position statements and resolutions, but none of these appear to address the relationship of anthropologists and legal practitioners. "The Canadian Anthropology Society in its role as a national association of anthropologists has articulated position statements on topics that directly concern our profession, researchers and students in our discipline and communities with which we work."

Section 18 of the Canadian Anthropology Society's bylaws (n.d.) reference termination of membership when expelled, and section 20 provides details of the terms of expulsion but not the content – that is, why someone might be expelled. Might expulsion include bending to requests by lawyers to stretch the facts or push an implication too far? Anthropologists, unlike those in some other disciplines, are not licensed but, rather, gain graduate degrees. I know of no cases of sanctioned Canadian anthropologists. My Brazilian colleagues, Gustavo Menezes and Stephen Baines, on the other hand, have mentioned the recent case of a Brazilian postgraduate-trained anthropologist who has been sanctioned by their national body for unethical behaviour, which has injured the interests of Indigenous communities.

Curiously, the National Association for the Practice of Anthropology (n.d.), in their Guidelines for Ethical Practice, do not list lawyers as stakeholders: "Stakeholders may include funders/sponsors/employers, colleagues, research participants, employees, consumers, and community members." Law is not included as a category. Perhaps law could be considered a consumer.

The Society for Applied Anthropology has its own code of ethics. A 1951 publication of the society's journal, *Human Organization,* noted in the abstract "that the applied anthropologist must take responsibility for the effects of his recommendations, never maintaining that he is merely a technician unconcerned with the ends toward which his applied scientific skills are directed" ("Code of Ethics of the Society for Applied Anthropology" 1951, 2).

This statement is notable because it contradicts the position of the Crown witness I described in a previous chapter, who claims he is disinterested in the outcome of trials in which he enters his work. The Society for Applied Anthropology connects to archaeological ethics in relation to colleagues, employees, employers, students, clients, and the public, but not in relation to lawyers. Some materials referenced on this website concern the law (as in what the law might be concerning pothunting or the Antiquities Act), but not lawyers. A review of the archaeological database turned up no articles or blogs on the issues I raise here.

In brief, the various North American professional associations offer limited guidance on the quite important relationship between anthropologists (including archaeologists) and legal practitioners. Law firms have posted online discussions of relations with expert witnesses, though not anthropologists in particular, but these discussions are from the perspective of lawyers, not anthropologists, and do not consider many of the issues I take up here. An exception is the National Association for the Practice of Anthropology. Their ethics guidelines do not mention work with lawyers, but the association's 1993 bulletin (see Kandel 1992 a, b, c) is aimed directly at this issue. This publication considers ethics but is not a code of ethics.

These facts show systematically that anthropology does not consider the law as a worthwhile object of ethics. Just as the court misrecognizes anthropology, anthropology at the institutional level misrecognizes the law and the close relationship between the two. There is almost the sense in these documents provided by national organizations that law is so onerous to even consider that anthropology's relationship to law is purposely ignored. But anthropology should consider this relationship more fully. It is important, as I have suggested, to consider our commonalities in background and training and our similarities and differences in logic, language, and ethics. We have been told why this is important; otherwise we become the law's anthropology and in Burke's (2011) envisioning, rendered and digested, or as Daly (2005) has it, we become traitors.

What Should Lawyers Teach Anthropologists?

University anthropologists often do not know basic things about involvement in litigation as experts. They do not know how much to charge, that they should keep track of expenses or billing hours, or whom to bill after giving a deposition. As mentioned, they may not think it is compatible with their appointments to educational institutions to do contract work. They may not realize that they might contribute to society through this work, forwarding the project of reconciliation in some cases, or protecting our environment or cultural heritage. (But note: these cases are not usually about reconciliation or cultural heritage and may simply be indirect consequences.) A number of people have called me to ask questions about these basic topics. Consulting anthropologists who have businesses, on the other hand, are very clear about these topics.

Ray (2011, 4) describes receiving a phone call in 1985 from a lawyer asking if Ray would appear as a historical expert in a treaty rights case. "I asked him what he expected me to do. He replied, 'You will be there to educate the court.'" Ray notes that he was completely unaware that he was being drawn into intensifying legal struggles. He describes differences in trials in which he has been an expert and the hostility and suspicion he encountered in several instances. However, he was alerted to the nature of trials and spent time with the lawyer who prepared him for giving his evidence-in-chief (direct testimony). He describes learning that he could not talk to anyone during recesses while he was still under oath and his consequent sense of isolation. Further, he could not consistently read the facial expressions of the lawyer who was cross-examining him (41–42).

In addition, Ray (2011, 73) describes his working relationship with lawyer Peter Hutchins, who introduced Ray to the plaintiff's legal team prior to the start of a trial in 2000 and explained their roles in the upcoming trial, including one who would address challenges to Ray's testimony by raising objections and serving as Ray's "protector" in court. Further, Hutchins introduced Ray to the work of an early anthropologist-expert, Alfred Kroeber, who testified in the US Indian Claims Commission, a court established in the 1940s specifically to hear unresolved American Indian tribal cases, and who kept detailed notes of his work and was meticulous in preparation for litigation.

In Ray's case, lawyers who hired him seemed to have informed him of their own theory of the case and how they would build it, which is a help in understanding what sort of cross-examination will transpire. Generally, more than one expert is involved in big land claim cases, for example, and there are more issues than those raised by a single expert. It helps to have an idea of the larger set of issues. Kandel (1992b, 59) calls for this exchange of information. In particular, case law that has produced specific legal tests for demonstrating Indigenous rights and title or other areas of legal contention could usefully be brought to the attention of anthropologists.

Ray (2011, 73) raises the issue of counsel as "protectors" during difficult cross-examination. This is another topic which deserves discussion because those otherwise unfamiliar with the court would not know how this might work. In one instance, feeling myself unfairly questioned and battered at length during cross-examination, I asked the lawyer afterwards why he did not object to inflammatory questioning. He responded, "Because it was going well." I would not have known. In my experience, legal counsel does not generally suggest that they will play this role.

Anthropologists are hazy about the boundaries between the roles of legal personnel and are particularly vulnerable to accusations by opposing counsel that they have overstepped their role into that of the presiding judge or other court official. In my experience, opposing counsel may make this charge even if it is unwarranted, because it is jarring and confusing to people accused of this who are not ordinarily part of legal processes. It can throw someone off their game and erode confidence in their ability to play out their own role in the courtroom. I provided an example above of such claims made about my own report to the *Blackjack* inquest.

For anthropologists, giving testimony derived from the range of topics they research may make it difficult to not draw conclusions about the implications for the case itself. But drawing conclusions from the data, for example, that someone was harmed or tribe X can fish in location Y, may rest with the court. Lawyers and anthropologists might meaningfully work together to avoid this issue, but typically this does not happen, at least in my own experience. In fact, as the examples from testimony in human rights tribunals and inquests show, questions are commonly put to anthropologists that push the authors of the reports into the domain of the judge. Burke

(2011, 25) observes that "the scope of anthropology makes it the only discipline that can assert an overlap between expert knowledge and judge." Further, he notes the "conceptually confused legal doctrine requiring experts to somehow avoid addressing 'the ultimate issue' that is rightfully the sole prerogative of the judge."

There are other routine issues in the anthropological relationship with legal practitioners. Anthropologists/experts have to rely on the lawyers to give an accurate representation of the schedule of events – when reports are due and when hearings are scheduled, if they can. Otherwise, one can be locked in place, unable to schedule vacations, for example, which might end up during court dates. These trial dates often move around as the parties change their schedules, court room schedules are booked, and new pretrial issues arise. Many lawyers seem to believe, or find it convenient to believe, that the schedules of the experts are always fluid and malleable to their needs, although they, too, are subject to changing schedules. Generally, after engagement as an expert, it is "hurry up and wait." Ray (2011, 28) describes submitting an expert report and hearing nothing back for a couple of years. In my experience, lawyers sometimes demand responses – to opposing experts, to the court, and so on, with almost untenable timelines.

In one instance, while working in my office I was called on the phone to be sworn in and, right then, to testify over the phone in a criminal matter regarding a member of an Indigenous community with whom I work. The testimony I provided concerned whether the group was a tribe and, therefore, had rights as an Indigenous people to fish. Part of this problem is that Indigenous people often have to rely on *pro bono* lawyers who do not have enough time to fully prepare themselves and who need to earn billable hours to keep their offices open, if they are not otherwise funded.

The Nature of Language and What Is Accepted in the Field

Another important area where lawyers could usefully work together with anthropologist-experts is the nature of language (Kandel 1992b and Rosen 1977 are among those exploring this issue). Some terms have specific meaning in law (a term that has a precise and specialized meaning in law is a term of art), but a different meaning in anthropology, and yet still another to the public. An example is the phrase "time immemorial," which denotes a particular date in a given jurisdiction (for example, before signing a treaty or the time of first recorded contact) but might just mean a long time ago, or when "traditional culture" was practiced. Other examples are the terms ownership, use-rights, clan, house, kin, and commerce. The reason this is important is that an anthropologist using terminology in court with a specific legal meaning who does not specify that they are using an anthropological meaning will find they have given testimony other than what was intended.

Further, during cross-examination over a long period, perhaps a number of days, opposing counsel may drop terms with distinct legal meanings into their questions hoping that the expert will fail to pick up on what precisely is being asked. In addition, judges may not understand terms common in anthropology, such as "material culture," which take on greater meaning in trial. Lawyers might scrutinize draft opinions for potential problems in language without interfering in an expert's opinion, or appearing to. The lawyers, particularly those with specialty practices, presumably know the end users, the judges, the relevant case law in which these terms are used, and how the terms might be read. In some instances, I have experienced and appreciated this help on the language problem.

A related issue is the idea of what is "accepted in the field." Anthropology and social sciences do not easily accept the notion of agreed-on core concepts; even "culture," the key concept around which the discipline emerged in North America, is a hotly debated concept in anthropology, which some argue should be abandoned (I am not one of these). There are related but distinct questions of what approaches (theories) are accepted in a field, including anthropology, and what facts are known. In law, the idea of fact is what emerges from a contest of ideas and data and what is subsequently accepted by the court. In social sciences the route to fact or what is accepted generally in the field is entirely different. Consequently, legal facts may not be the same as anthropological facts. What is "accepted in the field" is itself a contested domain in law, with debate over reliability, relevance, methodology, and the extent of data (Haack 2008).

An example concerns testimony I gave in US federal court regarding tribal treaty shellfishing, a phase of *United States v. Washington* following the original salmon fishing case. The treaty in question, signed in 1855 between the United States and several tribes in northern Puget Sound, in what is now the state of Washington, reserved resource rights to the tribes. In time, and after a series of subsequent rulings, the US Supreme Court refused to hear an appeal and the judgment in favour of the tribes remained in force. A long-deceased chief of the tribe in question, the Upper Skagit Tribe of Indians (their formal name), had given testimony in federal court in the 1970s that there were ten historical villages of his tribe. He had not included a village near the saltwater where the shellfishing takes place because he had come from an upriver village, miles upstream, and did not feel entitled to speak about a village that other people had the right to represent. After his testimony, "ten villages" was a legal fact but not an anthropological fact. The anthropological fact was that there were eleven historical villages. I was able to give testimony to this effect in a later trial and now eleven villages is a legal fact – and an anthropological fact, at least at the time of the treaty the ancestors had signed.

Debates over the number of villages, or any set of facts, is a minor version of debates over what is accepted in the field. In legal settings, generally accepted theories, methods, and conclusions carry weight, and anthropologists may be asked about what is generally accepted. Burke (2011, 21) notes that Australian courts have used the terminology "reliable body of knowledge." On a number of occasions I have been asked on direct examination if what I had testified was accepted in the field. How this question might be answered could well be a useful conversation between counsel and expert.

In the shellfishing phase of the *United States v. Washington* case, an expert expressed in some detail a pet theory regarding an Indigenous form of food production on beaches, which was tangential to the legal issues and not yet accepted by anthropologists (in due time it was accepted and embraced). Her comments created a firestorm of shock, and a recess in the court proceedings was called. A group of lawyers from more than a dozen tribes commandeered me, and we huddled in a conference room. They asked me if this expert was attempting to disrupt the unity that the tribes had achieved to win their case in federal court. I explained that I thought she was simply unaware what she was saying might favour some tribes and disadvantage others, but more significantly she was unaware of the significance of what is accepted in the field. It would have helped if a lawyer had explained this to her. Court is not necessarily a good place to advance a new theory. I do not mean here to contradict the idea that new concepts emerge from legal struggles but rather to suggest that how they are introduced is sometimes problematic.

I have referred to the work of the most eminent anthropologists writing about oral history, for example, Cruikshank (and others); their approaches ought to be considered the standard in the discipline. My practice shifts the focus somewhat and, I think, makes a stronger claim to the standing of particular scholarship and conveys a less passive sense of the discipline.

Cruikshank and others moved the academic field of oral history forward with their emphasis on a non-rigid understanding and on contemporary use of oral histories to give guidance in addressing the issues faced in the present day and operating on multiple levels simultaneously. In this sense oral histories can operate as theatre; as connection to ancestors; as guidance, with motifs known around the world; as myth; and also as a record of the past of the community, for example. Cruikshank (1992, 2006) and others moved away from using oral histories in an academic search for facticity, that is, simply mining oral histories (or traditions) for sets of facts independent of the context. Ray (2011, 122), as I have noted, uses a literature review in an expert report to show what he calls "current knowledge" in his field. His approach may be particular to history.

Similarly, the concept of inference in a legal setting and from an anthropological perspective is the sort of issue anthropologists face. Experts are permitted to draw inferences from data if they can explain the support for this. Lawyers often ask anthropologists to draw specific inferences from established data. Here is where entanglement and difficulty can arise, because inferences might be either useful and pertinent or in the gray zone of uncertainty. Legal scholars Ranjan Agarwal, Faiz Lalani, and Lalaini Boutilier (2018, 37) commenting on a Supreme Court of Canada decision in *Latif,* note the importance of social scientists giving evidence in human rights cases in Canada to "spell out the chain of inferences they wish to draw from circumstantial evidence and explain how the expert evidence increases the strength of those inferences."

Duelling Epistemologies

Part of this problem of language, and the nature of fact and truth, lies in the use of dated anthropological models in court because they lend a sense of finality, of firm and conclusive truth, that is attractive to the law. Partiality, anthropological insights being *a* way of understanding rather than the only way, is the anthropological dilemma. Stated another way, anthropological findings may be useful or proximal and ways of understanding or providing explanation rather than facts as they are understood in law. But this is at odds with legal practices. These are problems in duelling epistemologies.

There are theoretical ways of understanding the relationship of anthropology and law. Geertz (1983, 170–71) has famously written about an overlap in forms of reasoning between lawyers and anthropologists, noting the *skeletonization* of facts in law to narrow issues to determine what rules should be applied and the *schematization* of social action so that it can be understood in cultural terms in anthropology. Skeletonization and schematization, however, are both part of the "task of seeing broad principles in parochial facts." The schematization of social action, then, corresponds to the practice in law of relying on what is generally accepted in the field of anthropology and finding principles in facts.

Kandel (1992b, 1–4) provides insight into "how lawyers and anthropologists think differently." The first of these differences is that law seeks judgments so that liability can be assigned, and anthropology practices some version of relativism and nonjudgmentalism. She notes the concreteness of law – applying rules to particular cases as opposed to the holism of anthropology and the interest in abstract models. There are differences in the meaning of fact and truth in the two disciplines. In law, she writes, truth resides in the story told by human witnesses (sometimes with the help of technology), and a fact is a finding made in the legal process.

There are, in brief, two different worlds, and one is more important than the other in legal settings. If Indigenous people's interests are to be served in the courts, lawyers and anthropologists need to understand this and each other. This issue became clear when I and others explored the workings of the British Columbia Human Rights Tribunal.

Part 2

The Tribunal

6

The British Columbia Human Rights Tribunal

IN MY ROLE AS A classroom teacher, I have directed successive classes of undergraduate students in their studies of the British Columbia Human Rights Tribunal (BCHRT) decisions regarding an array of topics. These students have wondered: How does the tribunal work for Métis people in comparison to First Nations people, or for gay and lesbian litigants? Does the size of awards assigned to winning cases favour certain categories of cases? They ask, as new categories of those who may bring cases are created, Is the tribunal more likely to find in the favour of members of these categories? What are the discernable trends? The students have uncovered surprising features of the tribunal, but their research has been limited to examining decisions. Most of the students have not been on site to observe the tribunal in action and, as is my case also, have not observed tribunal staff at work answering inquiries from the public about whether and how they might bring an action.

Curiously, it became clear to me over several years that the students were disturbed by the tribunal processes and rulings, and although they had almost uniformly been advocates of human rights and presumably of tribunals, as I have been, they had come to view the tribunal negatively. Partly through their work on a range of topics, I have come to understand features of the tribunal as it actually operates, not as it exists on paper, which worries me and has led me to believe that tribunals are more limited in their effectiveness than one might hope. (See Kahlon, n.d., for views of the tribunal held by BC citizens.)

My understanding of the BCHRT also builds on other sources. As I noted, I read all the BCHRT decisions involving Indigenous people in the period from 1997 to 2015 and sorted them by outcomes so that I could get a quantitative sense of the tribunal decisions. Anthropology student Maeve McAllister (2020) extended this examination to 2020, in an analysis based on intersectionality. I consider some of these results below and the conclusions drawn in Indigenous scholar Riley Bertoncini's study of 194 randomly drawn cases (Bertoncini 2016). Note that McAllister, Bertoncini, and Joey Weiss, discussed below, carried out their studies of the tribunal as my students at UBC. Their writing and thoughts are original to them, but the intellectual framework came from our collaborations. I give their work some emphasis because their studies are distinct and directly fit the purposes of this book.

I have talked with various personnel involved with the tribunal as the various cases proceeded and I discuss their insights. And I consider the pertinent literature about tribunals, this one in particular. I take particular note of a recent study commissioned by the BC Human Rights Tribunal about Indigenous people's experiences with the tribunal (Walkem 2020). Amber Prince, in a public talk, observed that the *Menzies* case led to action by the tribunal regarding treatment of Indigenous people and specifically led to ordering the research and report (Prince 2020). This valuable report, written by Walkem, an Indigenous lawyer and a QC (an honour noted as Queen's Counsel), relies on survey data and deploys a legal perspective. The tribunal website states:

> On January 15, 2020, the British Columbia Human Rights Tribunal released a report addressing serious access to justice concerns for Indigenous Peoples bringing human rights complaints to the Tribunal. The report, entitled *Expanding Our Vision: Cultural Equality & Indigenous Peoples' Human Rights,* makes far-reaching recommendations that could transform human rights in this province. The Human Rights Tribunal is being joined by Indigenous, legal and human rights organizations in a shared commitment to transform human rights for Indigenous Peoples in the province.
>
> Report author Ardith Walpetko We'dalx Walkem QC surveyed over 100 Indigenous People about their experiences with discrimination

and the Human Rights Tribunal. Overwhelmingly those interviewed reported pervasive levels of discrimination. Many Indigenous People had no idea that the Human Rights Tribunal existed, or how to access it. Many said that their experiences of racism as Indigenous Peoples were so widespread that they did not believe it would make any difference to file a complaint with the Human Rights Tribunal. (BCHRT n.d., para. 1–2)

The report makes nine recommendations arguing for structural changes. Most significantly, Walkem (2020) points to the problem of the tribunal as a gatekeeper and the resulting difficulties in accessing the tribunal, the limited awareness of Indigenous people of the tribunal, problems in language (and the need for plain language on the website and in the tribunal's processes), problems in obtaining legal representation, and the lack of Indigenous perspectives and personnel in the tribunal, among other issues. I have also found all these to be serious obstacles for the participation of Indigenous people.

My work here serves to support this perspective and to add another lens, which I emphasize here as a description of the hearings themselves, the role of experts, and quantitative data about Indigenous participation. My primary purpose is not simply to undertake a formal analysis of decisions rendered by a human rights tribunal, but rather to look holistically at the human experience of the tribunal. I am not attempting a legal analysis of a tribunal but rather an anthropological understanding of the way a tribunal is experienced by those people engaged in its processes. Still, the quantitative materials yield their own insights and I include them here.

Using data from and about the BC Human Rights Tribunal, I find that the tribunal process fails Indigenous people on several grounds. It is too distant from their experience, requires too much legal assistance, and places them in disadvantaged positions and power imbalances relative to others, among other issues. The tribunal experience creates fear and is traumatic in many cases. Very few cases result in decisions, only 158 over twenty-three years. But, significantly, the tribunal allows for important judgments that substantively and positively change the circumstances for Indigenous people of the province. Some cases are presumably mediated successfully in favour of the Indigenous complainant, although the details are not released.

Background to the BCHRT

Enacted in 1967, the initial *Human Rights Code* of British Columbia consolidated existing antidiscrimination laws and established a full-time administration and a commission. At this point, human rights complaints could be brought to a dedicated site. Later, from 1983 to 1997, the Code was administered by the BC Human Rights Council. With the closure of the BC Human Rights Commission, formal complaints were filed directly with the BC Human Rights Tribunal, without the intervening investigation formerly provided through the BC Human Rights Council and BC Human Rights Commission (Froome 2007, 6–7; CAUT 2002).

Human rights tribunals are a recent development in the Canadian legal system, following from the logic of the 1948 Universal Declaration of Human Rights, promulgated in the postwar United Nations. The human rights concept seems to hold considerable promise for individuals, groups of individuals, and possibly "peoples" burdened by discrimination. "Today the BC Human Rights Tribunal is an independent, quasi-judicial body created by the BC *Human Rights Code*. The tribunal is responsible for screening, accepting, mediating, and adjudicating human rights complaints and offers the parties to a complaint the opportunity to try to resolve the complaint through mediation. Respondents have an opportunity to respond to a complaint and to apply to dismiss a complaint without a hearing. If the parties do not resolve a complaint and the complaint is not dismissed, the tribunal holds a hearing." Under the Code, cases of discrimination can be brought under the following categories: publication, accommodation, service or facility, purchase of property, tenancy, employment advertisements, wages, employment, unions and associations. In each case, the discrimination may be based in the race, colour, ancestry, place of origin, religion, marital status, family status, physical or mental disability, sex, sexual orientation or age of that person or that group or class of persons (BCHRT, n.d, Personal Characteristics Protected in the BC Human Rights Code).

New legislation has changed these categories over time; for example, sexual orientation is a recent addition. Eliadis (2015, 491) writes that "the staggered sequences of rights recognition, starting with race, colour, and religion, followed by sex, disability, family and marital status, nationality, sexual orientation, and, most recently, gender identity, have been the rule in Canada and elsewhere."

The British Columbia Human Rights Tribunal annual report (BCHRT 2019, 2) provides statements concerning what the tribunal hopes to accomplish:

MANDATE

Our mandate is to further the purposes set out in section 3 of the Human Rights Code:

a) To foster a society in British Columbia in which there are no impediments to full and free participation in the economic, social, political and cultural life of British Columbia;
b) To promote a climate of understanding and mutual respect where all are equal in dignity and rights;
c) To prevent discrimination prohibited by this Code;
d) To identify and eliminate persistent patterns of inequality associated with discrimination prohibited by this Code;
e) To provide a means of redress for those persons who are discriminated against contrary to this Code. Our mission is to resolve human rights complaints through fair, effective, timely, and accessible dispute resolution services. The Tribunal's process is governed by its Rules of Practice and Procedure.

VALUE STATEMENTS

Appropriate Resolution
We will provide dispute resolution services that are proportionate and appropriate to the issues in dispute. Our services will accord to the highest standards of adjudicative integrity. Our decisions will be issued within a reasonable time frame.

Public Confidence
We will be accountable and transparent. We will be impartial and independent in our decision-making. We will enhance full and informed participation of parties in our process, whether or not they have legal representation.

Service Excellence
We will exhibit the highest standards of public service integrity and professionalism. At every stage of our process, we will be responsive,

flexible, and sensitive to the needs of the public who seek our services. We will continually innovate and improve our public service.

Access to Justice Innovation
We are committed to improving access to justice in British Columbia. We proudly endorse the Access to Justice Triple Aim. We will be leaders in administrative justice that reflects best practices across Canada."

Weiss (2007, 2) noted that human rights have been treated in distinct ways:

What the [UN] Declaration set out were, in essence, general, moral guidelines for its signatories. These are not, in and of themselves, legally binding. Later, optional covenants to the UDHR do allow for such legal structures, however, which Canada has ratified. We thus have a three-tiered system that allows human rights to be transformed into 'legal rights which can be claimed by individuals or groups who can provide evidence to show that their human rights have been violated' (Kallen 1995, 6). Our concern here is with the bottom tier, statutory Human Rights legislation, provincially specific and applicable to relationships between individuals and organizations. In order to function, this legislation must create 'a legal framework of human rights protection [that] allows those whose rights have been violated to bring forward claims for legal redress and recompense' (Ibid.) for example, The Human Rights Code and its Tribunal.

There are several preliminary points to consider regarding the data from my and McAllister's studies of decisions of the BCHRT. First, in the Canadian Human Rights Tribunal many complaints could not be brought by Indigenous people against their own bands and elected council until Section 67 of the *Canadian Human Rights Act* was repealed (Canada 2014, 5). This change occurred in 2008, which allowed complaints to be brought against the federal government, although suits against bands and council were delayed for three years so that bands and councils could prepare for such actions. However, the Canadian Human Rights Tribunal commonly recommended that those Indigenous people bringing suit against BC bands and councils also bring suit to provincial human rights tribunals so that questions of jurisdiction could be determined, in the event that the Canadian tribunal lacked jurisdiction. For this reason, a number of suits involving federal jurisdiction (over bands and tribal councils) were also introduced to the BCHRT, and preliminary decisions regarding jurisdiction were rendered there. It was a safe course of action to file in both tribunals.

For my purposes this dual filing was helpful. I was able to see the cause of the action because this was recorded in the decisions concerning jurisdiction. It is important to note that the BCHRT did not exclude cases brought against Indigenous band councils and organizations prior to 2008, as happened under the *Canadian Human Rights Act*. In addition, the British Columbia Human Rights Tribunal had a provincial human rights commission until it was abolished under the *Human Rights Code Amendment Act, 2002,* which came into force on May 31, 2003. Instead of a commission, BC instituted a "direct access" model.

Changes in procedures followed the loss of an associated Commission: "Complaints are currently filed directly with the Human Rights Tribunal[;] ... the investigation stage is eliminated. Instead, the Tribunal Rules of Practice and Procedure requires the parties to disclose relevant information to each other. However, mediation and other forms of dispute resolution remain a part of the process, and many of the same policy considerations that [once] related to the Commission process are also relevant to the new Tribunal process" (Bryden and Black 2004, 76).

The BCHRT established special programs so that institutions accepted into the program are deemed *not* to have violated the BC Human Rights Code for a set period. These institutions are then free to treat historically disadvantaged individuals or groups differently, to advance equality and eliminate discrimination. An example is an Indigenous-based program that may practice Indigenous-only hiring, or schools that seek Indigenous-only faculty for some positions. This program was shifted to the Commission as of April 1, 2020 after the commission was reestablished.

Further, the tribunal directs many cases, far more than are heard by the tribunal itself, into mediation in order to attempt to resolve issues prior to a hearing. Mediation, however, is not my major concern here, because observers cannot attend mediation, although in mediation there exists a problem of power imbalances between self-represented complainants and defendants with legal counsel. Mediators try to correct this imbalance. In addition, Bryden and Black (2004, 76–77) write the following concerning the original commission, in the period before its restoration.

It is useful to emphasize five features of the early mediation model employed by the Commission. The first salient feature was that the Commission only offered early mediation in respect of selected complaints. The Commission decided not to offer early mediation where the complaint appeared to be complex or to have a significant public interest component. Nor was early mediation offered where it appeared from the face of the complaint that this was the type of complaint that the Commission was likely to dismiss prior to investigation. This screening process ... still left a significant majority of complaints eligible for early mediation. From the sample of 494 files we reviewed, 296 (60%) were screened into the early mediation stream and 198 files (40%) were screened out and addressed in the regular case processing stream.

A note on recent case settlement is detailed in the annual report of the BCHRT (2019, 7):

> Human rights complaints may resolve for a number of reasons. First, they may not be accepted for filing. Of the 1,228 closed complaints, 31% of the complaints were closed because they were not accepted for filing.
>
> After being accepted for filing, the vast majority of complaints resolve through mediation or adjudication. Last year, of all cases closed, 47% were closed due to settlement. 8% of complaints closed after a dismissal decision without a hearing, and 3% closed after a hearing on the merits of a complaint. 11% of complaints closed because they were abandoned or withdrawn by the complainant, and for other reasons. This category includes complaints that were previously deferred for other proceedings and settled by the parties on their own.

The tribunal reported 426 preliminary decisions in that year (BCHRT 2019, 9). Further, the tribunal reported that the parties were able to resolve their dispute in 74 percent of cases in which the tribunal provided assistance. In addition, "the Tribunal issued 23 decisions after a hearing on the merits last year. The complaint was found to be justified in 8 (35 percent) of those cases" (BCHRT 2019, 10). This indicates that very few decisions are made following a hearing for all causes. Bear in mind that these figures do not account for the very many initial inquiries made to the tribunal that are abandoned before an effort to submit a complaint is made.

Generally, it was not difficult to determine which BC filings I examined involved Indigenous people. Often the cause of the action was discrimination on the basis of race, ancestry, or colour. Sometimes, though, I had to read the body of the decision to find clues as to whether an Indigenous person was involved. Frequently I had hints: names that are common to Indigenous people of BC, or the institution the action was brought against. Friendship Centres are obvious First Nations–linked institutions, as are band businesses and governments.

I include cases brought by Indigenous people based on discrimination against them as Indigenous people and cases when this was not the issue. And, generally, suits against Indigenous institutions brought by Indigenous people were not brought on the grounds of race, colour, or ancestry, although in some cases they were. Further, I use the term Métis, which is somewhat problematic. There is no way of knowing how the self-identifying complainants themselves use the term, but it is probably used to mean both those with mixed Indigenous and non-Indigenous heritage and those who are descended from specific historic Métis communities that arose in the nineteenth century, in Canada.

Quantitative Analysis

I start with a quantitative analysis of the cases for which decisions have been rendered between 1997 and 2015. These are not all final decisions, and, in fact, most are preliminary decisions made within the body of the hearings. These preliminary decisions concern such matters as whether the tribunal has jurisdiction to hear the case, whether particular evidence can be entered, and, importantly, whether a case filed late will be heard because it is in the public interest to do so. That latter category is especially important for Indigenous people with complaints of discrimination because the time limit to file a case was originally only six months, and a significant number of Indigenous cases have been filed late. The time limit has since been changed to one year.

In all, over the eighteen-year period, a total of 125 decisions were published regarding distinct cases brought by 137 Indigenous people (there are cases in which more than one decision, preliminary or final, was rendered. I have not counted these twice). Of these complainants, 15 were people who

TABLE 1
Areas of discrimination under which cases were brought

Employment	63
Service	48
Accommodation	10
Union membership	1
Criminal record	1
Political beliefs	1

TABLE 2
Personal characteristics of complainant bringing suit on the basis of

Race	82	Family	12
Ancestry	65	Marital status	6
Colour	44	Religion	4
Mental disability	22	Age	4
Physical disability	21	Sexual orientation	2
Place of origin	20	Retaliation (for filing)	1
Sex	17		

self-identified as Métis and 122, First Nations people. In some instances, but not most, complainants mentioned their membership in a specific First Nation. Sixty-three percent of cases were brought by women and thirty-seven percent by men. In one instance, a case was brought by a self-identified two-spirit Indigenous person.

The tribunal requires that cases be brought within specified categories of cause (note that cases are commonly filed under more than one category) by complainants with particular characteristics, and here I provide a breakdown of the data concerning both of these.

Further, Indigenous people brought seventeen cases against Indigenous institutions of various sorts, and non-Indigenous people, primarily women, brought thirty-five suits against Indigenous institutions.

Temporal Patterns

It is difficult to establish patterns of use over time because of significant underlying changes such as the shift in the *Canadian Human Rights Act*, mentioned in Chapter 6. Generally, there were very few decisions rendered regarding Indigenous people and otherwise in the early years of the BC Tribunal. In 1997, for example, there was one decision concerning an Indigenous case.

TABLE 3 Number of decisions regarding Indigenous cases by year

1997	1	2002	2	2007	11	2012	10
1998	2	2003	6	2008	13	2013	7
1999	1	2004	11	2009	13	2014	7
2000	1	2005	12	2010	13	2015 (January)	0
2001	0	2006	9	2011	8		

Table 3 shows that the number of decisions gradually increased starting in 2003, reaching a peak of thirteen in the years 2008–10 and then declining. This decline probably reflects the changed federal rules allowing suits against Indigenous band councils, which came into effect in 2011. Note that prior to this change, some actions of First Nations governments were subject to the *Canadian Human Rights Act,* and some forty cases were brought each year against these governments by the Canadian Human Rights Tribunal. These complaints concerned decisions of band councils and administrators concerning human resources, such as hiring and dismissal, and decisions of band councils and administrators relating to infrastructure, such as accommodating persons with disabilities (Canada 2011, 10).

These data reveal that there are few cases brought by Indigenous people that culminate in actual final decisions. There are few final decisions of any sort. And of the decisions, many go against the person(s) who brought the action. On this basis, one might conclude that tribunals and commissions are of limited value to Indigenous people. It is unknown how many cases are initiated by Indigenous people to the BCHRT, although I sought to access this information from the chair of the tribunal.

The Critique of Human Rights

There are other ways to understand the data regarding the number of decisions. First, law and society scholarship (for example, Ewick and Silbey 1998; Engel, 2012) makes clear that a major reason many complainants enter into legal or quasi-legal proceedings is to have a venue to articulate their concerns, even when their concerns do not meet the criteria for evidence. The chance to speak one's concerns out loud is an important function of a legal system. Some Indigenous people, including two in whose cases I testified, approach the experience this way. Human rights are conceptually broad categories, perhaps even more than law itself, and can be drawn on rhetorically to mean far more than what might be legally actionable. Menzies' deployment of human rights as a category beyond the limited meanings provided in the provincial human rights legislation was a rare case of speaking back to colonialism, which the tribunal member did not stop or thin out. But ordinarily, in the other cases, thinning of the complainant's issues, as I will show in *McCue* and other cases, is the more usual outcome.

Bryden and Black (2004, 96), in their study of the BCHR Commission in an earlier period, noted something significant regarding mediation:

Many of the arguments against mandatory human rights mediation are based on the premise that the Human Rights Code sets out rights that are fundamental. Critics of mandatory mediation argue that fundamental rights should not be subject to compromise. A complainant or a respondent may be more interested in vindicating a particular human rights principle than in particular settlement terms.

Further, Bryden and Black (2004, 101) found a relatively low rate of successfully mediated cases in the category "race / colour / place of origin / ancestry cases," albeit only twenty-six cases with thirteen settlements.

It remains unclear if human rights tribunals are created in a way that allows them to meet the goals they espouse. For anthropologists, there is a need to create a framework for study that "can apprehend the ways that human rights are simultaneously enabling and constraining" (Wilson 2006, 78). The notion of human rights itself, at all levels (international, national, provincial; economic or social), has been criticized as existing solely within a Western, Eurocentric frame of reference. Human rights commissions and tribunals have been said to be unable to remedy problems facing non-Western communities, especially those organized collectively or whose members hold views of the world outside of the highly individualistic and materialistic premises of modernity. Million (2013, 4) notes that "human rights law appears to empower self-determination claims and then act as a buffer between any Indigenous peoples' ontological will to be and any nation-state's self-determined right to uncompromisingly thwart that will." Relatedly, one line of critique of the Waitangi Tribunal of New Zealand is that it cannot escape the logic of neoliberalism, despite the use of Maori spaces and Indigenous identities in the proceedings. New Zealand legal scholar Fiona McCormack (2016, 231) writes that the tribunal process is directed to affirm human rights abuse rather than deeper social structures that produce transgression.

For Jensen (2019, 202), however, "Human rights history has been providing some of the strongest empirical evidence to underpin the notion of universality and to counter the idea of human rights as a Western project." He holds that colonization was such a transformative historical process – the largest transfer of sovereign power in world history – and impacted the world at so many levels that "I do not see what defined human rights as having a clear place of origin or a home or care-of address. Rather, human rights emerged as part of intersections and interactions linked to other and quite diverse historical processes."

A counter to Jensen (2019) is that because human rights are framed within the system of states, members of societies not included among the states admitted to the United Nations are thought to be inherently disadvantaged. This includes the Indigenous people of North America and elsewhere. Canadian scholar social work scholar Delores Mullings (2009, i), for example, puts it bluntly: "Some [visible minorities] who have filed a claim [in the Canadian Human Rights Tribunal] feel that the institutions that were created to protect them have instead perpetuated discrimination." She argues that racism is reproduced at the tribunal level; further,

> the perspective of the Tribunal adjudicators, which deeply influences how they hear and respond to complaint cases, allows them to ignore everyday racism in the workplace, normalize racist action and policies, and blame the complainants for their experiences. I conclude that until the way in which these cases are heard changes, including the standard for accepting evidence, visible minorities will continue to be re-victimized" (Mullings 2009, ii).

The Walkem (2020) report confirms these findings regarding the BCHRT. My own ethnographic studies of the BCHRT provide examples of the ways in which the tribunal can reproduce racializing behavior.

Complaints and critiques about Canadian human rights tribunals come from non-academic sources as well. In 2015, senior Aboriginal leadership organizations led by then-National Chief Shawn Atleo, for example, lodged a complaint against the Canadian Human Rights Tribunal (albeit joined by the Canadian HR Commission):

> The Assembly of First Nations, First Nations Child and Family Caring Society of Canada, and the Canadian Human Rights Commission forced a three-day judicial review in federal court Feb. 13 to Feb. 15 to argue against a decision by Canadian Human Rights Tribunal Chair Shirish Chotalia. In 2011, Chotalia dismissed a claim that accused the federal government of discriminating against on-reserve people by underfunding child welfare services. Core to the argument was a comparison with the provincial funding provided for those same services

offered to the off-reserve population. The federal government argued that the comparison could not be made because the services were delivered by two different levels of government and to different clientele. Chotalia agreed. First Nations were appalled that the tribunal review of the matter was scuttled by what amounted to a technicality. (Narine 2012, 10)

Further, the Native Women's Association of Canada (2011, 73) pointed to problems of tribunals: "Legal systems and dispute resolution processes that presume their own neutrality despite the exclusion and silencing of indigenous values and perspectives constitute a continuation of the colonization process."

Bertoncini (2016, 3), a Métis scholar, raises another sort of question:

How can human rights be ever changing [in the enabling legislation] and at the same time fundamental? If they are fundamental how can we parse them from the stereotypes of any time and see past our own tendencies to discriminate? If they reflect the contradictions of any one time and some of these contradictions come from widely held stereotypes might they be behind as it takes time for codes and even cases to be passed and heard?

He adds that if stereotypes are thought to be characteristics of groups, why do human rights cases in British Columbia based on discrimination through these stereotypes primarily involve individuals?

Human rights tribunals seem to be simultaneously and, perhaps, paradoxically both largely invisible and irrelevant to the public at large and the object of occasional scorn for tribunals' apparently outlandish rulings in favour of people perceived as undeserving complainants. Misguided newspapers and journals regularly feature columns about the purported absurdity of litigation, the lack of common sense of the tribunal, the reliance on political correctness, and the triviality of cases brought. Here is one example of a headline: "Guilty of Sexual Thought: A Case against a BC Professor Sparks Demands to Trash the Human Rights Industry" (O'Neill 1999, 24). And a second (Yirish 1997, 18): "A Modern-Day Star Chamber [Procedural Irregularities in Human Rights Cases in BC]" that claimed

B.C. human-rights laws allow for none of the standard legal defences. Neither the truth of the statement in question, nor the absence of any demonstrable intent on the part of the speaker to promote hatred, can lead to a human-rights complaint being dismissed. The plight of defendants is further complicated by the B.C. Human Rights Tribunal's ability to set its own procedures.

Another publication (De Cloet 1998, 16) complained about the "lesbian activist" building her own empire at the commission, accompanied by the worry, "If Mary-Woo Sims has her way, religious schools in B.C. may soon be prevented from firing a male teacher who shows up for work in a dress and high heels."

Following my participation as an anthropological expert in the BCHRT in the *Radek* case, I received emails and phone calls from several Indigenous women hoping that they could follow in the footsteps of Gladys Radek and receive a favourable judgment by the tribunal. They believed that I could facilitate this. They were unclear about the process, and I explained the grounds on which a suit could be brought to the tribunal, noting that they needed, at this point, legal rather than anthropological advice to put together a case – including, potentially, finding witnesses and legal counsel, writing their brief to the court, and so forth.

None of these women who consulted me made it to the point where a ruling was rendered. My sense is that they found the process, so technical and legalistic from the viewpoint of a layperson, frustrating and disappointing. They had hoped, they said, to tell their own stories of racial discrimination, harassment, and mistreatment. These communications, to me, suggest that some Indigenous people are aware of the possibility of bringing a human rights complaint, but how this works has not clearly filtered down to the public, including Indigenous people. The Walkem (2020) survey noted the lack of visibility of the tribunal for Indigenous people of BC.

Nevertheless, there is simultaneously a problem of volume – the BC Human Rights tribunal receives twenty-four thousand phone calls per year, and tribunal personnel cannot give information on the complaint process over the telephone (Bernd Walter, Tribunal Chair, personal communication, February 17, 2015). The annual report for 2017–18 noted an astonishing 537,000 visits to the website (BCHRT 2018, 4). The annual report (BCHRT 2019, 4) for 2018–19 noted a new process to address the volume of complaints.

> Complaints are filed directly with the Tribunal which is responsible for all steps in the human rights process. The Tribunal received a total of 1,736 new complaints during the past year. Of those, 1,445 new complaints were accepted for filing, and 291 complaints were in the screening process at year end. Screening ensures complaints are within the Tribunal's jurisdiction, are timely, and set out a contravention of the Code. Three years ago, we implemented a new screening process to improve the quality, consistency, and timeliness of screening decisions. Our screening process now involves review by a team consisting of the Registrar, screening manager, Chair, and when necessary, legal counsel. Prior to this, there was no centralized process for screening human rights complaints. This past year, the Tribunal accepted 78% of complaints for filing.

The reinstated British Columbia Human Rights Commission has among its duties public education about the tribunal. Perhaps this will increase the visibility and public comprehension of the function of the tribunal.

Yet from another perspective, human rights and Indigenous rights are indivisible and are essential in a world still built on racist values and practices and colonial frameworks. Canadian political scientist Joyce Green (2014) and contributors, in fact, argue that the path from colonialism to reconciliation goes through Indigenous human rights. One scholar even writes that US treaty rights might be appropriately protected in human rights tribunals (Venetis 2013–14). Another scholar argues for an "anti-stereotype approach for the European Court of Human Rights, noting that stereotypes are both cause and manifestation of the structural disadvantage and discrimination of certain groups of people" (Timmer 2011, 707). This anti-stereotype approach would ostensibly mitigate the problem of everyday racism in the tribunal itself noted by Mullings. Timmer (2011, 737) takes note of a problem, however: "A likely objection will be that an anti-stereotyping approach is incompatible with the valid desire of the Court not to lose legitimacy by appearing 'activistic.' The Court, so the argument runs, cannot afford to be too far ahead of its time." Although Canadian law prohibits stereotyping, the public may be behind the pace of legal developments. This reasoning may be the cause of the bad press the tribunal suffers. At least on some occasions, the various human rights tribunals are clearly ahead of the public. To foster a society free of discrimination is one of the stated goals, however, so the tribunal must lead.

Perhaps the most significant recent development regarding Indigenous human rights was the activity of the Commission on Human Rights at the United Nations and the push for "Advancing the Human Rights of Indigenous Peoples," in the form of the United Nations Declaration on the Rights of Indigenous Peoples or UNDRIP (United Nations Commission on Human Rights 2005). The *Declaration on the Rights of Indigenous Peoples Act* was passed into law in British Columbia in 2019, with details of implementation to follow. In Canada, the federal government pushed human rights as a way forward in addressing differences in the lives of Aboriginal peoples and others. The *Report on Equality Rights of Aboriginal People* (Canadian Human Rights Commission 2013b, 4) made clear the gaps in the categories that overlap with those included in human rights legislation: "The *Report on Equality Rights of Aboriginal People* presents a national portrait of Aboriginal peoples compared to non-Aboriginal peoples based on the seven dimensions of well-being widely considered critical from an equality rights perspective. The seven dimensions of well-being are economic well-being, education, employment, health, housing, justice and safety, and political and social inclusion."

Many around the world clearly believe that human rights tribunals offer hope, as suggested by the increase in the number of cases brought to the attention of tribunals and commissions operating at many levels. The European Court of Human Rights, for example, received nearly 64,500 petitions a year by 2011, up from some 10,000 applications in 2000 (Hillebrecht 2014, 1101). International tribunals are thought to provide an "external stimulus for reform, convincing skeptics to buy into reform and promote the commitment of the state to human rights. Further, the rulings themselves are thought to legitimize reforms" (Hillebrecht 2014).

Ashwani Peetush, a professor at Wilfred Laurier University in Canada and an expert in human rights, takes note of the contradictory nature of human rights discourse as it relates to Indigenous people worldwide. He observes that the discourse helps Indigenous people articulate claims for cultural recognition in their struggle for self-rule. My work with Indigenous people who have brought cases forward certainly confirms this perspective. However, Peetush (2009, 190) notes that human rights bring along with them "powerful theoretical underpinnings, assumptions, and institutions that are at odds with and that undermine what most Native communities in Canada take to be an essential component of their cultural identities and self-understandings." He describes human rights concepts as "biased towards Western liberal ideals" which are not universal, even when they are described as such. Further, the dialogue must be recast within Indigenous perspectives for it to be fruitful (190).

Further, Peetush (2009, 192) describes imperialism as acting most forcefully in the "colonization of the realm of ideas or consciousness as opposed to physical space. It consists in the uncritical and illegitimate universalization of a narrow and specific perspective of human experience to all of humankind." Diversity, he writes, lacks legitimacy. The struggle for self-rule, an important part of decolonization, is a struggle for difference. The "Native challenge to human rights involves just this: It is about having the power to articulate, balance, and specify cross-cultural and universal human values within the structures of native self-understandings" (193). I disagree with Peetush to the extent that he understates the use of spatial segregation in the construction of colonial regimes, yet he touches on an important perspective (see Mawani 2009 concerning the use of segregation of Indigenous people in Canada).

Part of this problem is that individual rights discourse is built on human rights so that, to Peetush (2009, 194), rights can act as a "social, political, and economic Western Trojan horse ..." The state acts as a referee between individuals with differing interests and is neutral regarding questions of religion and morality. But aside from limited purposes, such as policing, fixing roads, and so on, the state relies on individual action. This, one can suppose, opposes the collectivist orientation that underpins Indigenous life (see Christie 2003). Further, the idea of human rights seems to exclude the nonhuman entities (everything from animated trees and rocks to anthropomorphic spirit beings) that are part of Indigenous cosmology.

There are objections to making these distinctions between Western and Indigenous thought, and Peetush (2009, 197) notes that Aboriginal people themselves often use the discourse of human rights (see also Isa 2014). This may not be because they wish to travel the road to becoming westernized and liberal but, rather, because they have no other possibility for bringing their issues and complaints forward. Further, Peetush (2009, 199) notes that the adoption of human rights principles "brings along with it such liberal ideals as axiomatic," such as land is private property and private property is a basic human right. Second, secularism is closely bound to liberalism, and religion is sometimes seen as irrational and primitive. Meanwhile, First Nations foreground their spiritual views, in part to draw distinctions with the mainstream society (for example, see legal scholar Borrows 2002). However, Peetush (2009, 201) notes that Aboriginal groups have specific laws and ethical codes that constrain political power yet are based on spiritual teachings.

Finally, Peetush (2009, 201) takes note of the critique that accommodating and recognizing cultural difference and diversity leads to disunity and disintegration. With self-government, as this logic would have it, Indigenous people no longer affirm a common identity with the rest of Canada. And while it is true that this discourse arises (see Audra Simpson's, 2014 book *Mohawk Interruptus*, for example), it conflates unity and uniformity, and disunity and cultural diversity. He notes that it is the attempts to impose uniformity that create disunity, rather than the emphasis on distinction.

Here, Green (2014) and contributors overlap with Peetush (2009) regarding accommodation and cultural difference. But can the BC Human Rights Tribunal move in the direction of reconciliation, and is it an obstacle to the aspirations of Indigenous people if it cannot?

Others have taken up their own analyses of tribunals in Canada, and British Columbia in particular, pointing to specific issues and problems. Canadian legal scholar Rosanna Langer (2007) provides a discussion of similar difficulties faced by Canadians entering the tribunal generally and, in particular, of the gap between the real and the ideal, that is, the public understandings of discrimination and the actual administration of human rights bodies. Eliadis (2014), too, points to the high expectations and frustrations associated with human rights institutions. Clément (2009, 43–58, and see 2009, 2012, 2014) notes that the human rights movement in Canada cannot be assumed to be progressive.

Eliadis (2015, 492) comments on Clément's work to report, "What lies in-between are the precipitous and recurrent rise and fall of human rights law in BC, displaying a volatility unique in Canada. Repeated and politicized efforts to pare back human rights protections and institutions and then subsequently reinstate them are what most distinguish BC from other jurisdictions. This has occurred with little regard for the Supreme Court of Canada's landmark decision in *Heerspink,* a BC case that found that human rights legislation is not to be treated as another ordinary law of general application" but rather as a "fundamental law" (Ibid.).

Further, Howe and Johnson (2000) note the expanding human rights consciousness in Canada. The expanding caseload, together with fewer resources, has made it difficult to deliver human rights, and criticism has followed. These authors, in their otherwise comprehensive work, do not address the key concerns of Indigenous critics that Indigenous thought cannot be accommodated. Shelagh Day, Lucie Lamarche, and Ken Norman, (2014, 11), however, gained a foothold in addressing the issues I raise here, writing that the situation in BC is "dramatic" and that the public feels the loss of the commission in 2002. Day, Lamarche, and Norman note that "governments have concluded that Canada's statutory human rights system should have little, if any, applicability to large, persistent patterns of inequality that Aboriginal peoples ... experience" (35). They argue that "Aboriginal women and girls have effectively been abandoned ... by public institutions" (47).

A more anthropological interpretation emphasizes that treating state-derived concepts as universal has the effect of naturalizing the underlying assumptions and practices while suppressing and perhaps making unthinkable alternative forms that they helped undermine (Nadasdy 2017, 9). State-derived concepts, including human rights, and state-derived practices need not be regarded as the only possibilities. A human rights tribunal, by this logic, forces Indigenous people into the courts of the colonial.

In sum, critiques cluster around the purported inability of human rights codes and tribunals to escape their origin from state-centred, Western, individualistic, universalizing, and neoliberal discourses. Tribunals, according to these perspectives, perpetuate everyday racism and discrimination and remain incompletely aware of the biases of the members. Tribunals falsely presume neutrality and serve as a Trojan Horse for non-Indigenous values. Further, tribunals suffer from the high volume of complaints, inadequate funding for low-income complainants, poor public visibility, and popular notions of the foolishness of the human rights approach. For some, human rights is inherently adverse to Indigenous values and cultures. Others, however, suggest that tribunals are contradictory and provide a vehicle for reconciliation and a way to articulate Indigenous values. These critiques concern human rights and their tribunals at a variety of levels – from international agreements to state and provincial codes. Next, I look at the BCHRT in particular.

On the Ground Issues

Difficulties in the Process for Potential Complainants

Lawyers who have worked for the BCHRT as members, or who represent clients, note several distinct issues from their perspectives. During my work regarding the tribunal, I spoke with Tim Timberg, a lawyer I worked with during the *Radek* case, Bernd Walter, the former chair of the tribunal, Lindsay Lyster, the tribunal member who heard the *Radek* case, and Amber Prince, the Indigenous lawyer who hired me for the *Menzies* case. Here I summarize some of their comments and my own observations. Evidence that might be transmitted orally is lost in the process of writing out the case. This act is an important moment in the transformation of a case from the issues troubling an Indigenous person into the legal categories acceptable to the tribunal but no longer recognizable by the litigant. Anthropologists Ewick and Silbey (1998) describe this significant process of cases moving through multiple lenses in the various phases of framing the case for trial, finally becoming transformed beyond meaning to the complainant.

Further, tribunal members have oddities of powers that are assigned by statute and are less than the broader powers of ordinary courts. The members are limited in their ability to control disrespectful counsel and maintain order in the courtroom, for example, when counsel refuses to sit at the table and makes horrible allegations about clients. All of this has the effect of intimidating those who bring suit and are heard by the tribunal. In my own experience, in the *Radek* case, Gladys Radek suffered through weeks of demeaning commentary from lawyers for the respondents, which affected both her and her child. While the tribunal does not have contempt power it does have "costs power," which can be applied in instances such as lying under oath, improper accusations, and abusive language.

An equally significant, but less obvious issue, for Indigenous people is that it is hard to talk about discrimination, and few topics are so personal and linked to the core of one's identity. Racial oppression affects one's being, but in the tribunal process it only has to be *a* factor, not the only factor, which might alleviate the stress experienced in bringing a case. A very significant issue is how to turn experiences of racial discrimination into evidence. Those people who prepare their own application to the tribunal struggle with their emotions and often make emotionally driven applications that either are not accepted by the tribunal or contain within them a weakness and are easy to undermine by the respondent's lawyers. Giving testimony, or the fear of giving testimony, can trigger post-traumatic stress syndrome, an issue that almost led one complainant to drop her case, for which I served as expert. As I noted regarding *Radek,* parts of the process are aimed at undermining the credibility of an Indigenous person or persons who have brought an action, which disempowers those who hoped the tribunal would be a place they could tell their own story.

The Prospect of Significant Decisions, BC

Another way of viewing the data regarding the limited number of decisions rendered and the difficulties of the process is to emphasize the cases that radiated past the tribunal itself, bringing significant decisions and helping to establish or affirm legal rights of Indigenous people. Even though there are few of these sorts of cases, all of them pushed the case law forward. The *Radek* decision is an example. It was heralded in the media and has come to be referenced in Canadian senior courts beyond the human rights tribunals. Testimony in *Radek* was relied on in other tribunal decisions and by the BC Supreme Court in a 2015 ruling regarding how to understand discrimination in *Pivot v. Downtown Ambassadors,* in which the BC Supreme Court chided the BCHRT for insensitivity regarding discrimination against Aboriginal peoples (a ruling, however, that was overturned in the BC Court of Appeals).

The *Radek* case was described succinctly by the *Georgia Straight,* a popular, then widely distributed Vancouver journal:

> In 2005, Radek won a major victory before the B.C. Human Rights Tribunal. The decision came down four years after she and a friend were harassed by security guards at downtown Vancouver's International Village, also known as Tinseltown, in 2001. She also complained in the suit that this incident was part of the systematic discrimination against aboriginal and disabled people resulting from the practices and policies of the mall and the guards it employed. The tribunal awarded Radek $15,000, at that time the highest-ever payment for damages in a case involving race and disability. (Pablo 2009)

I believe that Gladys Radek, based on my own days with her during and after her hearing, underwent a transformation going through the process and became a significant national Indigenous leader. The ways in which the human rights process transforms individual Indigenous persons is an important issue not reflected in the numbers, nor referenced by Walkem (2020) in her report. In a November 29, 2010, CBC News Website, Radek described her experience: "The first time I used my voice was proving systemic racism through a human rights tribunal in 2005. This case was based on witnessing abuse toward aboriginal, poor and disabled people at Tinseltown Mall in Vancouver. It took four years to win this precedent-setting case." Radek has created a significant profile in the Indigenous world since this case, in part because of the case but perhaps more so because of her central role in the national controversy over missing and murdered women. Radek was a central leader in the widely publicized march to draw attention to the issue and became one of ten CBC nominees for the national "Champion of Change" (see Milward 2012; Chartrand 2014).

Weiss (2007, 4) observes:

> There are, I suspect ... a number of reasons why Gladys Radek was able to arrive at this profoundly affirming result despite the inherently alienating qualities of the BCHRT. One, which should not be underestimated, is Ms. Radek's own considerable strength of character and dedication. Another, which she emphasized over and over again to me, was the trust and belief that her lawyer, Tim Timberg, placed in her: "He [Timberg] believed in me, and made me feel it was worth it to go the distance" (Gladys Radek: personal communication, February 12th, 2007). Ms. Radek also saw herself as fighting for her whole community as well as for herself, symbolically appointing herself as "an advocate for all people" (Gladys Radek: personal communication, February 12th, 2007) and drawing resolve from that.
>
> The most important consideration here, however, is also perhaps the most obvious one. Gladys Radek's experiences with the Tribunal were ultimately positive because she was successful ... She and her legal team successfully mobilized the schematized language of the Human Rights Tribunal ... Had Ms. Radek not had the support of excellent and understanding legal counsel, or had she not been successful in her case, I do not know how her experience with the Human Rights Tribunal would have been.

Fromme (2007) points out other implications of *Radek*:

The successful resolution of this complaint has led to the Coalition's development of training tools and materials for security personnel, based on provincial human rights legislation. This training will also be integrated into the core curriculum of the Justice Institute of British Columbia and its approved training schools, and to the development of a training package for the security industry's in-house trainers. (BC Human Rights Coalition, September 2006, and BC Human Rights Coalition, October 2006)

Clara Menzies, the complainant in another case I describe, was disturbed by the prospect of giving testimony, but when the occasion arose did so with very considerable power. (I use a pseudonym for the name of the complainant and obscure the name of the case for privacy reasons.) I believe that she found it important to provide her critique of Canadian society, the police, and the nature of racism. I believe this, in part, because during the hearing she assertively interrupted the tribunal member several times and spoke forcefully, and directly, to her own concerns, pointing to a larger context into which her experience should be placed. Hers was a dramatic display of what is sometimes called speaking truth to power. Her responses were so forceful, in fact, that I feared the tribunal member would find her testimony disruptive and lacking credibility (note, I did not believe that she lacked credibility). The member found quite the opposite, in fact.

Equity in Judgments

An unpublished quantitative study (Bertoncini 2016) addresses an altogether different set of issues regarding the BCHRT, namely equity in decisions and compensation. The tribunal publishes annual data on the numbers of complaints, on both grounds and areas of discrimination, on the number of cases that enter into judicial review, and on other information, but the tribunal does not present the data Bertoncini developed. Using the BCHRT search engine, Bertoncini randomly sampled 194 decisions of the BCHRT from 1997 to 2016 "for the grounds of discrimination brought up in them as well as the success they had, i.e., whether they were dismissed, were given a non-monetary compensation (usually an order to stop contravening the code), or were given a monetary compensation." He computed the average compensation and success rate for each of the grounds of discrimination and rank ordered the results. He differentiated by sex and gender and accounted for claims based on multiple grounds. Bertoncini (2016, 6–7) found,

Large inconsistencies ... when looking at average compensation and average percent [of success]. While sex[uality], ancestry, disability, religion, age, marriage, and sex garnered low compensation and had little success, gender and sex both had high compensation and success over half the time [Bertoncini distinguishes sexuality and sex in this analysis].

Table 1 Analyses of cases based on ground of discrimination, compensation, and success (*n*=194)

Ground for discrimination	Average compensation ($)	Success percentage (%)
Sexuality	838	10.5
Race/ancestry/place of origin/colour	340	12.0
Disability (physical and mental)	980	12.0
Religion	1,550	8.0
Age	847	8.0
Marriage status/family status	453	12.0
Sex	5,540	58.3
Gender	5,359	61.5
Sex + gender	5,446	60.0

Table 2 Breakdown of gender cases by type of complainant

	Successful	Unsuccessful
Women	11	6
Men	0	3
Trans women	4	0
Trans men	1	0

Table 3 Breakdown of gender cases by ground for complaint

	Successful	Unsuccessful
Pregnancy	1	1
Sexual harassment	5	1
Sex	5	7
Trans	5	0

In the closer analyses of the gender/sex grounds men were found to never win. Teeple explains how women have been historically very disadvantaged even within human rights (2005, 48–59). This is not found in the data. Here ... [the] absence of any men earning compensation and women being successful 11 times out of 17 shows that ... women were more successful than men in the BCHRT. (Bertoncini, 2016 11)

Bertoncini (2016, 12–13) writes further,

Looking at the analyses based on types of genders under the sex/gender ground we find that 100% of trans cases are successful ... On July 28, 2016, the tribunal added gender identity or expression to their code. While the trans cases ... did not explicitly state gender identity as their grounds of discrimination ... this recent change has given way to more trans cases. What is startling is the success these cases have had ...

Here we see human rights in the BCHRT responding and evolving to social awareness of a new type of discrimination. [Note that continued innovation is one of the tribunal value statements.] The success of these cases, while heartening in its' [*sic*] connection to the prevalence of transphobia, is also disquieting in its' [*sic*] disproportionate relationship to other grounds of discrimination. This can be explained either, like the results of women's cases versus men, by a response by the tribunal to prevailing social injustices or, more problematically, as a reaction to mainstream beliefs and values. Either way it is against some of the founding aspects of human rights as well as more ideal and practical theory regarding human rights and their implementation.

Bertoncini (2016, 14–15) concludes:

Human rights seem still to be based on group identities often brought up in comparison with stereotypes but claim and use language aimed at individual rights.

Table 4 Rank order by average success

1 Sex/gender
2 Race/ancestry/place of origin/colour, disability (mental and physical), marriage status/family status
3 Sexuality
4 Religion, age

Table 5 Rank order by average compensation most to least

1 Gender/sex
2 Religion
3 Disability (mental and physical)
4 Age
5 Sexuality
6 Marriage status/family status
7 Race/ancestry/place of origin/colour

These critiques of the concept and practice of human rights in many jurisdictions and of data specific to the BCHRT raise questions about the viability of the BCHRT as a legal instrument to fulfill its mandate and practice its values in regard to Indigenous people. The questions about the tribunal can be answered, in part, by an ethnographic approach of observing and participating in the processes themselves.

7

McCue v. University of British Columbia

IN PROVIDING COMMENTARY on what transpired in the tribunal I make observations of various people, including the complainants, based on my interactions with them and on listening to their words, their tone, and the volume of their voice, and on observing performative aspects – their expressions and body language in the tribunal – which I describe in detail in some instances. My observations here are based on field notes I recorded in pen, in notebooks, during the *McCue* hearings. I wrote subjective statements in the notebooks about my sense of the proceedings, and I wrote some brief objective descriptions of the material environment and data such as the day, time, who was speaking, and so on. These are separated from the recording of dialogue by their placement in the margins. This chapter, and Chapter 8, which concerns the *Menzies* hearing, are narratives in which I include the content of my field notes, transcripts of dialogue, and interpretation and analysis of the hearings both in regard to the specific hearing processes and the larger issues about the nature of the tribunal. The field notes contain descriptions of the physical setting and the ways in which it may affect the hearing processes.

In part, I hope to convey a sense of the events in real time as they unfolded, evoking words, sights, time, and even smells. For this reason, I use the present tense in these passages. In order not to interrupt the dialogue I have placed most of the commentary at the end of the chapter.

Several of the cases described in previous chapters re-emerge here and in Chapter 8, as do several issues, in particular the problem of the unexpected twists and turns, the issues of qualification of experts, the efforts at thinning my own testimony through *voir dire* and other processes, and the issue of who controls anthropological field notes. In addition, the stereotypes, demeaning language, and other forms of diminution I described earlier are present in these chapters. Note that the *Radek* case before the BCHRT was considered in Chapter 3.

But first, I introduce briefly the facts of the case.

The *McCue* Case

June McCue, formerly head of the First Nations law program in the Peter A. Allard School of Law at the University of British Columbia, brought a case against UBC following her denial of tenure and promotion. An important issue is that she was self-represented, and although she was a professor in the law faculty, she was not a courtroom lawyer. This was a problem for her, as I detail below, and self-representation can be a barrier for people attempting to bring their suit successfully. The several weeks of hearings and the preparations required would incur significant legal fees if one were to hire a lawyer. The BCHRT (2019, 10) annual report for 2019–20 notes a correlation between having a legal representative for the complainant (but bearing in mind that the sample size is too small for firm conclusions) and the complainant's success in the case. But this had not been the case in the reporting year, when fifteen of twenty-eight of complainants (54 percent) had lawyers. In the two preceding years the numbers were 32 percent and 29 percent. The respondents, on the other hand, had lawyers in 77 percent of cases in the reporting year and in 74 percent and 90 percent of cases in preceding years. But one case is not a statistic, and in the McCue case her lack of a legal representative to do the cross-examination and later to help write a summation with case citations was highly significant. McCue, however, developed her own legal strategy for her case.

The case was initially brought into the tribunal on the grounds of employment discrimination based on race, colour, ancestry, place of origin, marital status, family status, and sex. Marital status and family status were later excluded. In brief, Lorna June McCue argued not that the tenure system is discriminatory but rather that she met the terms in an Indigenous manner, particularly involving the idea that oral presentations and community work constitute scholarly work. Prior to the hearing, which I partially describe here, a preliminary hearing resulted in a decision of January 15, 2016. Paragraph 3 notes that "Ms. McCue closed her case on June 24, 2015. The evidence of Ms. McCue, Dr. Frances Henry, Dr. Marie Battiste, and Dr. Jo-Ann Archibald was received" (*McCue v. UBC* (No. 3), 2016 BCHRT 9).

I asked the UBC lawyers if they could provide me with copies of the reports by three experts, assumed to exist given the phrase "was received." UBC refused. I then made a request to the BCHRT on April 29, 2016, for the expert reports. The tribunal registrar sent me a letter on June 3, 2016, refusing my request. This letter notes that the presiding Tribunal Member "exercised his discretion to deny access to expert witness reports." The letter also states that my request was considered a request for access to records under the *Freedom of Information and Protection of Privacy Act* and "disclosure by the Tribunal is presumed to be an unreasonable invasion of a third party's privacy because the personal information in the Tribunal's files includes medical, psychiatric, or psychological history." I did not, however, request files, just the three expert reports. I note that the references to the testimony in the tribunal decisions did not engage any of the privacy issues raised in the letter. The body of the hearing proper had nothing of this sort. Later, June McCue told me that there were no written reports, just unrecorded oral testimony. It is not clear why I was denied reports that did not exist. These incidents reflected an atmosphere of secrecy at the tribunal.

The preliminary decision picked up an issue important to McCue, namely that "Dr. Henry testified that the narrative style is very common in indigenous societies being one of the main tools by which members of those societies communicate" (paragraph 335). Further, among many comments, "Dr. Henry testified that the most important work indigenous scholars do is research on their own or similar communities. An important concern for them is research that aids their community. They do not generally conduct research in areas that do not immediately affect their community. Further, for indigenous scholars, that research is oral. Unfortunately, it is not valued by the university because it is not part of the traditional topic of research. Often, such research has been requested by the community," (paragraph 347).

Paragraphs 120–122 of the preliminary decision give a good sense of the case, what McCue needed to prove to win her case, and brings the *Radek* case into focus regarding how discrimination is determined:

> [120] I repeat that, in order to establish a *prima facie* case of discrimination on the grounds of race, colour, ancestry, place of origin and sex, Ms. McCue will need to prove that she exhibits

the characteristics of each of those grounds, that she experienced an adverse impact with respect to her employment and that it is reasonable to infer from the evidence that the prohibited grounds of discrimination were a factor in that adverse impact: *Moore v. British Columbia (Education)*, 2012 S.C.C. 61, para. 33.

[121] In *Radek v. Henderson Development (Canada)*, 2005 BCHRT 302, the principles applicable to racial discrimination and analysis were established as:

a) the prohibited ground or grounds of discrimination need not be the sole or the major factor leading to the discriminatory conduct; it is sufficient they are a factor;

b) there is no need to establish an intention or motivation to discriminate; the focus of the inquiry is on the effect of the Respondent's actions on the Complainant;

c) the prohibited ground or grounds need not be the cause of the Respondent's discriminatory conduct; it is sufficient if they are a factor or operative element;

d) there need be no direct evidence of discrimination; discrimination will more often be proven by circumstantial evidence and inference;

e) Racial stereotyping will usually be the result of subtle unconscious beliefs, biases and prejudices. (para. 482)

[122] It is clear that the evidence supports that Ms. McCue exhibits membership in all five classifications of prohibited ground advanced in the Complaint. It is also clear that she experienced an adverse impact with respect to her employment in that she was denied tenure and promotion, and ultimately that resulted in the loss of her assistant professorship. The issue, therefore, is whether any of the prohibited grounds of discrimination upon which this Complaint is based were a factor in that adverse impact.

The Hearing: *Lorna June McCue v. University of British Columbia*, BCHRT, November 14, 2016

Eltringham (2012, 433) describes the entryway into a tribunal as a "distinguishing strategy more than a matter of security." However, at the BCHRT offices there is no security. He adds (441), "The need for the presence of a validating public at trials is enshrined in many constitutions and built into the very fabric of court complexes throughout the world." But strangely, not here. Meanwhile, as with all courts and tribunals, hearings are open to the public unless explicitly closed. On the many days I have been there, I have never seen more than a few people attending, simply to observe or to report in newspapers or other media. The light of day does not seem to penetrate the tribunal offices and hearing rooms nor, apparently, are people encouraged to attend. This is a paradox regarding the very place where Indigenous people's complaints of discrimination are supposed to be aired in public. The concept of public, as it is practiced here, is limited and technical rather than broad and expansive. Perhaps this will change with the creation of a Human Rights Commission in British Columbia and efforts at public education (Kahlon n.d., considers the possibilities of change with a commission). The British Columbia Human Rights Tribunal "Public Access and Media Policy" of 2006 was amended on January 13, 2020 (BCHRT 2020). The statement concerning the announcement of the policy notes that hearings are open to the public and provides rules regarding access but still emphasizes restrictions.

The *McCue* hearing is held in Hearing Room 2, on the twelfth floor of the tribunal offices at 1270-605 Robson Street, a downtown Vancouver business tower. Most of the floor is devoted to the BCHRT. Visitors enter into a hallway with a single reception window. To the right are the several hearing rooms and conference rooms for lawyers and clients to meet. The hallway bends around a corner, creating a complicated maze of space. There are schoolchildren's posters about human rights on the walls. It is very clearly a different realm one has entered. The hearing rooms themselves are small, perhaps ten by seven metres, with tables arranged into a rectangle. There are a great many documents placed on the large table in the centre of the room. The hearing room is high up in the skyscraper, with large windows taking up most of the southern wall. There are nine chairs by this wall, in front of the windows. There are six chairs on the north side of the room, and June McCue occupies one of these. The UBC lawyers sit across from her. There is a large calendar behind her and a closed whiteboard. Next to the whiteboard is a small table with three more seats, and I sit there, and in a recessed area along the east window are a few more chairs, occasionally occupied by the few visitors. The room is well lit.

Unlike Australian anthropologist Amelia Radke's observations in the Australian Murri Aboriginal sentencing courts (2018, 50), I do not register smells – there is no smoking, nor scent of perfume or sweat. Nor are there enough people for their placement on one or another side of the tribunal room to suggest loyalties (52). Radke (198) notes "the different layout of the Murri courtroom, the use of Indigenous art and insignia, the reciting of WTC and Acknowledgement rituals, and the recognition of Aboriginal English distracts the observer from the deep colonising practices that permeate these specialist courts." But there is no art or decoration within the BCHRT tribunal hearing room to obscure colonizing practices.

Ray (2011, 146) observed that when giving testimony in federal court, he was unsure whether he should face the judge, who sits far off to the side, on the margins, or the lawyers directly in front asking questions. He writes that by addressing the lawyers he did not know how he was being engaged by the judge. I have had the same dilemma. But here in the BCHRT, these problems are eliminated. There is no seat placed higher than others, as in a courtroom, nor is there a special door for the tribunal member to enter and depart the hearing, as in a conventional courtroom. There is no "bar" separating officers of the court and everyone else or an official seal on the wall behind the member's chair. Tribunal members do not wear judicial robes nor do lawyers bow as they enter and exit. Instead, everyone sits around the tables, with the exception of the few (usually none) visitors. The person giving testimony sits directly across from the tribunal member, face to face but about six metres apart. Clearly, an effort has been made to relax some of the formalities of the Canadian legal system. There is no jury, and the tribunal member will render the decision. There is no stenographer or note-taking machine or transcript. The member generally records their own notes. Despite these differences with other courtrooms, lawyers Prince and McCallum register the hearing rooms of the tribunal as still conforming to an idea of non-Indigenous space (McCallum 2020).

Even the rules concerning expert witnesses are different from those for other legal venues, which I have discussed in Chapter 4, and are purportedly softer. In this case, a written statement of qualifications "is proof that the expert has those qualifications, unless there is evidence to the contrary and a member finds otherwise" (BC Human Rights Tribunal Rules of Practice and Procedure 2003, 29). In my experience, though, there is no difference in practice, and in the *Radek* case, counsel for the defendant gave significant time and effort to exclude or limit me as an expert. As always, the member or judge will determine the weight given to expert testimony, even after an expert is accepted and permitted to testify.

Other than June McCue, I am withholding names of the public figures there because particular persons are not the issue here. I understand my statements do not provide a full picture of the views of the people who participated in the hearing. But I attempt here to depict the atmosphere and dialogue of the tribunal as it occurred in the *McCue* hearings, and its implications, in particular the ways that Indigenous people face demeaning and symbolically violent processes. The confrontation in the discourses of the UBC lawyers, McCue, and the tribunal member, based on starkly different premises, will become apparent. Three representatives, lawyers, for UBC are in attendance before 9:30 a.m., the starting time, as is June McCue, representing herself. One friend attends with her, and later an elderly First Nations woman enters and sits at the back. No members of the UBC law faculty or anyone else from UBC are in attendance except me and the witnesses. The tribunal member is a white man with previous experience with a national law firm and expertise in labour, employment, human rights, and administrative law, according to the tribunal website. He received a law degree in 1973, so he is likely in his early seventies. He is vigorous and alert.

An issue that I identified at the McCue hearing and develop here was the tin ear of the UBC officials and, sometimes, the tribunal member, regarding Indigenous perspectives and Indigenous people's place in society. There is no sense of Indigenous protocol in this hearing, and "human rights" organizations such as the BCHRT represent, dominant colonial social forms even as they disguise them with the language of universal humanity. Not a lot seems to have been thought through, although the officials seem unaware, or institutional restraints make them unable to consider. Or both. A second issue is the browbeating McCue faces, and efforts at ridicule and intimidation, including interruptions and mockery. Excerpts from my notes and my discussion of the McCue hearing focus on these issues because they provide a specific rationale as to why Indigenous people may find the human rights tribunal experience alienating and difficult. My point here is not that everything about the tribunal is racist – it is not – or that there are no good faith efforts to make the tribunal responsive to Indigenous people and their perspectives – there are. Recently, the Walkem report, commissioned by the tribunal to study problems for Indigenous people, recorded similar issues. Other tribunal efforts have aimed at making the process more accessible. Indeed, the *Menzies* case started with a smudging ceremony in a separate room before the hearing (note: this woman was from the Canadian Prairies and her community has historically practiced smudging). Then, local Coast

Salish elders gave prayers in the hearing room itself and sat next to the tribunal member throughout a portion of the hearing. The lawyer for the complainant and the complainant herself held eagle feathers. Further, in this case the tribunal member had a very well-developed sense of the injustices Indigenous people have suffered and the way discrimination is carried out in the streets and in real life. This was made clear in her ruling. Things are different in the *McCue* hearing. The member here seems more experienced with labour issues.

There are telling issues related to the material environment. In McCue's case, she relies on four oversized suitcases filled with documents she intends to rely on during the hearings. As I get to know her by talking with her during the breaks in the hearings and during the lunch periods, I begin to help her haul these heavy suitcases in and out of the hearing room every day. In the mornings, the suitcases are transported a few blocks from a parking garage. In the late afternoon the process is reversed. In total, the suitcases may weigh fifty kilograms, far too much for one small woman to manage. But most significantly, during the hearings McCue searches through the suitcases and the many dozens of documents to find the ones she needs to carry out cross-examination or to respond during her own examination by the university's legal team. Documents and the difficulty of organizing them and transporting them constitutes an obstacle which McCue struggles to overcome. There is a significant element to the materiality to the tribunal processes in this issue of hauling and managing documents by a single person, just as there is in the appearance and arrangement of the tribunal hearing rooms. Another note: through most of the days of the hearings, the member busily records notes as the testimony proceeds. But at one point by the afternoon of November 25, he largely stops taking notes. Has he come to his conclusion and knows how he will rule?

Former UBC president Stephen Toope is there to give testimony. I use his name here because he is a well-known public figure. I note to my surprise that Toope has a conservative dark suit, but colourful, bright red socks. The trend for colourful socks has just hit, but I am as yet unaware of it, so to me it seems incongruous. It is the only bit of colour in the plain, rather drab room. While previously at UBC I had approached him only by email, now I am sitting perhaps just three feet away for the entire day. I greet him, introduce myself, and he amiably mentions the email I had sent. We chat until the hearing is ready to get underway. But he is not there to talk with me.

Stephen Toope is the first witness. Toope's testimony primarily concerns his role as the final authority on promotion and tenure cases and SAC, the senior appointments committee, which reported their findings to him. I notice that in his direct testimony about the ill treatment McCue suffered from non-Indigenous law students she taught, acknowledged by Toope, and in questions about difficulties faced by Indigenous and female faculty, he makes no reference to intersectional analysis, including race, class, gender, and the ways in which these and other variables impact a minority person. But Toope mentions his desire to see Indigenous minority scholars succeed. The dean, he says, did more than expected to help McCue. Toope, a noted legal scholar, stays tight in his testimony, sticking to describing the university policies and practices in his answers. In a question near the end of his direct testimony, Toope is asked about his final letter to McCue, in which he says he set out the criteria and specifics and considered culturally appropriate paradigms, Indigenous approaches within the framework of the binding collective agreement between faculty and administration.

> Toope's testimony-in-chief establishing his work history and credentials ends at 3:30 and at 3:32 June McCue begins her cross-examination of the witness. McCue asks whether Toope looked at seven [First Nations] community letters of support for her. Toope responds by saying he read her entire file including the letters and,
>
> A (Toope) Letters saying 'this is a good person helping the community' are not helpful. They don't show impact. The file needs impact, not a statement of work being done.
> Q (McCue) Did you think you should inquire? [about the nature of the work mentioned in the letters]
> A No, the president is given materials, and is not an advocate for more evidence. It is up to the candidate to say 'I have more to present.'
>
> The Member intercedes, "The evaluation is based on what is in front of you."
>
> A Yes, I make hundreds of decisions. It has to be brought forward.
> Q In computer science, everyone knows what to expect with quantitative evidence. What about an emerging field of knowledge?

UBC Counsel intervenes, This is not a question.

Member intercedes, This is hard to follow. It wants a succinct question.

> Q Let's try it again, What happens without a degree of regulation to get at impact?
>
> A [There are] many fields like this. Today there are mixes with traditional assessment. It is not unusual with degrees of flexibility. Indigenous scholarship is not unique in this sense. It is emblematic of changes in the academy. All were flexible. An attempt was made in good faith. Your case is not unique.

* * *

> Q When reviewing my application, did you think peer review might be inappropriate?
>
> A No. Peer review has stood the test of time, across all disciplines, in many cultures. I'm not saying it is perfect.

The Member intercedes, doing a bit of work for the former President – "You are saying peer review is not restricted to publications but you have to be able to evaluate the work."

> A Otherwise you go on the candidate's own view of their work.
>
> Q You have read my file and professional contributions. What impact did I have?
>
> A My role is not to substitute my view for [that of] others. My reaction to the reviewer's report – your work is very personal but not analytically grounded, and therefore would not affect the work of other scholars.

NOTE: My view of this exchange with the President is that he is not fully grasping, or, more likely, is unable to accept, McCue's approach because of UBC institutional ground rules. Indigenous work is often very personal, or intimately linked to an Indigenous community, but this does not mean the work has no impact on other scholars or communities. I discuss this in more detail below.

The next witness was the Dean at the time of McCue's tenure review. Her direct and cross-examination, I believe, reveal a failure on the part of the university to accommodate and enhance Indigenous peoples and forms of knowledge. More significantly, I believe, at heart, some of the testimony shows a lack of interest and a lack of preparation to understand some of the underlying issues. A question arises concerning whether these issues are relevant to the tribunal and whether the tribunal is an instrument able to measure and weigh the issues. In either case, the Dean's testimony contributed to the diminution of Indigenous people's lives and practices, although she likely did not intend that.

The Dean began her testimony on the morning of November 16, 2016, with the usual questions about background, training, and academic positions. Much later, still on direct examination, the Dean begins a discussion of McCue's request during the tenure review process to make an oral presentation to the faculty committee concerned with her tenure case. This has never been done before and the Dean says it is unclear how it would be evaluated. McCue wanted to bring a mentor for support and wanted a guarantee of enough time. The Dean says that her response to the request was that she could bring a tenured faculty member as her support person, who would then be bound by confidentiality. And, regarding time limits, she would get thirty minutes to make a presentation and fifteen minutes for questions. McCue had requested that her written materials be reviewed first, but, the Dean says, it is not in the Collective Agreement to do this. The university here asserts that they've adhered to the letter of the union rules while ignoring their spirit.

NOTE: *My response to this exchange is to suggest that the Dean's accommodation was not friendly to Indigenous practices. Later, still in direct testimony, the Dean asks whether oral presentations create a record or creates an academic debate, implying doubt about either. I suggest here that this perspective is entirely uninformed of Indigenous practices.*

The Dean responded to questions to state that McCue had a strong sense of her own voice, and that some of her work is controversial and might create difficulties.

These opinions, I suggest, are characteristic of the views of people who are unfamiliar with the voices of minority peoples and who experience these voices as rule-breaking.

At one point the Member, in considering the category of professional contributions, which are the oral products, intervened to ask the Dean "Are you suggesting her work was inferior?"

In questioning after a short break, the Dean is asked about the approach of the university and the Dean herself to Indigenous faculty and students. The Dean's foot is tapping up and down. She appears impatient.

> Q What supports, initiative, and policies to recruit, retain and support Aboriginal faculty and students are there?
>
> A The Dean responds by mentioning a "strong, long-standing commitment. UBC was one of the first to teach Aboriginal law topics" and provide support for research and training. She says "It is an important priority in my role as Dean to focus on actions in support of people, programs, and activities related to Indigenous legal issues and studies." She listed various programs at the law school. She mentions honoring Indigenous communities, especially Musqueam [a First Nation on whose unceded grounds UBC is located]. She describes programming with "respectful dialogue" and "highlighting supportive environment." The law school, she says, became a model to the university. Despite this claim of engagement with Indigenous law and peoples, a few minutes later the Dean is asked:
>
> Q How many Indigenous tenure track faculty are there in law?
>
> A Three.
>
> *The Dean specifies that this includes two Indigenous and a Métis. She is apparently unaware, at least in this exchange, that Métis people are Indigenous, and that in Canada, by law, the category Indigenous includes First Nations, Métis, and Inuit. It would be accurate to say either three Indigenous faculty or two First Nation and one Métis faculty. It's an odd mistake.*

This ends the direct examination of the dean, and McCue begins her cross-examination of the dean at 11:52. The UBC lawyer is drinking coffee through a straw and has on a checked shirt with a sports coat and no tie. His appearance is a measure of the apparent informality of the tribunal, which stands in contrast to the occasionally harsh and jarring dialogue.

McCue next addresses some of the questions to the Dean's background in Indigenous history and law and the preparations she may have made when she moved from the United States to take up her position as Dean at UBC.

Q What specific experience did you have with Indigenous law – training or learning?

A My closest experience in[sic] my role as Associate Dean Academic at the University of Houston.

Q What role?

A [In] admissions, efforts ... to ensure diversity of students.

Q Your experience at UBC, did you have any training in Indigenous law and oral traditions?

Member intercedes – what's the question?

A Awareness? No specific course or program in [Aboriginal] law or oral tradition.

Q Indigenous knowledge?

A No.

Q Community based research? Scholarly activity?

A There are many forms of community-based research and many types of involvement. I'm trying to be helpful. Most of my research is not community-based. Health law at the University of Houston, public policy in Texas could be considered community-based.

NOTE: what the Dean proposes as community-based is not what McCue is talking about. Her responses suggest a misunderstanding or lack of awareness of the sort of deep community engagement and commitment which McCue is bringing up, and which in my experience goes far beyond what academics often consider community engagement. This exchange has a hostile quality.

Q What was your understanding of the UBC First Nations Law School program? Did you try to understand when thinking of coming [to UBC from the University of Houston]?

A It is a very important part of UBC. There were areas of stresses; and it needed careful attention to continue to develop the program.

Soon afterwards, McCue asks about an initiative, the Centre for Indigenous Legal Studies (CILS), to create a more significant element of research in the program, and which was "not successful."

> A Why was it not successful? It is not in my domain, it's in the past, I didn't examine why [the program was not successful].
> Q Who funded the CILS project?
> A The Law Foundation of BC – it was before my time.
> Q What was the size of the grant?
> A It was a significant grant.
> Q What was the nature of the grant?
> A That is not part of my work as Dean.
> Q Did the Law Foundation offer a matching grant?
> A Not part of my work as Dean.
> Q So when you arrived as Dean in 2003, what understanding did you have? Had the faculty matched the grant? Was the CILS program going anywhere?
> A I understood the effort was unsuccessful.

In my view, this series of exchanges shows at least here in the BCHRT, a Dean with no training in Indigenous affairs or law, and who did not undertake training when she moved to British Columbia, who confuses foundational Canadian concepts of Indigenous people, and who was notably lacking in curiosity about how a signal Indigenous project had worked. She had failed to look at the details of a substantial grant to the law school. She testified that she had not seen the First Nations Legal Studies Plan of 2000, which is described as a blueprint for consultation with students. This stands in opposition to her statement a short while earlier about the importance of Indigenous people and programs. It signals that Indigenous people and their programs are not significant, a form of diminution.

McCue, after addressing questions to the part of the dean's engagement with Indigenous programming, turns to the issue of the dean's local knowledge and her awareness of the Indigenous presence in the law school.

In McCue's cross examination of the Dean, continued, she shows a photograph of a Coast Salish spindle whorl (a device used for spinning wool) mounted on a wall in the law school building.

Q Do you know what it is?

A I am not qualified to analyze it.

Q It is in the Indigenous room at UBC [school of law].

A I don't want to overstate my knowledge.

Q The Musqueam Declaration?

A I don't recall receiving it.

Q Musqueam support for the CILS project – ?

Member intercedes, and asks "why explain this?"

The Musqueam Declaration, mounted on a wall in the UBC law school[,] is a statement of the Musqueam Indian Band "aboriginal rights and a basic, universal human rights." It is signed by Chief and Council, it identifies Musqueam territory, and contains a map of that territory and signatures of many Musqueam citizens.

At this point, the cross-examination largely left the rails. The Member became visibly annoyed and the Dean responded to several question by answering "I don't recall" or "no recollection." In fact, a whole series of questions produced an answer of no recall. The Member interrupts McCue to tell her, following McCue's question to the Dean, "[It] could be for all sorts of reasons." (Note: it is well within the Member's scope of duties and his authority to interrupt the examination and ask his own questions in order to better understand the issues or to move the hearing forward. Here I am raising the issue of how it is done and how often and the degree to which it breaks the flow of the examination. Performative gestures and interruptions maintain hegemonic power in the courtroom, even when speech is ostensibly respectful.)

Less than a minute later, the Member tells McCue, "It is all set out below [the answer to the question]. That's what it says. Why are you asking the question?" and one minute later, the Member says "Ms. McCue, I'd like to say I'm confident you have a reason for asking these questions, but I'm not. These are established in evidence, your own and this witness. You don't need to ask a question established when cross-examining ... I'm going to be very annoyed if you go through all the evidence of this witness ... It's hard to shift gears. Either challenge the evidence or get at new questions. Not to reinforce evidence already solidly in place." I note, however, that going through evidence to reinforce its'[sic] relevance from their perspective is precisely what UBC did earlier in the direct examination of the witness.

Then, a few seconds later, McCue asks the Dean what she recollects about a letter in evidence. The Member, annoyed, interrupts. He takes his glasses off. The cross-examination continues and he interrupts again, saying "You are allowed to ask leading questions [on cross examination]." The UBC lawyer in response mimics "Leading questions!" He points animatedly at McCue and says in a mocking voice, "I'm trying to help." A few minutes later, the Member repeatedly undertakes to ask McCue's questions for her, asking the Dean, "What do you recall of that discussion?" and then, "Do you remember if others were present?" and after a one-sentence response by the Dean, the Member asks her "Do you remember if you said anything to lead McCue to believe she could rely on presentations?" The Member asks the next question of the witness as well, concluding with this statement, "Ms. McCue, at the risk of patting myself on the back, that's the way to get at information you need." McCue continues on with her questioning, unfazed.

A few minutes later, the Member re-engages, interrupting to ask yet another question, but his tone here is different. He tells the Dean, "She's asking, were her concerns of racialization of student evaluations such that these should be set aside?" (this concerned student evaluations of McCue's classes which contained racially-charged comments).

NOTE: *here the Member is picking up that the Dean is not giving proper answers and is evasive.*

Later the Dean repeats her response to questions, "I don't know how to interpret your questions," and "I have difficulty with the question." Later on, the Member speaks sharply to McCue, "She [the Dean] hasn't answered you. How many times do I have to say that?"

I am a bit confused and my fieldnotes say, "Who is he [the Member] frustrated with?"

Later, the Member says to the Dean, "I think the answer you gave didn't respond to McCue's question."

My notes say, "The Member has good concentration and memory and control of docs [documents]," and he appears to expect this of others.

From these passages, I want to suggest that the tribunal cross-examination process is difficult, to say the least, or perhaps nearly impossible for non-courtroom litigators. And, the Member repeatedly expressed his frustration with the process, concerned by the time limitations on the hearing in total. There are very many interruptions, including five within the space of about ten sentences and five questions by McCue.

At one point, the Member resorts to shouting at McCue, "You are giving evidence! What is the question? I'm getting quite impatient" On many occasions, he cuts McCue off. On one occasion he commiserates with the witness, "Mr. [UBC lawyer], I appreciate your frustration."

And on another occasion, the UBC lawyers taunt McCue, giving her their instructions as to what she should do.

In response to a question one faculty witness replies that in the faculty discussions of McCue's tenure case "No one was suggesting it was wrong to take into account Aboriginal identity and use a different, broader lens."

My notes record, "The flexibility they, UBC officials, offer isn't the same as understanding how to use this broader, different lens. But do they, UBC, know how to use this lens? No. Can the HRT grasp this?"

On page 116 of my notes from the hearing, I record a significant exchange between a male faculty member who had been part of the tenure decision process and the Member on November 23, 2016. My notes say, regarding this retired faculty member, "Older man, gray hair, very large mustache, baggy khaki pants, checked shirt, blue vest. Soft spoken, slow speaker. About 5'10'. The Member is late, [arrives 9:32]. Is jolly today." A later note recorded during the examination of this witness observes that the Member enjoys direct testimony by UBC more than cross-examination by McCue. My notes record that the Member was "jolly today" again on the morning of November 25, as the tribunal prepared for direct examination of another retired UBC faculty member.

UBC counsel asks,

Q You had heard before the notion that oral publications could be scholarly activity?

A That was the first time. [At the meeting in which McCue was permitted to make a thirty minute statement].

Member intervenes, "You accepted it."

A An Indigenous person's oral tradition plays an important role. Whether that means every oral presentation counts as scholarly activity caused me to pause because a critical part of each assessment is the ability to assess — rely on external reports or yourself. Unless you have recordings made, listened to, transcribed, which would be ways of accepting these. It was clearly impossible to assess. It was a new submission, I had to accept it with some caution. Conferences, symposia, that all makes, factors in — more of quantity of how many, what contexts. It must be done on paper — a record of it.

Member intervenes — Assess in quantity. But in terms of treating as a publication, some information is missing that is needed?

A Yes.

Member (laughs) *Thank you!*

This exchange is curious because the faculty member, one of the people who voted on McCue's tenure case, has admitted here that he isn't sure how to assess a file like McCue's and found it "clearly impossible." An unspoken issue is whether McCue's file was incomplete and therefore impossible to assess or the nature of the file and its newness made it impossible to assess. The Member's laughter and response "Thank you!" suggests the former and he seemed relieved that a key issue of the trial was clarified for him.

There is another, later, day in the McCue hearing which merits attention and which provides insights into what can only be regarded as a significant affront to Indigenous people, namely an apparent effort to discount an Indigenous person's identity, and legal standing, as an Indigenous person. I anticipated it to be an exciting day. A witness for the University, a biological anthropologist based in Arizona, is expected to testify that there is some issue with June McCue's status as an Indigenous person. He will testify remotely. Robert Williams is a retired professor of anthropology at Arizona State University.

Williams is the author of many publications, including: R.C. Williams, A.G. Steinberg, W.C. Knowler, and D.J. Pettitt, "Gm3; 5,13,14 admixture: independent estimates of admixture in American Indians." American

Journal of Human Genetics *(1986) 39:409–413. And this: YF Chen and RC Williams "Estimating non-Indian genetic admixture in American Indians."* American Journal of Physical Anthropology *(1999), Supplement 28, 106. JD McAuley, et al. RC Williams is the last author given, an indication of his senior status in the field in science journals. Another paper is "Evaluating high volume HLA class I DNA typing with serologically defined alleles."* Human Immunology *(1998) 59, Supplement I, 12. Further, R.C. Williams, "The HLA distribution of Paleo-Indian."* American Journal of Physical Anthropology *(1992), Supplement 14:174. Williams received a grant on genetic admixture: R.C. Williams, NIDDM and Genetic Admixture in the Cherokee Indians of Oklahoma. Subcontract to an NIH grant, Dr. Elisa Lee, Principal Investigator. January 1, 1995 to December 31, 1999, $123,951. He has been an expert witness in paternity testing in Arizona, Nevada, and Texas. These details are taken from his c.v. as a faculty emeritus. (https://isearch.asu.edu/sites/default/files/cv/williams%20cv.pdf, accessed May 17, 2020.)*

I provide these details because I am told that Williams had submitted an expert report to the court which indicates that June McCue is not an Indigenous person, according to what McCue told me. Further, Williams' publication record shows his academic expertise lies in part in determining "admixtures" of Indigenous people, a field which considers the population outcomes of various groups, such as Europeans and Indigenous North Americans, encountering each other. And, this is the topic of previous expert testimony he has given. Disputing McCue's Indigenous status based on data relating to admixtures is untenable, an approach I critiqued in Invisible Indigenes *(2007). I presume this idea would be used to suggest that her idea of achieving tenure through Indigenous oral practices would then be undermined. I was not able to access this report, despite a written request to the Registrar of the BCHRT (who did not reply), although McCue had read it. I am certain that Williams was scheduled to testify but not about what he was going to say. The idea of his purported testimony puzzled me because June McCue is a hereditary chief of the Lake Babine First Nation, and as an enrolled band member, an Indigenous person under Canadian law, a settled matter in law. Previously McCue had not called a rebuttal witness to Williams, but manages to enter a request in the nick of time, at the end of the last day she could make a submission for a witness. (McCue's only witnesses in this hearing were UBC employees – faculty members of tenure committees, the former President, the former Dean.) Arranging for witnesses is part of the large burden of work for a single person attempting to put on a case.*

This expert rebuttal witness would be Sherene Razack. I am anticipating a battle between the perspectives of Razack and Williams. Razack, a retired professor and author of nine books, is a distinguished scholar of post-colonial studies, formerly at the University of Toronto/ Ontario Institute for Studies in Education. I had once worked with her on a university committee and observed her sharp intelligence and wit. One of her early books (1998, and see 2016), reprinted several times, is Looking White People in the Eye: Gender, Race and Culture in Courtrooms and Classrooms. *I fully anticipated that she would indeed look white people in the eye in the tribunal room. (https://www.oise.utoronto.ca/ sje/People/695/Sherene_Razack.html, accessed June 17, 2020.)*

This would be a titanic clash between two distinguished scholars from fields as far apart as humanly possible, with entirely different premises about identity, membership, and group. I took the bus to the tribunal from my home with great excitement and trepidation. Soon after entering the hearing room I heard; neither witness would be called. My notes for that day say: "UBC removing witness –because June McCue has brought a counter [witness]?" Next, I provide a more detailed look at this day in the tribunal.

November 29, 2016, BC Human Rights Tribunal office. There were no Monday hearings.

9:25 a.m.: June McCue unpacks three suitcases to bring out the document books, her daily routine in the trial. The next witness is in a black jumpsuit, red scarf, brown boots. She is an important witness because she wrote the guide to tenure processes. She is an acquaintance and greets me and the UBC team, today including a woman lawyer, chats happily about movies, then is quiet. Everyone is dressed in black but me. McCue's friend has not arrived. We have the usual view of skyscrapers but also of the waterfront, cranes, and the North Shore. The other day, I smiled at the tribunal clerk as I entered the offices and she frowned in return. Today she manages a half-smile, perhaps before remembering that I am an intruder (who she refers to as "that guy"). June has told me that tomorrow, when Williams testifies, there will be several others here to watch, but they do not show. She takes up her chair in the new row of seats near the door, facing the window and next to the member's seat. I have my $1.05 coffee from 7–11, cheaper than $2.25 at Blenz downstairs, and just next door. I read the free *Metro* paper while waiting for the hearing to begin. There are eleven volumes piled up in front of McCue. The member comes in exactly at 9:30 [starting time] (he told me previously that he works three days per week by contract). An articling student is here with UBC.

The hearing starts up again. My notes:

> 9:30 start. Member says news! UBC will not call expert Williams in rebuttal, nor scope of evidence. Evidentiary part of hearing to be done today. I wonder why [Williams is not called]!!
>
> [The tribunal continues, nevertheless; the next witness] is sworn in. Two questions in the swearing-in: Tell the truth, whole truth? Do you understand ... if you break that oath it violates Canadian law?
>
> [next her qualifications are given], retired from UBC law in 2015.
>
> Q Were you on SAC [UBC senior appointments committee]?
> A 2009 appointment as member two years; co-chair of subcommittee; 2009-chair until 2012.
> Q Tab 141 ...
>
> The witness gives her direct examination until a break from 11:06 to 11:23. My notes say "[witness] is very calm, answering questions deliberately."

The substance of her testimony concerns SAC, the senior appointments committee that oversees a tenure decision prior to sending the case up to the president of the university. The process starts by determining the witness's qualifications (although she does not need to be "qualified" to be a witness; it is a fact that she chaired SAC and, therefore, is or was aware of the McCue tenure case). In addition, she will be cross-examined by McCue.

The witness speaks about the collective agreement, which sets the terms for tenure decisions, between the university and the faculty. There is a guide booklet to this agreement.

> Q Does it [the guide booklet] change?"
> A Every year, not to a great extent, from consultation, SAC with Deans. I used to invite members to give feedback based on cases. For clarifying and refining.

The direct questioning establishes the principles on which SAC makes recommendations to the president concerning tenure. The witness calls these principles "excellence, the Collective Agreement, procedural fairness." There are discussions of how SAC members are chosen, when meetings are called, the number of files per year.

Everyone fiddles around to find documents. My notes read, "no interrupting today" of McCue's cross-examination of the witnesses. Later, I write in my notes that the questions and answers sound "like appeals court," referencing the fact that human rights tribunal decisions can be appealed. Sometimes a legal strategy is to put into evidence information that might be helpful at a later date, if the ruling is under appeal.

At one point the member interrupts to clarify the limit of tribunal authority:

> "As indicated, I have no jurisdiction over the process [of tenure review] unless it leads to discriminatory behavior. I'm not interested in whether the Collective Agreement is followed as discretion to decision-makers as long as it doesn't lead to discrimination. I don't have the appropriate expertise."

McCue, still cross-examining, points to a pivotal issue in her case, namely, what constitutes a peer in an Indigenous case. She is arguing that the chiefs and members of band councils and other Indigenous officials, and also the UN experts she worked with, are her peers.

> Q May 25, Go to Tab 215, 72, What are SAC understandings of McCue's proposal of Indigenous peer review?
> A To disseminate knowledge, receive feedback, reflect on field.
> Q Did SAC have an appreciation for just who are my peers and the places I was disseminating knowledge?
> A A reading of this document, yes, SAC appreciated you were taking seriously your responsibility to Indigenous communities. In part this is valuable to UBC – scholarship and relationship to communities, especially in hiring Indigenous scholars. The committee heard your words and how you saw whether they agreed on how you define peer review. University norms of peer review [have to be followed].

> *Q* By paying attention to university norms. Is it true that university standards were followed?
>
> *A* Especially knowing this was a file of an Indigenous legal scholar, a more holistic approach was needed to be taken but standards of the Collective Agreement, we still have to have an eye to the Collective Agreement.
>
> *Q* Peer review, was it double blind?
>
> *A* Yes, it is the norm in all faculties – some form of anonymous peer review. We wanted impartial assessments, tried and true.

Member, "Somebody expert in the field." [More a statement than a question].

> *A* Yes.

NOTE: this exchange between McCue, the witness and the Member gets at the fact that the Collective Agreement can be understood as a road-block. The issue is, what constitutes an expert in the field?

The member put his finger right on this point about the Indigenous peer review concept later in the cross-examination:

> "Would you expect members of the committee to use a sliding scale? What process were you using and what do you expect the rest of the committee was doing [concerning her work] with the United Nations and CILS?" Following the response to this question, he tries again, "Is there a broad, impressionistic basis [to faculty evaluations of work] or a science, for example nine out of ten?"
>
> McCue follows this lead a few minutes later in her cross-examination:
>
> *Q* Did you ask for oral presentations to be considered like publications – a global consideration of that?
>
> *A* Not to my knowledge. Like any oral contribution in the file as one form of the dissemination of knowledge – harder to assess. When I go to a conference and present a paper it is rare to get feedback, and oral presentations are harder to assess.

NOTE: here the witness has made a category confusion. McCue is not talking about oral presentations at conferences. Instead, she is talking about oral presentations to Indigenous communities, perhaps tribal

148   WITNESS TO THE HUMAN RIGHTS TRIBUNALS

councils, or tribal delegates to an inter-tribal meeting, those she considers her peers. A few minutes later the Member brings this point up.

Member, "She wants to know how do you factor in her status as an Indigenous scholar and not as just another presentation?"

My notes read, "Ask, are the standards incompatible with Indigenous practices, and you [UBC] offer no accommodation?" Of course, I am merely speaking to myself. My notes read further, "UBC – all [those giving testimony] are vague about accommodation. UBC uses the vagueness strategically!" There isn't a science to tenure case evaluations.

Later on in the cross examination, the UBC lawyer interjects following comments by the Member, "[We are experiencing] frustration, we are going through the same thing; it [the answer to McCue's question] was explained by a previous witness."

Following the UBC comments, the Member says "The problem is SAC doesn't decide, just makes recommendations, and this issue is ultimately immaterial in showing discrimination. Also, [there are too many] details ... right now I am having difficulty understanding why we are doing this."

> Q All [Indigenous] customary law requires – permission [for research and publication] must be sought.

Member intercedes, "How do you get around evidence ... that if you are restricted in publications, then it is not appropriate as a vehicle for Promotion and Tenure? The purpose of the university is to disseminate." McCue, responding to the Member, says "Is the goal of the project tenure or research?"

My notes read, "UBC guys gasp!" McCue is making her point that dissemination as the university understands it and tenure cannot be the primary goals of Indigenous research.

Member, "Somehow you [McCue] will argue this is discriminatory. I have trouble, you are about to ask a question that it wasn't allowed to be disseminated, but the President says it isn't eligible and shouldn't be included in a cv. It's a concern to me. Make a note to address it. You've got forty-five minutes to finish the witness."

McCUE v. UNIVERSITY OF BRITISH COLUMBIA 149

Still later, McCue asks the witness,

> *Q* In reviewing my file, did SAC consider if an Indigenous law
> expert could come in and help make recommendations?
>
> *A* No, it is not a practice permitted to follow under the Collective
> Agreement guidelines. And we assume experts have reviewed
> the file earlier [in the process].

Member, What I want to do now, reopen file 215 – If you can look at
paragraphs 18–20, what do you see there?

> *A* A list of presentations.

Member, On the basis of the information in the cv, would anybody be
able to evaluate it for quality and significance?

> *A* No, we noted [the term] "invited" [to give a presentation] as a
> marker of quality, as respect for the candidate.

A few minutes later my notes read, "Member takes over." He asks a
series of penetrating questions of the witness. The member is apparently
trying to get his own questions answered now, very near the end of the
hearing, in order to make or clarify his decision.

> Member, to witness: "Wouldn't you agree with me, for the sake of argu-
> ment, that if publication in a written sense is not possible and you elim-
> inate other kinds of review, you disqualify anybody [for tenure], correct?
> If you have oral presentations and requirements in the Collective Agree-
> ment of quality, significance, how would you measure those oral
> presentations?"

And underlying here is McCue's contention that some presentations
made to Indigenous communities cannot be published, because doing so
would violate cultural norms.

> In response to the Member's question, the witness proposes that
> Indigenous scholars publish on why they cannot publish their research.
> To this, the Member responds "That would be limited." The Member
> and witness discuss other means of publishing through digitization,
> virtual journals online and so on.

Notes: "Member gets Charley Horse." Following his recovery, there is a discussion of SAC procedures, my notes here record my observation that there is "No real place to add new, different materials or paradigms of metrics" [to evaluate a c.v.].

> At 4:12 the cross-examination ends. The Member tells both parties that there will be written final submissions rather than oral submissions. He says he wants them to be coherent, concise, on point, with the legal issues raised. The UBC lawyer says "I don't know what she [McCue] is arguing. I will have spent time trying to figure this out. There are maybe thirty topics she might argue." The Member tells McCue, "I can tell you, it is unacceptable if you arrive without written arguments with a chance to supplement orally. The document must be fully developed in writing with authorities [legal decisions], citations to the binders." This presents a serious obstacle for McCue who must cite all the relevant decisions she uses to support her case. She is given until December 20 to make her submission. UBC, on the other hand, has until January 17 to respond to McCue. It is November 29, 2016.

McCue has only three weeks to produce this document on her own, which is little time working by oneself but enough for a legal team. McCue tells me she asked for an adjournment but did not get it. Regarding case law, she has to rush to pull together the authorities, the key cases. She has to produce three sets of her evidence and the expense is considerable to copy the materials. The UBC lawyers ask for full versions of the decisions, not just the paragraphs relevant to the hearing. She has to highlight the details in yellow marker.

Note: I recorded some two hundred pages of notes while attending the three weeks of hearings, recording elements of the material environment. I observed that McCue carried out her work organizing her materials quietly during the hearing, with her own agitation and discomfort clearly expressed on her face and later in comments she made over lunch. This contrasts with the university legal team, which had documents organized, no doubt by staff, and ready to use and submit to the tribunal member. In brief, the mere volume of documents and the difficulty of organizing them and transporting them constituted an obstacle that McCue struggled to overcome. These problems eroded the patience of the tribunal member and damaged the efficacy of McCue's presentation of her issues.

Analysis and Commentary

Regarding former UBC president Toope's testimony, I submit that he gives a narrow view of scholarship and the ways in which people are affected by various forms of work, which creates a difficulty for McCue. A great deal of Indigenous work is aimed at particular modes of knowing and knowledge that the president does not acknowledge here, in this short response. This exchange in the tribunal mirrors the differences between Western science and Indigenous traditional ecological knowledge, which appeared to be non-analytical and merely stories before scientists and elders began to learn how to work together, as noted by anthropologist Julie Cruikshank (2006), in her book *Do Glaciers Listen?*. She presents some of the issues that have arisen regarding differences in modes of knowing and forms of expression and the difficulties in hearing one another. In her book, she describes the dilemma facing scientists who hoped to get elders with traditional knowledge of glaciers to present the information in a clear, discrete manner. Instead, their understanding is embedded in story and a larger worldview and is inscrutable, at least initially, to scientists.

And Toope sets a false dichotomy between being personal and being analytic. McCue is trying with her line of questioning to make the point that UBC had not geared up to actually have a way to assess the impact of her work in communities, and letters written by nonacademics from these communities were, no doubt, dismissed as inconsequential. However, the renowned Indigenous legal scholar John Borrows (1992), among others, has written a number of books that concern his family and their oral traditions and, yet, are analytical.

Please note, my intent here is not to render an opinion regarding the merits of McCue's case, or to compare Borrows and McCue, but rather to identify issues in the operation of the tribunal and, in this case, the university. Also, my discussion here is not meant to imply that Indigenous faculty do not produce significant scholarship. They do, a great deal of it. And I do not mean to assess the degree to which Indigenous practices and knowledges are uniform across nations or individuals, or to suggest that Indigenous beliefs run counter to the idea of writing. This is not inherently the case. See Sarris (1993), for example, for a discussion of the fraught relationship of oral and written knowledge from an Indigenous perspective.

I wish to show here the struggle McCue faced in attempting to address issues of emerging fields of knowledge and their scholarly impact. Indigenous studies is one such emerging field and has recently established itself as a stand-alone field, with its own major scholarship, leading lights, and national organization. Women's studies in the 1960s and 1970s similarly had its own struggles to establish itself as a legitimate field of study, with its own research methods and questions, and I watched that difficult process unfold as an undergraduate and graduate student. As with women's studies, Indigenous studies is an intellectual undertaking but with elements of a political or social movement, a situation that does not sit well with university committees. The responses to questioning in the BCHRT, at points, failed to differentiate between McCue's particular case and these larger issues. Again, a question is whether the issues McCue was raising (about impact, in particular) can be appropriately heard by a tribunal or whether Indigenous perspectives are stymied and ignored here.

* * *

One measure of the difficulties of taking on a university and their lawyers in a human rights tribunal is the heavy workload. June McCue mentions to me that she and a friend stayed up all night preparing documents and were tired. And she could not take notes the previous day because she was managing the documents.

* * *

Through the testimony of the various witnesses, not all of whom I consider here, it became apparent that the collective agreement between the administration and the faculty of UBC was either an obstacle to a proper evaluation of Indigenous contributions to scholarship or, alternatively, used as an obstacle. An example of this occurred during the dean's direct examination, when a question arose about how a decision is made to include a report on "professional contributions" to be sent to reviewers. Professional contributions, in this case, included documents about McCue's work with the United Nations and with Indigenous communities, which is oral. To not include material on this would be an inherent obstacle to McCue's case. In addition, the dean, who sends out the cover letters for the law faculty tenure cases, was asked how cover letters sent to reviewers of tenure files are written. The dean replied that Tab 35, a document, is the standard letter sent out, and in McCue's case the letter included language specific to the review of professional contributions. The dean commented that McCue had requested unpublished work also be evaluated and that the letter let the reviewers know the standards to apply. Letters of appraisal ordinarily must be standard, to create fairness between faculty being evaluated for tenure and because the language is the result of negotiations between the university and the faculty association. The dean's response does not make this clear but sounds potentially prejudicial if she had informed reviewers that materials and standards were different for McCue in the inclusion of unpublished materials. Different could sound like "lesser."

* * *

I contrast the decision regarding a support person, which McCue requested in presenting her case for tenure to the faculty committee, with the BCHRT's arrangement in the *Menzies* case, where elders gave prayers in the hearing room and remained next to the member throughout the first part of the hearing. It is possible that McCue or another Indigenous person might want a community elder as a support person. This is a practice I have witnessed during dissertation examinations of Indigenous PhD candidates at UBC. The time limits (thirty minutes to present, fifteen for questions) imposed on McCue's comments to the faculty group about her tenure case seem artificial and much too short to build a case for one's professional career, especially since McCue was building her case on oral methods. Many Indigenous people, I suggest, would want to start with a prayer or other spiritual practice, a common event, which might take much of the thirty minutes. It seemed to me that the accommodations were either designed to be inadequate or were created with little understanding of the request.

Further, the faculty association asked for clarification of the basis of the promotion and tenure review, which the dean responded was "traditional and professional." But I do not think she meant Indigenous traditions, for they are not spelled out, but rather those of the academy, which had been detailed through the responses of the president and dean. There is no apparent allowance for an Indigenous perspective in this response.

* * *

The arguments about the importance of impact in assessing a tenure case make the claim that oral presentations do not "create a record," as in President Toope's words and are, in that sense, ephemeral. This is not the situation in Indigenous communities, at least regarding certain categories of information. Archaeologists (Edinborough et al. 2017; and see Martindale 2014) recently published a scientific paper establishing that particular oral histories about a battle have lasted for more than a millennium. Anthropological archaeologists Bill Angelbeck and Eric McLay (2011) published a paper about the Coast Salish battle of Maple Bay in the 1830s, and I, along with them, heard accounts in the present day about battle specifics from almost two hundred years ago, accounts which Indigenous people reference in the history of relations of their own nation with other Indigenous people and with Canada. *Oral History on Trial* (Miller 2011a) takes up issues of orality that make this case for the relevance of oral presentations to debate. It is beyond question that oral presentations, at least in some circumstances, can create a record, in this case an oral record, and establish the grounds for debate and have a lasting and profound impact. The tribunal, however, is an institution that, presently, is not equipped to address the issue that McCue tried to raise here (the nature of how oral materials create impact in communities), and this illustrates the limits of the BCHRT for Indigenous complainants.

* * *

The dean stated the oral historical style of teaching as is does not account for students' learning styles, a view that indicates to me that at least some Indigenous practices are not welcome in the halls of academia. And why do majoritarian practices make alternative forms of pedagogy unacceptable? This is a logic of exclusion, albeit probably unwitting. I recall watching Rabbi Robert Daum teach a course at UBC in a highly effective rabbinical style, well known among Jewish people, and which has been crafted over the hundreds of years since the loss of the second temple. No one, I presume, wishes to exclude this practice. Likewise, Indigenous oral teaching methods have been honed over time. This is another subtle point of Indigenous practice and pedagogy that the tribunal, at least in this case, might well have missed.

* * *

The dean's testimony reveals a disconnect with the Indigenous presence in the law school. This is important because McCue, in her cross-examination of the dean, attempted to show that the dean was unaware of Indigenous culture and practices and, ultimately, how this would affect her understanding of McCue's tenure case. UBC has made a considerable effort in recent years to connect with the local Musqueam people and to make the presence of Indigenous people visible on campus. When the Peter A. Allard School of Law building was opened in 2011, during the dean's tenure, special attention was given to acknowledging and honouring the Indigenous people and culture. A large totem pole was placed outside, facing the street. Inside, there is a Coast Salish spindle whorl art piece. The spindle whorl is an object used in spinning wool, but more importantly here, the spindle whorl is emblematic of the Coast Salish culture. The Coast Salish people are the local Indigenous cultural group, and the university, as noted, sits on unceded Musqueam Nation (a Coast Salish band) historical territory. The Musqueam tribal centre is perhaps five kilometres from the university and eight kilometres from the tribunal. Indigenous art is located in display cases and on the walls around the building.

The Memorandum of Affiliation that hangs on a wall in the law school affirms Musqueam Aboriginal rights and title to the lands identified, including the site of UBC. It is dated June 10, 1976, and a copy was later gifted to the law school. UBC and the Musqueam Nation signed the Memorandum in 2006 that together with the Declaration symbolize the place of Musqueam in contemporary Vancouver, BC, and in Canada. One of the stated benefits of this memorandum is that "the Musqueam Nation will benefit from a more visible presence at UBC" ("Memorandum of Affiliation" n.d., 2).

In her exchanges with McCue during cross-examination, the dean showed little or, perhaps, no awareness of the the spindle whorl and the Declaration, key, and widely displayed, public symbols of the Coast Salish and, in particular, the Musqueam Nation. This is so even though UBC signed the memorandum three years after the dean's arrival. (She served as dean from 2003 to 2015.) Independent of the merits of McCue's case, the dean, distinguished in her service and her scholarship, nevertheless knew little regarding Indigenous affairs, at least as evidenced in the tribunal hearing. What is important here is that the dean's testimony is an example of evidence that is deaf to Indigenous understandings but which an Indigenous complainant must endure in a hearing establishing whether Indigenous human rights have been violated.

The tribunal remains a hostile environment for an Indigenous complainant for reasons particular to Indigenous people and also for reasons that would bother any complainant unrepresented by counsel. My field notes read, "McCue just can't get her argument out." And on another field note page, "The tribunal requires a certain kind of personality, aggressive. Other types just aren't tolerated here." I record in my notes, "McCue isn't, can't be, aggressive; she can't shake the Dean out of her stance of refusal." And "the Dean doesn't answer questions, but gives her own narrative in support of her own position." There appears to be a certain circularity to the UBC position, at least as presented in responses to questions at the tribunal hearing; community work cannot be established as scholarly because it has not been established as a scholarly category. There is no way to get there from here.

* * *

The member's approach here appears to give priority to things "done on paper," and from this viewpoint those things on paper have higher standing than oral materials. For McCue, the tribunal's requirement for written documents is layered on the university's requirements of paperwork. This perspective is reminiscent of the position taken by the Crown expert regarding oral history evidence after the Canadian Supreme Court ruled in *Delgamuukw*, 1997, that oral history would have the same footing as written history. The Crown then took this to mean that oral history would stand as evidence if subsequently recorded and treated as any other form of document corroborated by written material. It reflects an inclination in the law, and in society in general, to privilege written over oral.

This point echoes the earlier discussion about different understandings of expertise and fact in anthropology and the law. The epistemological questions that undergird the text show through here in different but important ways – how do we apprehend Indigenous knowledge, anthropological knowledge, and legal knowledge when they are brought together in the courts or law-like settings, when the stakes are so high?

* * *

A number of granting agencies, admissions processes, dissertation exams, and other administrative processes and practices have moved towards allowing, even requiring, the inclusion of Indigenous community members as peer reviewers, in recognition of their expert knowledge of their field of work, which may be as a chief of a band, tribal administrator, cultural advisor, or other similar position. It is not clear that McCue's effort to include letters from Indigenous community leaders was regarded in this light in the tenure process. I think they were not. McCue described herself as feeling an obligation, as a fundamental Indigenous practice, to consider the opinions of community leaders in her work. But it does not work like this at UBC, apparently, and therefore not at the tribunal. The member had previously stated he could not rule on UBC tenure processes unless they were discriminatory. Seen from one angle, that is, to not consider community letters as expert opinions, if they are more than the kind of letter Toope described, is discriminatory. Perhaps we are not that far along in our understanding of human rights in the area of employment for Indigenous people. This cannot be the fault of the tribunal member, who can only follow current understandings. But human rights codes, including that in British Columbia, continue to evolve, and must be regarded as works in progress. Both the university's academic policies and the BCHRT could become more inclusive of Indigenous knowledge so that a claim like McCue's, and the role of Indigenous community experts, could be better understood and incorporated into the practices of both sorts of institutions. Both claim a willingness to change in this direction.

* * *

Cross-examination was a big problem in this case, particularly as it manifested in interruptions of McCue's questions to witnesses. McCue had been a law professor and is a legal scholar, but common with many law professors, she is not a courtroom legal practitioner and this showed in her cross-examinations of the various university authorities who had a role in her denial of tenure and whom she had called as witnesses. In two pages of notes, I recorded that McCue was interrupted three times in just a few minutes by the tribunal member hearing the case; other pages reveal many other interruptions. The significance of interruptions and the ability to interrupt and control turn-taking has been identified by John Conley, a professor of law, and his colleague William O'Barr, an anthropologist, as gendered expressions of power (1998). McCue, in my observation, was visibly distraught by the repeated interruptions but, nevertheless, remained calm and controlled and soldiered on, her line of questioning and effectiveness undermined.

The case resulted in a defeat for the complainant. However, it is worth noting that June McCue brought up issues of great importance, among these the relevance of oral scholarship to the work of university professors and the tenure process. Another is the significance of the requirement of scholars working with Indigenous communities to follow existing Indigenous protocols, the constraints that may place on publishing in a conventional sense, and, therefore, the need to understand community work in a broad sense. Failure to adhere to the protocols undermines trust. The third issue is the possibility of a role for community leaders in tenure decisions. The tribunal did provide space for these issues to be aired, yet in all three instances their importance to the case itself was negligible.

I found it unconscionable that UBC considered challenging McCue's status as an Indigenous person, however that argument might have been made, and that a report was entered to this effect. Indeed, the concept of human rights, in part, prohibits discrimination based on one's person, including race and identity. Here, the university has done this in reverse. The intent of this testimony seems to have been to dismiss the first grounds on which discrimination might occur and the complaint be brought. Approaches like that come at a cost for the complainant, and, I believe, place the university in a precarious position in their relationship with Indigenous people. Even in victory for the university, there is a cost. The hearing put McCue in a position to be confronted by sometimes obstinate witnesses who manifested a denial of Indigenous culture and the presence of Indigenous people at the university, despite saying otherwise. Taken together, the process McCue faced has the characteristics of some features of symbolic violence, in particular the sense of injustice and not being heard, of being demeaned.

Next, I consider a case in which the Indigenous complainant won; however, the trauma inflicted on the complainant was a very high cost.

8

Menzies v. Vancouver Police Department

TO REMIND THE READER, the *Menzies* case concerns an event that transpired one evening while Clara Menzies happened upon her teenage son as he was being arrested. She attempted to talk to him and give him a cigarette to see how he was and calm him down. But police blocked her view and after an exchange of words carried her away from the scene before throwing her on the ground. Trauma was interwoven throughout this case, right from the beginning, before I met her.

I served as an expert witness in the *Menzies* case, submitted an expert report, and gave testimony the first day of the hearing. In addition, I attended the remainder of the hearing, recording detailed notes of the proceedings and also my subjective responses, as I did with the *McCue* case. I was contacted regarding this case by an Indigenous lawyer acting for Menzies, Amber Prince, from the nonprofit Atira Women's Resource Society. Prince received a law degree in 2005 and describes herself in a law journal as a "left-leaning feminist of Aboriginal heritage" who offers "legal assistance and support services for marginalized women ... Sometimes the most important thing is that the woman is being heard. Being listened to and also believed. To feel supported is sometimes the most important thing, and that's been a big lesson for me" (quoted in Milstead 2010, 23–24). Her self-description fits the lawyer I worked with.

In a public lecture, Prince (2020) provided important insight into the backstory of Menzies' hearing and my own participation. She noted that Menzies was skeptical about the human rights process and wanted a white man to serve as an expert, feeling that the tribunal would be more receptive to such a person's opinion. Menzies and Prince both wanted female Indigenous lawyers to argue the case and undertake the cross-examination of the members of the Vancouver Police Department (VPD). A trauma-informed lawyer specialist, Myrna McCallum, was selected. Prince noted her engagement with the performative aspects of law in this case, with the use of Indigenous women lawyers, eagle feathers, elders, and opening prayers. She also made the important observation that the *Radek* case demonstrated that anger is an appropriate response to racism, and in testimony in the BCHRT, Menzies was openly angry, at points. Prince described Menzies as fearless and honest and that these qualities helped lead to the member's judgment in her favour. It is this anger that reflects a response to the symbolic violence of Menzies' experiences in the tribunal.

Prince (2020) also mentioned in the lecture that the efforts at mediation in the *Menzies* case went nowhere and resulted in four decisions over three-and-a-half years; hence they proceeded to a hearing. In addition, Prince added that the ruling in the *Menzies* case was the first time the Vancouver Police Department was held accountable for racism. This outcome and the subsequent Walkem report, she added, led to a number of Indigenous women approaching her to take on their prospective cases. She became a *de facto* gatekeeper for the tribunal, unable to represent all the women who came forward to her. In addition, Prince expressed the view that the tribunal member who heard the *Menzies* case was able to see the social context of Menzies' life and her role as a mother. One might presume that the social context, including the diminution of Indigenous people subjected to systemic racialization, would be, without question, part of the work of the tribunal, but Prince suggests that it is not. She wondered aloud if the fact that the member herself is a mother may have helped her see this context. Finally, in her talk Prince (2020) emphasized what she understood as the arrogance of the police who were cross-examined, and the testimony exposed how much power they assume – even when they are the accused – while giving testimony. My discussion of the tribunal hearing in Chapter 3 reveals this police arrogance in questioning why he had to testify and Prince's rapid and ironic response, "Thank you for the lesson in criminal law." Prince noted that the testimony also exposed the insufficiency of police training in dealing with Indigenous people.

Prince (2020) expressed concern that the VPD may have learned nothing from the case and that Menzies is still wary of police. And Menzies received cash for winning her case but not effective reassurances for her safety. In addition, the award of cash implies that the VPD paid for their behaviour in the case, and nothing further in improved relations with the Indigenous community would result in practice.

At Prince's request, there were Indigenous prayers, smudges, and use of eagle feathers in the tribunal hearing. In her talk, Prince (2020) considered the case from the viewpoint of the police who were called to testify about their own actions. For these people, she observed, the ones whose behaviour the tribunal wishes to alter, the Indigenous measures had only a temporary effect on their use of power. But the Indigenous features had an important positive effect on the complainant and her Indigenous lawyers (McCallum 2020). Prince credits the tribunal member for allowing these Indigenous practices, for the first time, in the tribunal.

The individual complaint form Prince submitted to the tribunal states that the case was brought on the basis of discrimination resulting from ancestry, race, colour, and family life. The complainant asked for a settlement meeting and wrote that the adverse impact of her episode was linked to the issues of colonialism over five hundred years and the lack of regard for her by the VPD in their action. She noted that all Indigenous people would be affected by the remedies requested. As I have detailed, following the demand for my interview notes under the discovery procedure, the complainant considered withdrawing her case. The negotiations to keep the notes out led to the withdrawal of portions of my expert report.

Now to the formal process itself – the hearing.

I indicated in Chapter 7 where the BCHRT meets in Vancouver. This hearing is at the same address and in Hearing Room 6 (not all hearings are at this site; the tribunal sits in other locations as needed). The hearing was scheduled to begin on the morning of September 9, 2019. Three water jugs are on the table, with paper cups and Kleenex. There are three people in the gallery and a Vancouver Police Department (VPD) lawyer and a VPD human resources officer. The VPD people sit along the table on the south side, as usual for the respondent's team. There are two lawyers acting for Menzies sitting along the north side of the table. One represents an Indigenous organization, the Union of BC Indian Chiefs, which obtained intervener status, allowing them to make a statement in the hearing. Meanwhile, a man on scaffolding outside is cleaning the large windows, adding a rather strange element to the hearing. I sat on the north side, near the lawyer acting for Menzies and next to the witness.

The tribunal member is present but the complainant is late. The member, Devyn Cousineau, is a young woman who graduated with a BA in 2003 and a law degree in 2006. She served as legal counsel to the BCHRT and worked at a nonprofit doing anti-poverty and human rights law.

At 10:08 a.m. the complainant arrives.

Unlike at other human rights hearings I have attended, Indigenous rituals are enacted. At 10:09 a.m., two Indigenous women sit in the front, along the table where the member sits, holding cedar boughs and eagle feathers. Introductions are made. At 10:10 a.m., two more women come in, one sitting in the audience area and another next to the member. A smudge, an Indigenous ritual in which smoke is used to purify participants, has occurred in room 207. Now there are nineteen people in attendance. All of this is recorded. Elder Roberta Price gives an opening talk. She mentions she is Coast Salish and Musqueam. She speaks for five minutes about the unceded Coast Salish lands and notes that the late Vince Stogan, of Musqueam, and a Tseil-Waututh elder were her mentors. (I fail to hear the latter name). The other elder speaks in Cree and thanks the Musqueam, the local Indigenous people. These women perform a welcome and prayers.

Menzies mentions three names she goes by, one Coastal [Coast Salish], and the other two from the prairies. Menzies, she says, is a colonized name.

> The Member says, how do you want to be addressed? Menzies says her first name.

Menzies holds a pipe wrapped in a bright red cloth. Then introductions are made around the central table but not including others gathered in the room.

> The attorney acting for Menzies makes her opening statement. She starts by mentioning distractions, including the recent victory of a Canadian woman in a major tennis tournament. This, she says, is celebrated as a Canadian moment. She contrasts this with the circumstances of Menzies and her teenage son. Menzies, she says, is denied the ability to ensure her son's comfort. She was mistreated on the basis of her race and ethnicity. Then, the lawyer creates a larger context, referencing the abuse Indigenous people experience in prominent cases. The Stonechild Inquiry (2009) concerned a seventeen-year-old who was removed by police from his city and dropped off outside and left to

freeze to death in a Canadian winter. This practice of removal by police and leaving people in frigid weather has been called "Starlight Tours" in the media and the Inquiry resulted after an inadequate investigation of the death by police. The lawyer references other cases and a recent report of street checks by the VPD which found that 21% of those stopped and checked were Indigenous women even though they represent only 2% of the population. She mentions disproportional rates of incarceration of Indigenous people. Most significantly for this hearing, the lawyer references the *Red Women Rising* report (Martin and Walia 2019) a study in which only fifteen of the 157 Indigenous women who participated said they would go the police if they felt unsafe. The lawyer mentions the National Inquiry of Missing Women, which found violations of human rights and genocide against Indigenous women. There is little reason for confidence in reaching out to the police, she says.

The lawyer turns to the case at hand, observing that the complainant would have reason to mistrust the police and that there is a power imbalance when Indigenous women encounter the courts. She provides details of decisions in other cases and concludes that "this is the social context and why Indigenous women are underreported in the BCHRT." The lawyer concludes by saying that the BCHRT says it is alive to the history of Indigenous people, that Menzies faces trauma in telling her story. The social realities, the lived experience, she says, are all evidence and she will show racial discrimination in the VPD encounter.

She ends her opening at 10:52 a.m., spending eighteen minutes in all in what I found to be a powerful talk with her contrast of a tennis player cheered on by Canadians and the experiences of Indigenous men and women as reported in the Stonechild Inquiry and *Red Women Rising*.

Next, the representative of the Union of BC Chiefs speaks. She acknowledges the Musqueam and Tseil Waututh First Nations, on whose ancestral, unceded lands the tribunal is located, and states that since the founding of Canada the state has been controlling and genocidal. She speaks of the trauma against the whole community, which is not understood by the non-Indigenous community. Trauma, she says, is historical and personal. The police services in a city with the third largest Aboriginal population of Canada must act in a non-discriminatory way. The tribunal must implement the UNDRIP (United Nations Declaration of the

Rights of Indigenous Peoples), just recently passed into law in BC. In every interaction police must have in mind the colonial history. The traumatic history of the destruction of spiritual practices, relocations, enforced confinement, prohibitions on practices, residential school, on-going conflict, is a degradation. In each interaction [with Indigenous people] the police must consider how the interaction will be perceived. This, she says, will require unlearning police practices. She concluded at 11:05 by thanking the tribunal for the opportunity to be an intervenor. She speaks for twelve minutes. At this point, the elder sitting next to the Member thanks the tribunal and departs.

At 11:06 the lawyer for the VPD makes her opening remarks, and as my notes say, speaking in a "formal voice." The lawyer takes the position that it was a specific event, not systemic racism, that Menzies was not singled out as an Indigenous person, and any adverse impact was not connected.

There is a ten-minute break at 11:08 a.m.

Then it is my turn as witness. In direct testimony I talk about stereo-typing, discrimination and its effects on Indigenous peoples. I provide a history of how this developed in the region. The cross-examination is shorter and less intense than I had expected from previous encounters on the stand. The Member asks me what "mainstream" means. My notes state, "She [lawyer for VPD] asks me about why I substitute 'police' for 'security guards,'" noting that I had similar portions of written testimony in *Radek* and in this case. One of the VPD lines of attack on my report on systemic discrimination is that I included these similar materials in *Radek* and *Menzies*. I respond to this question by noting that I had read a thousand pages of internal documents regarding the VPD when I prepared a report for the BC Commission on Missing Women, and that on those grounds I concluded that the behavior was the same – both groups were responding to the same set of historical stereotypes and forms of discrimination. I am cross examined until 12:30.

After lunch, at 2:02 p.m., the next witness is Menzies, for her direct examination. She is holding a large eagle feather as she takes the chair for witnesses.

Menzies says the feather is the bible, and she couldn't act dishonorably while holding it. Lawyer Prince says that it is difficult for Menzies to give testimony, meaning the trauma she experiences and the fear she has. Menzies, a short woman, switches chairs, and quips "to be on the same level of everyone else." She is asked to give her name, and responds with a statement about Indigenous naming and colonized names. She speaks of her obligations as a mother. The lawyer, also an Indigenous woman, and holding a feather herself, questions her about the evening in July of 2016 when she encountered officers of the VPD. She describes the encounter in detail, including points of dispute about whether she spoke abusively to police, their claim, and whether she was told to leave the scene of her son's arrest.

Menzies is asked about the constable's demeanor. She demonstrates while sitting in her chair, moving from side to side with her arms stretched out, attempting to show how she was blocked from communicating with her son. She describes how in the encounter an officer "left finger prints on me," from his forceful grip. She says that the officer's attitude was that she was stupid, and that Indigenous people are over-policed and profiled. She says she is doing this case for all Indigenous, poor, homeless, for everyone. My notes say the complainant "is very agitated, [and energized, speaking] in a repetitive, strong voice." Menzies is asked about her treatment,

Q "Do you believe the VPD treated you because you are Indigenous?" and she responds, mentioning the "patriarchal, colonial system. It is holocaust today, people being killed."
Q How would you describe your own conduct?
A "I was tired, on my way home." My notes state that she is "forceful" in her testimony.

Menzies describes her attempt to get the badge numbers of the officers. They would not give them. Direct testimony ends at 3:10. The Member asks the lawyer one question, about why a film a neighbor had supposedly taken showing the event is not in evidence. She replies, "He was afraid because the police instill fear."

There is a ten-minute break. Standing near the door, as a courtesy I try to tell the member I will attend the remainder of the hearing and will be taking notes. She cuts me off to say she cannot talk to me off the record outside of the room. I stop talking.

The hearing resumes at 3:33 p.m. The member makes clear that the obligation to give true testimony created by holding a feather continues in this part of the ceremony, similar to swearing on a bible. Menzies is agitated and speaks of the colonial system to which she has not given consent and asks how can genocide be reconciled?

Menzies appears to be triggered by the member's comments.

> Later, Menzies asks again why she has to keep answering the same questions, and the Member is patient and says "this is how the process works – some questions will overlap. Keep answering the questions." Menzies remains in her seat and answers detailed questions from the VPD counsel, going over the same ground as in her direct examination. There is an interesting exchange, and the VPD lawyer says
>
> > Q I suggest to you, then you yelled. Constable [name] asked you to move away.
> > A No, I was told to leave.
> > Q You came closer.
> > A To hear about my son. This is Indigenous land!

Menzies, throughout both the direct and cross-examination, comes back to her sense that there are issues, such as the fact that the land is unceded Indigenous land, that must be reinforced.

At 4:04 p.m. there is a five-minute break. Menzies uses her eagle feather to brush off, an Indigenous practice to remove anything spiritually harmful. At 4:16 p.m. everyone returns from the break and the testimony is ended. On the next hearing date, the VPD constables would be examined.

A VPD constable takes his place in the seat for witnesses at 10:00 a.m. on Wednesday and swears to tell the truth. He is questioned about the incident with Menzies and gives his version of events. The constable is then questioned under cross-examination about his training.

> > Q Did you receive any training for serving Indigenous peoples?
> > A Justice Institute of BC (JIBC) – 2008. And on-going training for sensitivity.

Q Not much take-away about Indigenous people?

A How do you surmise that? I've taken numerous courses.

Q Not specific training – but any training on cultural competency, serving Indigenous people? The Truth and Reconciliation Commission?

A I've not heard of it.

Q The Missing Women's Inquiry?

A I've heard of it. If you are asking about the content taught – I can't [say what it is].

And then this question was posed –

Q What was your take-away?

A Treat people with respect as the situation unfolds.

This was an important moment because the VPD leadership had professed to account for Indigenous history in their interactions with Indigenous people. The Constable noted that he had served for four or five years in the Downtown Eastside of Vancouver, an area with a large Indigenous population. I note that respect for Indigenous people isn't enough; it fails to go beyond standard police rhetoric that includes all populations. In this sense, this position ignores and diminishes the Indigenous history of Vancouver.

Q Your take-away, over a long period, what have you learned about them [Indigenous people]?

A Treat them with respect, not 'broad strokes' people.

Q Is it fair to say you haven't learned anything specific about the perspectives of Indigenous people? "Respect" applies to any relationship. You haven't identified needs or special relationships with the VPD?

A I don't handle in broad strokes – but I have no animosity with Indigenous people. I never ran into that situation. I understand some historical events, and I have Indigenous friends. I'm not going to say ... I'd rather deal with a ...

Q What are these historic events?

A Missing and Murdered Women, residential schools, homelessness, poverty, in the criminal justice system. I'm not an expert on any of this. I don't know the years of the residential schools ... has created conflict with police.

> *Q* Do you know whether the VPD has ever communicated to all
> officers a *priority* in rebuilding relationships with Indigenous
> people?
> *A* I don't recall.
> *Q* Respect. Would you agree telling a mother of a youth in cus-
> tody to go home is not respectful? And asking for her ID?
> *A* It is respectful. I need to prove the relationship [between
> Menzies and her son].

My notes here say "witness is blinking rapidly. He looks nervous and
stressed." A few minutes later in questioning:

> *Q* Is calling someone a racist a criminal offense?
> *A* No.
> *Q* I suggest to you, you knew that the young male wasn't a sus-
> pect ... you knew his mother wanted information, she ID's
> herself as the mother. You were disrespectful, flippant.
> *A* I don't recall that interaction.
> *Q* Is it fair to say because Menzies was Indigenous, you could be
> disrespectful? If an upper-class white person, affluent, you
> would show respect to a parent interested in a child.
> *A* The assertation I would treat it differently based on race is
> incorrect.

During this period of questioning, the constable fails to try to pro-
nounce Indigenous names. He is unwilling. I note that these names
have distinct importance to Indigenous people and often link back to
specific, honored ancestors in the Coast Salish world. A few minutes
later there is an interesting exchange:

> *Q* Are you aware that the VPD has made a pledge —upholding the
> values of integrity ...
> *A* Yes.
> *Q* Are you aware that there is an Indigenous logo on patrol cars
> – do you know what it represents?
> *A* No.

There is a then a break. It is 10:50 a.m. The constable has been on the
stand for fifty minutes under cross-examination. During this break I remain
in my seat and the constable engages vigorously in a conversation with an

MENZIES v. VANCOUVER POLICE DEPARTMENT 169

audience member next to me. They talk about personal responsibility. He says, "If you put a group of people together ..." and indicates with a hand gesture, explosion, trouble. It is apparent that this constable understands events in terms of the individual instead of society, which is a way to escape responsibility for historical events. His notion of respect at the personal level does not account, or allow, for systemic properties of society, including racism.

> After the break, the lawyer queries the constable about how to pronounce the name of the young man the constable has called "the male." The Member asks if it would help to give a pronunciation. The lawyer sounds it out in three syllables.

Note: it is a classic sounding Coast Salish name, not uncommon here in Coast Salish territory and in a region where people from all over the world have come to live, bringing names that are new to Vancouver. The lawyer says the name right, the first time. This is an example of refusal to convey the respect the constable has claimed he practices. Menzies has already drawn a distinction between Indigenous names and non-Indigenous colonial names.

A few minutes later, the constable is blinking rapidly again and appears agitated. While being asked a question, he interjects:

> "Can I ask a question? I don't understand why I'm explaining policing matters to the human rights tribunal."

The officer is testy and gives a long discussion of VPD process and practices, but not referencing Indigenous people.

> The lawyer says, with irony, "Thank you for the lesson in criminal law." The VPD lawyer objects, and the lawyer for the complainant says "This is an example of over-policing."

At 11:30 a.m. the constable's testimony is complete. There is a fifteen-minute break.

> The lawyer says to the Member, "The client wants it confirmed for the record that *retaliation* is not permitted in the human rights code." The Member responds, "That is correct."

The constable sits down by me, energy pouring off, sitting askew, visibly disturbed. The complainant's lawyer is smiling for the first time as people mill around the witness. The constable's question about why policing practices might be a matter of human rights is astonishing in that it boldly reveals his failure to understand the issues and why he is here, that police, including himself, may have violated the complainant's human rights and he has to explain his behaviour. My notes read, "Wow! Weird."

The next witness is a VPD Indigenous liaison protocol officer. He is slim and is wearing a blue shirt, no coat, black polished shoes, and dark-framed glasses. His hair is a buzz cut pushed up in the front. He is Métis/Cree. He states that he has held his position for twelve months and previously had a similar title for nine years. He has been in the VPD for fifteen years and spent a year-and-a-half in the RCMP. He is questioned about his role in the VPD during direct examination:

> Q Walk through your activities of your role – the initiatives, activities of the VPD.
>
> A Sister Watch program in the Downtown Eastside – for women and girls, a sweat lodge community, a lodge, and I mentor youth – Indigenous girls.
>
> Q Any other VPD activities?
>
> A We hire Indigenous cadets, including young girls, for three months – they go out with units and experience policing, and go on a canoe journey for ten days. The rest of the time – they look after our vehicles, and clean them up.

The witness describes some of his other activities, not VPD related.

> Q Is there any cultural awareness training for the VPD?
>
> A There was a half day training session – an introduction to the territory with a forty-minute film about residential schools, survivors speak about the schools, drumming, singing, and regalia.

Cross-examination begins at 12:11 by the co-counsel. She shows a Maori necklace.

> Q You are in a liaison capacity?
>
> A Eleven years.
>
> Q Over eleven years, has the number of VPD sworn officers increased?

A Yes, there are 1400 sworn officers.

Q Are you the sole liaison?

A One works with Musqueam, one with the patrol, now one with the diversity section [of VPD].

Q With Musqueam, the liaison is not Indigenous ... in diversity, [name of constable] not-Indigenous; the Aboriginal policing centre – patrol officer, hasn't arrived yet. Not Indigenous.

This testimony reveals that there is one Indigenous liaison member for a fourteen hundred-member force, and later testimony provides the information that there are twenty-five Indigenous officers. "Close to half," he says, of these are women.

Q Are you familiar with *Red Women Rising*? [a study of Indigenous women's experiences with police in Vancouver]?

A I've heard of it. I don't recall.

Q Are you familiar with the Downtown Eastside Women's Centre?

A Yes, but I don't participate, men are not allowed ...

Q Your role with Sister Watch?

A No. I have sat in when invited involving the Memorial Pole, the last time was December, 2018.

Q Why were you invited?

A Just for the house [totem] pole.

Q What do you know about their [Sister Watch] role?

A They do advocacy for the Downtown Eastside, generally.

And a minute later,

Q Is it fair to say that Sister Watch is an advocacy group for the DTES with the VPD?

A Yes.

Q But you haven't read their report, *Red Women Rising*? One hundred and thirteen Indigenous women's stories. It documents that they don't feel safe with police.

A It is a fact for all our communities with residential schools, child seizures. There is a fear of police.

Q You educate colleagues [VPD] on this fear – does that require you to stay appraised of their perspectives?

A That's why they established the Advisory Committee in 2019.

Later on in testimony, the witness states that he is the primary contact with Indigenous organizations and that he encourages constables to go to Friendship Centres to learn. He described previously being marginalized in the VPD and that he advocated for a changed position. Now, he says, instead of "going through the Sergeant," he has gone up two steps in the chain of command. But he says "we're marginalized, and there is room for improvement in the VPD." Still later,

Q Cultural awareness training – you developed the curriculum. There was one half-day [of training] done only once, in 2015.

A We are looking for funding for more training. It should be every couple of years ...

Q What are you hoping they take away?

A They, the constables should understand history, build compassion, communicate better.

Q Would it surprise you that some VPD have very little understanding?

A I think the majority do.

Q Cultural training is the real issue regarding the police – the bias, harm done, systemic.

A There was none [of this training] before 2015. The Justice Institute of BC (JIBC) – it's new to members' training.

Q The online course – are they [VPD officers] aware of the contents?

A No.

Q JIBC programs –what are the contents?

A A film, two [residential school] survivors speak, there is singing, drumming, and smudging.

Q Do you think this is enough exposure to the historical and cultural? Are there other issues you wish are in? Other topics you should include?

A Maybe childhood family services.

Q Any mandatory training for all members [constables]?

A No.

Q Should there be?

A Yes.

* * *

> Q Do you agree with [VPD] Chief Palmer that the relationship
>   between Indigenous women and the police is a priority? Is it
>   expressed to members?
> A He is at every Indigenous event. My perspective is he com-
>   municates to officers.
> Q But you can't show examples.

*NOTE: the witness in these exchanges doesn't show a clear awareness of
the significance of the historical nature of Indigenous grievances with
the police.*

> Q Would you expect officers to have cultural competency in the
>   Downtown East Side?
> A I hope they would have training and take it upon themselves to
>   learn about the area.
> Q But there is no mechanism to ensure training?
> A No.
> Q There are no statistics, no metrics to assess the training?
> A I don't disagree with the perspective of *Red Women Rising*.
> Q Have you evaluated the baseline cultural competency of officers?
> A None that I am aware of.

The cross-examination ends at 2:28 p.m. The VPD lawyer raises questions briefly, asking if there is consideration to provide more training. The
witness answers that the issue is funding. The VPD lawyer questions if it is
a problem of timing and is told that the training is overdue. The witness
departs at 2:29 p.m.

The final witness in the case is another constable who was involved in
the incident. He arrives in a dark suit, black socks. He is about forty-three
years old, of medium height, with short hair and short sideburns and an
Eastern European accent. He is a fifteen-year veteran of the VPD, on patrol
for ten years and three-and-a-half years in surveillance. He has been in the
public services unit. During his testimony he seems to have a good memory
and does not consult his notes. There is a very slow direct examination.

> Q [Regarding] Cultural competency training, did you participate?
> A I believe so. There are constant updates and a four-year cycle
>   [of training], [including] pistol use, legal matters, and about
>   particular groups.

> Q Any training on your own in 2017?
>
> A I'm not sure.
>
> Q Cycle training?
>
> A There are four parts – fire arms scenario [is one]. The cycle changes.
>
> Q Some of it [training] is how to control a scene?
>
> A The priority is to make the scene safer for officers, [pauses] the public.

He makes no mention of any training in issues of working with Indigenous women. He is unsure if he did cultural competency training, or perhaps remembers nothing from it. Later in the direct examination he will not say the last name of the young man who was arrested, a strange act of refusal, and the second officer to so refuse. Direct examination ends at 3:44 p.m. and the cross-examination begins with the co-counsel for the complainant.

> Q Training – Did you take any Indigenous cultural competency or awareness?
>
> A I wouldn't be able to say.
>
> Q What do you know about working with Indigenous people?
>
> A From experience or media. I try to do the job without bias. I approach all the same way.
>
> Q What about history?
>
> A Abuse, violence, the settlers came. I am not an expert. I came to Canada in 1991. But all you can do is be unbiased.
>
> Q Have you heard of the Truth and Reconciliation Commission?
>
> A I don't know what it calls for.
>
> Q The Missing Women's Inquiry?
>
> A [It is something about] the highway of tears, the Downtown Eastside.

The "Highway of Tears" is the name given to a rural route where a number of Indigenous women have disappeared. The Downtown Eastside is a poor neighbourhood in Vancouver with a number of Indigenous residents.

> Q Are you aware of the contentious relationship between Indigenous women and the police?

A I don't see it day to day.

Q Did you hear of it from the Police Chief?

A No.

Q Are you aware of the Indigenous logo on patrol cars and the meaning?

A No.

At the end of the cross-examination at 4:28 the counsel for the complainant tells the Member "The client wants confirmation for the record that retaliation is prohibited."

Comments

From these police witnesses we learn that the police have no obligation to take training on issues of cultural safety, Indigenous history, and related topics. There was a half-day training program several years earlier that had not been repeated. There is only one Indigenous person who serves as a liaison between the VPD and Indigenous communities and people. These constables know very little about Indigenous people or issues and are largely unaware of the absence of and importance of this information.

The liaison officer, for example, mentions only contemporary programs and issues he would like included in training. Later on, in the cross-examination, he exhibits a conceptual confusion between generalizing about groups and understanding the notion of systemic properties of society, including racism. He apparently cannot comprehend systemic racism because he regards it negatively as generalization. He and the other officers do not understand their particular obligations to the Indigenous communities. This is the same problem the constable stumbled over earlier in his testimony, when he repeated he would not generalize about Indigenous people. Hearings like this are one of the few ways to make this problem public and apparent.

The member's decision foregrounds the trauma involved in her interactions with police and that it has not ended for Menzies. Cousineau (2019) writes:

"Finally, I accept Mrs. Menzies' testimony that the impact of the discrimination on her was severe. She never thought she would be so victimized by the police. She explains that, even three years later, she has an enduring sense of being unsafe. She feels particularly traumatized that this mistreatment happened at the hands of people who are supposed to be there to protect her and her family. She says that, in large part because of this experience, she does not feel comfortable calling the police if she needs help. This is a significant impact, given that such reluctance could place Ms. Menzies in danger in the future if she is unable to seek police protection for herself and her family. She feels fearful that the police could arbitrarily harm herself or her family: "if they wanted to, they could kill me right on the street." While this is clearly Ms. Menzies' own subjective belief, it is significant because it illustrates the depths of her ongoing distrust in the police" (paragraph 158).

Conclusion

BY LOOKING BEYOND one type of Indigenous case, for example, land claims, a stronger view, both in breadth and depth, of the anthropologist-attorney and court relationship emerges. This perspective shows how anthropologists and others might better enter their ideas into the legal system and produce more insight into legal problems facing Indigenous people. The various cases I describe in this book reveal, most importantly, the different dimensions and systemic nature of problems facing Indigenous people in legal proceedings, including the various forms of thinning occurring in court, the variety of issues in expert relations with lawyers, the way cases can be derailed at various points, and, simply, the range of legal questions facing Indigenous people, some of them largely unheralded. These cases reveal the difficulties of the judicial system in redressing wrongs experienced by Indigenous people.

The broad variety of cases examined, from treaty cases to private and criminal matters to tribunal cases, all contain in them symbolic violence and trauma, which undermine and poison Indigenous people's view of legal processes in Canada and the United States. In other words, human rights tribunals, which ought to serve the interests of Indigenous people, are too similar to other legal forums to do so. As the system stands, there are numerous conceptual and practical hurdles to overcome before tribunals can serve Indigenous people's interests.

First, there is a need for a clearer conversation between anthropologists and lawyers, both as individuals and collectively, as Kandel and others have stated. Anthropological organizations appear to have a blind eye to the practitioner's relationship with lawyers and courts, as measured by the absence of these topics in various codes of behaviour. Too many problems for experts in courts remain largely unspoken. In my own experience, and those of others who have put their thoughts to paper, this conversation is not often held. Lawyers, with exceptions, know too little about what anthropologists do and know, and anthropologists surely know too little about the courts. Anthropologist-experts may not understand their relationship to the legal system itself and their place in the proceedings. This is so even though legal anthropologists working in the domain of scholarship known as "law and society" have described characteristics and properties of law and legal proceedings. Most of these people, however, do not give expert testimony and do not see significant portions of this process in person, behind the scenes inside and outside the court. They are observers, not practitioners. There are exceptions here, too, of course; sometimes lawyers become familiar with the practice of anthropology and, even, of local ethnography, and anthropologists understand the social field of law in both grounded and theoretical terms. One interesting example is an anthropologist, Justin Richland, who has served as a judge in a US tribal court (Richland 2008).

The issues that need discussion include the differences between legal and anthropological language, specifically the epistemological difference in legal and anthropological reasoning and concepts of fact and truth and how these are arrived at. This is a concern because, as I have shown, experts sometimes do not understand how their testimony is received. Further, the simple issue of the way the trial or hearing will proceed needs discussion. Conversations about the theory of the case presented by the lawyer working with the anthropologists are important so that testimony can be specific to the case at hand.

The same is true for the process of qualifying and presenting evidence. The notion that law compels a clear story is understated in the lawyer-anthropology relationship. What will happen in direct testimony and cross-examination and the challenges one will face in a sometimes hostile and suspicious court with bias against experts or social science ought to be the topic of conversation. This is not to suggest that lawyers are necessarily aware of the twists and turns that cases often experience, but my experience suggests they have been through litigation more times and have a much stronger sense than anthropologists of the processes. Anthropologists might benefit from learning how to describe and explain their methods, other than saying, for example, that they are scientists and other anthropologists are post-modernists. This is important in a domain suspicious of research involving direct contact with the Indigenous communities whose causes have been brought to trial. The concept of "generally accepted in the field" should be considered before entering the courtroom. And we need to create a field of anthropological expertise in which the "small pool" problem is eliminated for all parties' mutual benefit by using a Master agreed upon by all parties, "hot-tubbing," a meeting of all experts engaged in a case to work to find agreements, or panels with experts from both sides.

The outcome of this poorly understood, labyrinthine social field of law is that expert testimony is not used to its fullest and is thinned, and the issues at hand are not properly explored in the court. Anthropologists entering the "strange classroom," in Ray's (2011) term, hoping to educate the court, risk becoming "digested," as Burke (2011) has it, wandering down a blind corridor and becoming merely law's anthropology, with their concepts misunderstood. Law's anthropology cannot fully do its job for the court. The alternative is anthropological testimony that is more effective in tribunal and court hearings concerning Indigenous people.

In the end, the problem is not so much that human rights as a concept and practice derives from the ideology of Western, state-based, individualistic societies, but rather that the process of the human rights tribunal has a particularly adverse relationship with the Indigenous people whom the law has not protected, in a dominant society that has eroded their lives and those of their ancestors. It is not so much what the tribunal and law are but rather what they do. In this sense, the tribunal is too much like any other court and there remains too much malign history. Indigenous people still undergo too much surveillance and too much exclusion, and they experience too much fear of public institutions, such as the police and the tribunal, for the tribunal to function fully and meet its mandates. In the tribunal process, although the proportions vary, the *rights* part of human rights predominates over the *humanistic*. My critique, then, veers away from the theoretical grounds to the pragmatic and more grounded, to that which is visible ethnographically. Given this situation, expert testimony can still aim to be of service in explicating the problems of discrimination in the current tribunal format, which I have tried to do here, and perhaps more so in a transformed format.

This book is conceived around the notion that legal processes involve a diminution of Indigenous people's lives in a period in which encountering systemic racism remains a regular experience for Indigenous people. For that reason, too, I have argued that it is useful to look at a range of cases brought by Indigenous people in the current period of resurgence and refusal. All the cases I have brought to attention here, from the simplest to the most complex, involve a misrecognition of Indigenous lives. The traditionalist Coast Salish family, whose son, a ritual worker, was killed in an auto accident, struggled to receive compensation because his contribution to the community was not valued in the dual sense of being understood and capable of being accorded a dollar amount, and of recognizing the spiritual practices he undertook. This case, then, is in common with the massive treaty fishing rights case involving teams of experts and a few dozen tribes, because those Indigenous people were in court to argue for the survival and restoration of their historic and culturally specific resource and associated spiritual practices. I have looked closely at the BC Human Rights Tribunal as a site of both amelioration of the pain of extracting oneself from discrimination and being forced back into it, where the process, itself, invokes stereotypes that undermine the credibility of the complainants. To do this, my approach has been to pay attention both to the emotional register of the narratives in the tribunal and to the play of power.

There are difficulties in making a successful case for discrimination in the BCHRT. Statistical issues can be brought to bear. Case data from 1997 to 2015 and from 2015 to 2020 (Miller research notes; McAllister 2020) show that the BCHRT attracts the interest of significantly more potential and actual female complainants than male complainants, which is notable because the cases I present show the important role Indigenous women play in bringing forward problems faced by Indigenous people. The particular significance of women's engagement of the tribunal references the assault on women's roles in the colonial process as a means of achieving assimilation and women's efforts to resist.

Many more cases end up in mediation, with its own problems of power differentials, than in the tribunal itself, and more cases still are simply abandoned. The tribunal is used against Indigenous institutions in cases brought both by Indigenous and non-Indigenous people. This analysis, however, shows that complaints brought on the grounds of discrimination on the basis of race, ancestry, and colour over a long period are by far the most frequent among Indigenous cases but are not the most successful (Bertoncini 2016). Bertoncini's (2016, 6) study suggests there may be a trend in which particular categories of cases win and are awarded the largest monetary awards, with newly established legal categories of identity most successful. He writes, "While sex, ancestry, disability, religion, age, marriage ... garnered low compensation and had little success, gender and sex had high compensation and success over half the time." This trend does not bode well for Indigenous users of the tribunal. Further, both the Walkem (2020) report and Prince (2020) show that many people do not realize a human rights tribunal might potentially be available to them, and if they do, they are dubious about the chances the tribunal will be helpful to them.

The very difficulties people who have faced racialization experience in creating an acceptable statement of complaint create the grounds for dismissal of a potential case. For these and many more reasons, the tribunal process is tremendously difficult for Indigenous people to navigate. Prince (2020) noted that at the time of the *Menzies* case, there were no legal sources helping people prepare their statements, and further, that it takes up to eight hours to research and write each statement. This constitutes a barrier to accessing the tribunal. Prince noted favourably that the tribunal allows case conferences by telephone, mediation by Skype, and tribunal filings online – developments in a positive direction. But still, Prince took note of the emotional difficulty of reliving stressful and dangerous situations: "It is traumatic for people to relive how they were treated" (Miller notes from online University of British Columbia class presentation).

The experiences of the lawyers acting for the complainants and of those who have served as members of the BCHRT, and the related evidence concerning Indigenous awareness of the human rights practice itself, suggest that the human rights tribunal does not adequately serve the needs of Indigenous people, however "needs" might be defined. Weiss, now a professor of anthropology but who worked with me on tribunal issues as a UBC student, points to the understanding of law as rule-based versus the understanding of law in relational terms and how this rule-based structure reframes and diminishes the complainant's issues and risks missing addressing the complainant's needs. Weiss (2007, 1–2) gives a vivid sense of the way people experience the tribunal and argues for a more relational approach in the tribunal:

> Say, for instance, that James, a white-male, were to encounter ... Saba, a middle-eastern woman, on the street and yell an insult at her as they passed, derogatorily referencing her gender and ethnic background. This, in British Columbia, is not a violation of Saba's human rights ...

Now say that Saba is going to interview for a job with James' company, 'hypotheticaltech,' and James makes the same comment to her as he rejects her job application. This, contrary to our first incident, is a violation of the B.C. Human Rights Code, and Saba could now make a complaint against James to the B.C. Human Rights Tribunal. The insult itself has not changed, nor have the discriminatory sentiments that underlie it.

... there is a disparity between the stated objectives of the B.C. Human Rights Code to "foster a society in B.C. where there are no impediments to full and free participation in the economic, social, political and cultural life of B.C." and promote "a climate of understanding and mutual respect where all are equal in dignity and rights" (BCHRT Pamphlet 1:1) and the way in which these objectives are enacted and operationalized.

The locus of this disparity lies ... in the way in which the B.C. Human Rights Tribunal categorizes what is and what is not a viable Human Rights violation and, in turn, how this forces potential Human Rights plaintiffs to schematize their experiences so that they fit into the categories that the Tribunal provides ... Thus, although the concerns of a plaintiff may be complex and emotional, bound up in relational concerns and moral claims, they must be made solely and strictly rules-oriented in order to be legally understood and accepted by the B.C. Human Rights Tribunal.

The difficulty inherent in the human experience of attempting to file and carry through with a case merits attention, as Weiss (2007) indicates in his narrative. The transformation of cases beyond what a complainant understood occurs in several ways. One way is apparent in *Menzies,* when the complainant was disturbed to be answering the same questions over and over in direct and cross-examination. Another version would be the alienation Weiss portrays in the passages above. The trauma of the process, even in the case of victory for both Radek and Menzies, is severe. For those who lose, as with McCue, there is an onerous, painful process and outcome. These Indigenous women experienced symbolic and structural violence during the process of being cross-examined and of sitting in the tribunal space from derogatory and snide commentary and from the foreignness of the process, even for a law professor. As I point out, the process was materially difficult, resulting from managing documents and witnesses and, significantly, the costs of conducting a case. These costs include hiring experts, preparing documents, the opportunity costs of lost employment income, and more. In addition, there is the variability in the perspectives and practices of the different tribunal members.

Prince noted that at the time she began to work with Menzies in preparation for her case, there was only the *Radek* case to provide guidance in referencing relevant decisions in the tribunal and which "really addressed discrimination" as Indigenous people experience it (Prince 2020). Now, she observes, there is also *Menzies*. Both Prince and McCallum found the *Menzies* case had a transformational effect on themselves personally and professionally. They movingly describe the pride and power they felt when three Indigenous women, the lawyers and the client, all wearing or holding Indigenous items – a feather, a necklace – and sitting together on one side of the tables in the BCHRT took on the police department and called out the behaviour of its officers. The experience has changed the direction of their legal practices to include those bringing cases to the BCHRT (McCallum 2020). These decisions in the BCHRT have carried over into senior provincial and federal courts regarding how discrimination might be understood and demonstrated (McCallum 2020). The facts I have presented here do not persuade me that the human rights tribunals must be viewed simply as eroding the possibilities for Indigenous people or merely as absorbing the energy of Indigenous people and deflecting criticisms of the state. There is more at play. Even though few cases reach the finish line, each case adds to the body of precedent. *Radek* and *Menzies* have transformative power, both in the life of Gladys Radek herself and in Canadian law in the human rights sector and beyond.

But, still, perhaps the most significant feature was the fear experienced by the complainants bringing a suit, especially fear and wariness of police. All three Indigenous women mentioned here can only be described as brave, willing to undergo the punishing experience. In one case, the police giving testimony refused to use Indigenous names when the issue of non-colonial names was of great significance to the complainant. Many other unknown people would not be willing to submit their grievances to the tribunal. The fear the process generates is perhaps the greatest weakness of the BCHRT in its capacity to serve Indigenous people.

Eliadis (2015, 492) points to the historic difficulties in establishing the grounds to bring suits based on discrimination in tribunals. She notes that tribunals do not create binding precedents unless confirmed by courts and often fail at that level.

In fact, many human rights commissions and tribunals had been crafting systemic remedies for years, only to be told by the Supreme Court of Canada in the *Moore* case that they were casting the net too wide. This is not a failure of human rights laws or systems, but rather a structural limitation in the ability of the courts to reconcile the role of administrative law systems designed to address the broader public interest, on the one hand, with traditional legal systems that only decide the issue between individual parties, on the other. Human rights protections in Canada reflect struggles to introduce new rights.

To the extent this is true, human rights tribunals fail at the first pass.

New Directions?

Signs of the direction in which human rights is going are contradictory. That concepts and practices of human rights institutions have evolved remarkably quickly to address critiques (Howe and Johnson 2000; Day, Lamarche, and Norman 2014) provides hope that further changes might enable a deeper engagement with Indigenous epistemologies and the problems Peetush (2009) details. The retreat of government from human rights towards a conservatism that disparages them, which Day, Lamarche, and Norman (2014) describe, suggests, however, a dimmer future for Indigenous people's engagement with the BCHRT. But the province of British Columbia has changed directions more recently with the recreation of the commission, the legal embrace of the United Nations Declaration of the Rights of Indigenous Peoples, and the creation of a new category of rights holder. Even though the Declaration has faced its own criticisms, for many of the reasons presented here regarding human rights regimes, it still offers possibilities as it is engaged in litigation. Further, the tribunal continues to attempt to be more accessible and accountable. All of these changes indicate possibilities for meaningful change. But the question remains, is it enough?

Goodale (2017, 136–38) observes that the anthropology of law reveals the ways in which law regulates features of the contemporary world. Law, he says, shapes understandings of nature, embodies and promotes values, suppresses other values, establishes categories in which one can seek empowerment and conceive of resistance and protection, and legitimizes or marginalizes group identity. All of this, he writes, occurs within the larger movements of history. Goodale asks, however, how and why law is able to act as an important regulator of social life. He references E.P. Thompson's notion that law contains logics independent of any of the uses to which it was put – "whether on the side of the powerful or on that of the powerless." And, further, "the logics of law regulates identity, value and belief in often contradictory ways." The BCHRT has these very qualities.

In this ethnographic study of the legal domain and the actors within it, including anthropologists acting as experts in courts and tribunals, my intention has been less to consider why and more to consider how law acts on those who come close. Looking at the *McCue* hearing, for example, one can find passages in the dialogue that appear to be simply cases of the university closing ranks and protecting itself and the system of promotion and tenure. But the tribunal also provides a space for resistance to the use of force by authorities, as in the *Menzies* or *Radek* cases and even the *Blackjack* case, in which the jury recommended a nurse-practitioner be assigned to her community. Often, neither closing ranks against the complainant nor resistance by the complainant, or both, can be said to have occurred. Concerning Indigenous identities and lives, the human rights venue remains mixed and contradictory in its outcomes and influences. In these cases, the legal rights component of human rights predominate; at other times, the humanistic, although the balance is different in each.

The Walkem (2020) report, *Expanding Our Vision*, provides a number of recommendations for reforming the BCHRT. Among these are the inclusion of Indigenous people throughout the tribunal – as members, clerks, advisors, guides, mediators, support workers – and elsewhere. Further the report calls for measures to incorporate Indigenous practice – protocols, spiritual practices such as smudging, Indigenous laws, and dispute resolution methods. These recommendations are unassailable. In addition, the report calls for monitoring, studying, and reporting on a variety of issues, including how the various processes of engaging the tribunal, mediation, adjudication, have worked retrospectively. The report calls for holding hearings in culturally safe locations such as longhouses or tribal centres. Also, the report recommends to "advocate to add Indigenous identity as a protected ground to the Code (Walkem 2020, 7). Current grounds of discrimination under the Code (including based on race, colour, ancestry or religion) do not adequately address the discrimination Indigenous Peoples report experiencing. This would send a message of inclusion and reflect the individual and collective nature of Indigenous human rights." Indigenous identity, then, is not yet in the Code and is not the grounds for bringing a complaint.

All these recommendations have great merit and are the result of careful study of the tribunal from the vantage point of law and Indigenous culture and through the use of survey methods. In addition to these recommendations, one might focus on those issues identified through ethnographic methods, as I have reported here. If a primary issue is the trauma and violence people have experienced before entering the tribunal process and the trauma and violence they experience within the process, as I have shown, then this can be a focus of reform. All the Walkem proposals would positively influence the experience of those bringing cases in this sense. But there are other potential avenues.

My interest here is to direct attention to issues that must be considered in undertaking reform of the human rights system and, secondarily, what this might involve. A linked issue, in common with other, more formal, court settings, is the use of intimidation, harassment, mockery, insults to one's character, and continual interruption during testimony. This might be called the underlying symbolic violence of the legal process, with particular resonance for peoples whose cultures and societies have been and continue to be so massively disrupted. A lawyer commented to me that all people experience these sorts of problems in courts. But they do not necessarily experience them as a member of a marginalized minority on the land that once securely belonged to their own ancestors and in a venue that is constructed to address these very problems.

The Walkem report (2020, 13) indicates that 37 percent of respondents in their survey did not file a complaint because they were afraid of retaliation. How many of those who did file were afraid of retaliation? That was certainly the case for Menzies, such that her lawyer, Amber Prince, asked the member at the end of every day of the hearings in which police gave testimony to restate that retaliation is protected against under the Code. If the focus of reform is on the inherent violence of the system and the fear that people experience in the process, what changes would be made? A critique of this position is that it might favour the complainant over the respondent, but I think this position allows the respondents to more fully explain the problems that complainants have brought to the tribunal.

CONCLUSION 187

How can the tribunal be altered so that potential complainants can enter without fear of those about whom they have brought complaints – especially the police? The tribunal regulations on retaliation are civil, not criminal law, and are helpful but inadequate. It would be interesting to study how the complainants feel in the months after their cases. Do they feel safe? Have they experienced subtle retaliation? How many people do not dare to present cases – and what studies can bring their experiences into focus?

How can the process of entering a complaint be transformed so that it does not require an emotionally difficult journey of reliving the discrimination that brought the complaint and without revealing elements of one's life, which creates more vulnerability? Prince and McCallum provide part of the answer to this question – lawyers and tribunal members should recognize the history of colonialism and the reality of the lives of marginalized Indigenous people and give the clients the space to tell their own story, what is important to them and in their own manner. For Menzies, she connected her experience with the police with the larger question of colonialism. BCHRT Member Devyn Cousineau gave Clara Menzies that space, treating her with patience, respect, and compassion, and allowing her to vent her anger, which the lawyers mention, and which I saw for myself. Prince described this as understanding "what is safety" for her client. Working with Clara Menzies, Prince and McCallum came to realize more fully the importance of a trauma-informed legal practice. In my experience, some tribunal members give this space and others do not.

In addition, these two lawyers described Menzies' emotionally difficult and frustrating effort to find lawyers who understand the nature of discrimination against Indigenous people, both arguing that non-Indigenous lawyers "do not see the discrimination and thought the case had no merit" (McCallum 2020). They encountered the problem of non-recognition, even in the tribunal, because the *Menzies* case "brought in issues not contemplated before" (McCallum 2020). A similar problem, the failure to recognize discrimination, arose in the *Vandu* case. The complainant lost in the tribunal but won on appeal to the BC Supreme Court, although it was overturned in the BC Appeals Court. The tribunal members do not always grasp discrimination even though the tribunal is created for this purpose.

Does the tribunal acknowledge that marginalized people may not feel enough a part of society to have the grounds on which to tell their story?

How can the hearing and prior processes enable a complainant to tell the story in their own way without the lawyers for the respondent picking the complainant apart as over-emotional and the grounds as ill-fitting with the implementation of the human rights legislation?

What can be done to buffer the Indigenous claimants from the almost daily assault on their person, on their credibility as people, and on their status as Indigenous people? A dramatic and explicit example is the aborted effort to challenge McCue's status as an Indigenous person, but all the cases contain this element, if not so explicitly and dramatically. Even cases that are settled and do not end up not being heard in the tribunal have this form of diminution, an example being the signage and letters to the editor in a small interior BC town associating Indigenous people with violence. In effect, all that happened for the complainants in the tribunal process was that someone stopped publicly calling them and other Indigenous people violent. That does not represent much forward progress.

How can people be buffered from the violence of ill-informed testimony, such as I heard from VPD officers who were strikingly unaware of their responsibilities to Indigenous people, and women in particular? The testimony of the officer who wondered why he had to explain policing practices to a human rights tribunal makes clear to the complainant the frightening fact that she and other Indigenous people must encounter powerful agents of the state who feel their actions are unaccountable and who remain poorly informed about Indigenous lives and histories but *are* deeply informed and motivated by systemic racism and discriminatory practices. She had to sit quietly and witness this. Is there a way to mitigate the violence of the emotional strain of long hearings and the sheer foreignness and non-Indigenousness as is of the process and hearings, without respite other than brief breaks?

Further, the problems facing Indigenous people who self-represent have been addressed by *Expanding Our Vision,* but in my view, it takes a person with considerable determination and resources to enter into the process. My observation of tribunal processes suggests that particular types of personality are needed to succeed – public assertiveness, even aggressiveness, to combat the verbal jabs of opposing counsel – that often do not fit culturally acceptable Indigenous forms of expression. Although they did not have to represent themselves, both Radek and Menzies had these qualities but McCue did not. What about the chances for other people who

CONCLUSION 189

experience proscribed discrimination? The tribunal must be reformed so Indigenous people raised within cultural practices to publicly express different characteristics can succeed.

And on the off chance that an Indigenous person wins a favourable ruling – how is this followed up? What have the companies that train and hire security guards learned from *Radek*? Do they conform to the terms of the judgment? What will the VPD learn from *Menzies*, if anything? What forms of award can be made in addition to requirements for retraining of security guards, for rewriting of training manuals, and awarding of money? Is there a way to make the judgment in the event of a successful suit appeal to and benefit Indigenous people broadly? I ask this, because all the complainants I have worked with hoped to achieve something for Indigenous people generally. The Walkem report (2020) notes "several lawyers identified that the BCHRT system is weighted towards 'privatized' instances of discrimination and less able to address instances of systemic racism" (15). This may partly explain the survey finding: "The most common reasons for not filing a complaint, even where people identified that they had experienced discrimination, were (in order of commonality) that they: Did not think that filing a complaint would make any difference (68%)."

Can the promise offered by human rights be reasonably met? One of the expressed mandates of the BCHRT, as Weiss (2007, 20, referencing goals of the tribunal) points out, is "to foster a society in British Columbia in which there are no impediments to full and free participation in the economic, social, political and cultural life of British Columbia." The monetary remedies in the *Menzies* case do not suggest that she is free now to enter fully in the life of the city of Vancouver and in British Columbia. Nothing seems to be altered for her in that respect, as the member pointed out in her decision. Even in the *Radek* case, which called for retraining of guards working at Tinseltown, the purported impact is small compared with the effort of getting to the conclusion.

If law depends on an audience to express its authority but also to bring to light and to restrain abuses and excesses, why do not more people attend hearings? Holding a hearing in a tribal centre or longhouse would have that effect. Courts have already acted on this possibility, including in the *Delgamuukw* trial.

Creatively envisioning what the tribunal might be could produce better outcomes. Is human rights the best term? If national law in several locations around the world now accept that mountains and rivers have the rights of citizens, is there an analogue for human rights being accorded the birds, bears, and fish from which some Indigenous people believe they are descended? Perhaps there can be a way in which Indigenous epistemologies are more adequately incorporated. What might follow from this approach? In anthropology-of-law terms, how can the process become less rule bound and more relational, beyond the current efforts to deconstruct legal formalisms but with limits because of the threat of appeal to a court?

A significant rearranging of the delivery of human rights might answer, at least in part, these questions. Some of the Puget Sound Coast Salish tribal courts I have written about (Miller 2001; see Milward 2012 for a discussion of the prospects for indigenizing in Canadian legal venues) allow for multiple avenues of adjudication in civil and criminal matters. If both parties agree, adversarial justice practices can be set aside and Indigenous protocols, such as reciprocal family feasting, followed. An equivalent could be created concerning the BCHRT. Could there be the possibility of multiple streams of tribunal processing? My study shows a significant percentage of cases brought by Indigenous people against Indigenous persons or organizations. These persons and organizations might find it suitable to enter a non-adversarial avenue beyond the Western-derived mediation services now offered by the BCHRT. Non-Indigenous business might find that doing so would fit their business model and their relations with the public.

These changes would require amendments to the Act, but there are possibilities well beyond the modest move towards a dispute resolution model suggested in the Walkem (2020) report. There could be proceedings in which the tribunal member is an advisor and is joined by Indigenous authorities, as happens in sentencing circles. But unlike sentencing circles, the process could meet Indigenous practices at the stage of entering a complaint and during the body of the hearing, not just at the end, in the sentencing phase.

I found that through the process of adversarial justice, the interior practice of thinning testimony diminished the likelihood that the anthropological contribution to the hearing would be as meaningful as it might be. This would not have to be the case in a format in which anthropologists could present their findings rather than respond to the questions initially posed to them in the question-and-answer format. The restrictions on what can be said are themselves a means by which the tribunal reproduces inequality. The *voir dire* procedure independent of the voice of the expert in question facilitates a misrecognition of the cause brought by the complainant.

In the end, I conclude that anthropology can play a role in Indigenous litigation, including human rights hearings, in two ways: first, by providing a critique of the existing systems, pointing out the flaws and strengths and advocating for other processes and the recognition of other epistemologies; second, by providing explanations to the "strange classroom" in the form of clear stories about the nature of systemic racism, everyday racism, and the associated stereotyping and discrimination that result in adverse effects for Indigenous people and communities. But we can do a better job if we understand the social field, the rules of the game, and, in F.G. Bailey's (1969) terms, the unofficial but acceptable rules to act successfully within the social field. We need not be, as Daly (2005) says, traitors to our discipline and subalterns to the law. We need not, as Bourdieu (1987) suggests, collude in the production of the misrecognition of rulings as impartial.

Case Law and Legal Materials

Blackjack v Yukon (Chief Coroner), 2018 YKCA 14.

Calder v British Columbia (AG) [1973] SCR 313, [1973] 4 WWR. [*Nisga'a*]

Citizens to Preserve Nookachamps Valley et al. v Skagit County, et al., (SHB No. 93–14).

Cousineau, Devyn. 2019. *Reasons for Decision. Menzies v. Vancouver Police Board* (No. 4), 2019 BCHRT 275.

Delgamuukw v British Columbia, [1997] 3 SCR 1010.

First Nation Child and Family Caring Society and Assembly of First Nations, 2016 CHRT 2.

Insurance Corporation of British Columbia v. Heerspink et al., [1982] 2 SCR 145.

Johnson v M'Intosh, 21 U.S. (8 Wheat.) 543 (1823).

Les Carpenter v Town of Faro. Yukon Human Rights Board of Adjudication. 2010. Board File #2008–03.

McCue v University of British Columbia. (No. 3), 2016 BCHRT 9.

McCue v The University of British Columbia (No. 4), 2018 BCHRT 45.

Menzies v Vancouver Police Board (No. 2), 2019 BCHRT (name changed and case number withheld).

Menzies v Vancouver Police Board (No. 4), 2019 BCHRT 275.

Miller, Bruce Granville. 2003. *Report to BC Human Rights Tribunal re: Gladys Radek.*

–. 2006b. Report to the Knucwentwecw Society Human Rights Complaint before the BCHRT.

–. 2008. Report to Yukon Human Rights Commission, "*Racism against Aboriginal People, Particularly in Regard to Employment Access Discrimination.*"

–. 2010. *Expert Report to BC Human Rights Tribunal, Pivot and VANDU v. DVBIA et al.* BCHRT File No. 62281.

–. 2013. *The Hwlitsum First Nation Traditional Use and Occupation of the Area Now Known as British Columbia.* Volume 2: Hwlitsum Marine Traditional Use Study: 2013, with Al Grove, Bill Angelbeck, Raymond Wilson.

–. 2012/13 *Expert Report concerning Usual and Accustomed Fishing in State of Washington vs. Stark,* Case No. 11–1-01225–8, Superior Court of the State of Washington, Whatcom County. October, 2012. Expert testimony, March 20, 2013.

–. 2012. *Supplemental Report, State of Washington v Stark,* Case No. 11–1-01225–8, Superior Court, Whatcom County. Report concerning Tsawwassen historical marriage patterns.

Moore v British Columbia (Education), 2012 SCC 61.

Pivot Legal Society v Downtown Vancouver Business Improvement Association and another (No. 6), 2012 BCHRT 23.

Quebec (Commission des droits de la personne et des droits de la jeunesse) v Bombardier Inc. (Bombardier Aerospace Training Center) 2015 SCC 39. [*Latif*]

R v Gladue, [1999] 1 SCR 688.

R v Van der Peet, [1996] 2 SCR. 507.

Radek v Henderson Development and other (No. 3), 2005 BCHRT 302.

Sharma, Madame Justice. 2015. *Reasons for Judgment, Vancouver Area Drug Users v. British Columbia Human Rights Tribunal.* 2015 BCSC 534. http://www.westcoastleaf. org/wp-content/uploads/2015/04/VANDU-v-DVBIA-BCSC-decision.pdf.

Tsilhqot'in Nation v British Columbia 2014 SCC 44.

United States v State of Washington, 384 F.Suppl. 312 [1994].

Yukon Blackjack Jury Verdict; Verdict Form H. January 31, 2020. [*Blackjack Inquest*]. https://yukon.ca/en/yukon-coroners-service/blackjack-jury-verdict-january-31 -2020.

References

Afshani, Reza. 2012. "Iran: An Anthropologist Engaging the Human Rights Discourse and Practice." *Human Rights Quarterly* 34, 2: 507–45.

Agarwal, Ranjan K., Faiz M. Lalani, and Misha Boutilier. 2018. "Lessons from Latif: Guidance on the Use of Social Science Expert Evidence in Discrimination Cases." *Canadian Bar Review* 96, 1: 37–57. Can LIIDocs 131, http://www.canlii.org/t/29zp.

Allen, Lori A. 2009. "Martyr Bodies in the Media: Human Rights, Aesthetics, and the Politics of Immediation in the Palestine Intifada." *American Ethnologist* 36, 1: 161–80.

–. 2013. *The Rise and Fall of Human Rights: Cynicism and Politics in Occupied Palestine.* Stanford: Stanford University Press.

Alvarez, Lynn, and James Loucky. 1992. "Inquiry and Advocacy: Attorney-Expert Collaboration in the Political Asylum Process." In *Double Vision: Anthropologists at Law,* edited by Randy Frances Kandel, 43–52. NAPA Bulletin 11. Washington, DC: American Anthropological Association.

American Anthropological Association. n.d. "AAA Statement on Ethics." Accessed May 11, 2020. https://www.americananthro.org/LearnAndTeach/Content.aspx?Item Number=22869.

–. n.d. Ethics Forum. Principles of Professional Responsibility. http://ethics.american-anthro.org/category/statement/.

Angelbeck, Bill, and Eric McLay. 2011. "The Battle at Maple Bay: The Dynamics of Coast Salish Political Organization through Oral Histories." *Ethnohistory* 58 (3): 359–92.

Asch, Michael. 1992. "Errors in Delgamuukw: An Anthropological Perspective." In *Aboriginal Title in British Columbia: Delgamuukw v. the Queen,* edited by Frank Cassidy, 221–42. Lantzville, BC: Oolichan Books and the Institute for Research on Public Policy.

Asch, Michael, John Borrows, and James Tully. 2018. *Resurgence and Reconciliation: Indigenous-Settler Relations and Earth Teachings.* Toronto: University of Toronto Press.

Bailey, F.G. 1969. *Stratagems and Spoils: A Social Anthropology of Politics.* New York: Schocken Books.

BCHRT (British Columbia Human Rights Tribunal). n.d. "Personal Characteristics Protected in the BC Human Rights Code."

—. n.d. "Indigenous Peoples and Human Rights." http://www.bchrt.bc.ca/indigenous/index.htm.

—. n.d. Front Page. http://www.bchrt.bc.ca/.

—. 2003, March 31. Rules of Practice and Procedure. http://www.bchrt.bc.ca/law-library/rules/index.htm.

—. 2018. *Annual Report* 2017–2018. July 2018. http://www.bchrt.bc.ca/shareddocs/annual_reports/2017-2018.pdf

—. 2019. *2018/2019 Annual Report.* July 2019. http://www.bchrt.bc.ca/shareddocs/annual_reports/2016–2017.pdf.

—. 2020. "Public Access & Media Policy." Amended January 13, 2020. http://www.bchrt.bc.ca/shareddocs/policies/public_access_and_media.pdf.

Bertoncini, Riley. 2016. "The Tangling of Human Rights: Contradictions and Inconsistencies in the BCHRT." Paper written for Anthropology 471, University of British Columbia. Copy in possession of author.

Borrows, John. 2002. *Recovering Canada: The Resurgence of Indigenous Law.* Toronto: University of Toronto Press

Bourdieu, Pierre. 1987. "The Force of Law: Towards a Sociology of the Juridical Field." *The Hastings Law Journal* 38: 814–53.

Boxberger, Daniel T. 2004 "Whither the Expert Witness: Anthropology in the Post-Delgamuukw Courtroom." *In Coming to Shore: Northwest Coast Ethnology, Traditions, and Visions,* edited by Marie Mauzé, Michael Harkin, and Sergei Kan, 323–38. Lincoln: University of Nebraska Press.

—. 2007. "The Not So Common." In *Be of Good Mind: Essays on the Coast Salish,* edited by Bruce Granville Miller, 55–81. Vancouver: UBC Press.

Browne, Annette J., and Jo-Anne Fiske. 2001. "First Nations Women's Encounters with Mainstream Health Care Services." *Western Journal of Nursing Research* 23, 2: 126–47.

Browne, Annette J., and Colleen Varcoe. 2019. "Cultural and Social Considerations in Health Assessment." In *Physical Examination and Health Assessment,* 3rd ed., edited by Carolyn Jarvis, Annette Browne, June MacDonald-Jenkins, and Marian Lucktar-Fluede, 28–45. Milton, ON: Elsevier Canada.

Bryden, Philip, and William Black. 2004. "Mediation as a Tool for Resolving Human Rights Disputes: An Evaluation of the B.C. Human Rights Commission's Early Mediation Project." *UBC Law Review* 37, 1: 73–112.

Bullock, Narida. 2021. "Pesky Polygamist Women: The Marginalization of Qualitative Data in British Columbia's Charter Reference on Polygamy." *Canadian Journal of Law and Society* 36, 1: 69–88.

Burke, Paul. 2011. *Law's Anthropology: From Ethnography to Expert Testimony in Native Title.* Canberra: Australian National University E Press.

Canada. n.d. *Overrepresentation of Indigenous People in the Canadian Criminal Justice System: Causes and Responses.* Ottawa: Department of Justice. https://www.justice.gc.ca/eng/rp-pr/jr/oip-cjs/p4.html.

–. 1998. *Federal Courts Rules,* SOR/98-106. https://laws-lois.justice.gc.ca/eng/regulations/sor-98-106.

–. 2011. *A Report to Parliament on the Readiness of First Nations Communities and Organizations to Comply with the Canadian Human Rights Act.* Ottawa: Minister of the Department of Indian Affairs and Northern Development.

–. 2014. *Report to Parliament on the Five-Year Review of the Repeal of Section 67 of the Canadian Human Rights Act.* Ottawa: Minister of Aboriginal Affairs and Northern Development.

Canadian Anthropology Society. n.d. "Position Statements and Resolutions." https://www.cas-sca.ca/about/position-statements.

Canadian Human Rights Commission. 2013a. *A Toolkit for Developing Community-Based Dispute Resolution Processes in First Nations Communities.* Ottawa: Minister of Public Works and Government Services.

–. 2013b. *Report on Equality Rights of Aboriginal People.* Ottawa: CHRC. https://publications.gc.ca/collections/collection_2013/ccdp-chrc/HR4-22-2013-eng.pdf.

Carlson, Keith Thor. 1996. "Stó:lō Exchange Dynamics." *Native Studies Review* 11, 1: 5–48.

Carr, E. Summerson. 2010. "Enactments of Expertise." *Annual Review of Anthropology* 39: 17–32.

Cassell, Joan, and Sue-Ellen Jacobs, eds. 1985. *Handbook on Ethical Issues in Anthropology.* American Anthropological Association. https://www.americananthro.org/LearnAndTeach/Content.aspx?ItemNumber=1942&RDtoken=4168&userID=6944.

CAUT (Canadian Association of University Teachers). 2002. "BC Government to Disband Human Rights Commission." *CAUT Bulletin* 49, 6.

CBC News. 2010. "Gladys Radek: Why I Volunteer." November 29. https://www.cbc.ca/news2/citizenbytes/2010/11/gladys-radek-why-i-volunteer.html.

Chartrand, Vicki. 2014. "Tears 4 Justice and the Missing and Murdered Women and Children across Canada: An Interview with Gladys Radek." *Radical Criminology: An Insurgent Journal* 3. http://www.journal.radicalcriminology.org/index.php/rc/article/view/25/html.

Cheng, Sealing. 2011. "The Paradox of Vernacularization: Women's Human Rights and the Gendering of Nationhood." *Anthropological Quarterly* 84, 2: 475–505.

Christie, Gordon. 2003. "Law, Theory and Aboriginal Peoples." *Indigenous Law Journal* 2: 68–115.

Clarke, Jennifer F., ed. 1991. *A Gathering of Wisdoms: Tribal Mental Health; A Cultural Perspective.* LaConner, WA: Swinomish Indian Tribal Community.

Clément, Dominique. 2009. "Rights without the Sword Are but Mere Words: The Limits of Canada's Rights Revolution." In *A History of Human Rights in Canada: Essential Issues,* edited by Janet Miron, 43–60. Toronto: Canadian Scholars Press.

–. 2012. "Human Rights in Canadian Domestic and Foreign Politics: From 'Niggardly Acceptance' to Enthusiastic Embrace." *Human Rights Quarterly* 34, 3: 751–78.

–. 2014. *Equality Deferred: Sex Discrimination and British Columbia's Human Rights State, 1953–84.* Vancouver: UBC Press.

Comack, Elizabeth. 2012. *Racialized Policing: Aboriginal People's Encounters with the Police.* Black Point, NS: Fernwood.

Commission of Inquiry into Matters Relating to the Death of Neil Stonechild (Saskatchewan). 2009. *Report of the Commission of Inquiry into Matters Relating to the Death of Neil Stonechild*. Regina, SK: Commission of Inquiry into Matters Relating to the Death of Neil Stonechild. http://www.stonechildinquiry.ca/finalreport/.

Conley, John M., and William M. O'Barr. 1990. *Rules versus Relationships: The Ethnography of Legal Discourse*. Chicago: University of Chicago Press.

—. 1998. *Just Words: Law, Language and Power*. Chicago: University of Chicago Press.

Cruikshank, Julie. 1992. "Invention of Anthropology in British Columbia's Supreme Court: Oral Tradition as Evidence in *Delgamuukw v. B.C.*" In "Anthropology and History in the Courts," edited by Bruce G. Miller, special issue, *BC Studies* 95: 25–42.

—. 1994. Oral Tradition and Oral History: Reviewing Some Issues. *Canadian Historical Review* 75, 3: 404–18.

—. 2006. *Do Glaciers Listen? Local Knowledge, Colonial Encounters, and Social Imagination*. Vancouver: UBC Press.

Culhane, Dara. 1992. "Adding Insult to Injury: Her Majesty's Loyal Anthropologist." In "Anthropology and History in the Courts," edited by Bruce G. Miller, special issue, *BC Studies* 95: 66–92.

—. 1998. *The Pleasure of the Crown: Anthropology, Law, and First Nations*. Burnaby, BC: Talon Books.

Daly, Richard. 2005. *Our Box Was Full: An Ethnography for the Delgamuukw Plantiffs*. Vancouver: UBC Press.

Darien-Smith, Eve. 1999. *Bridging Divides: The Channel Tunnel and English Legal Identity in the New Europe*. Berkeley: University of California Press.

—. 2007. *Ethnography and Law*. New York: Routledge.

Das, Veena. 2008. "Violence, Gender, and Subjectivity." *Annual Review of Anthropology* 37: 283–99.

Day, Shelagh. 2014. "Reflections on Government Hostility, Systemic Discrimination and Human Rights Institutions." In *14 Arguments in Favour of Human Rights Institutions,* edited by Shelagh Day, Lucie Lamarche, and Ken Norman, 19–55. Toronto: Irwin Law.

Day, Shelagh, Lucie Lamarche, and Ken Norman, eds. 2014. *14 Arguments in Favour of Human Rights Institutions*. Toronto: Irwin Law.

De Cloet, Derek. 1998. "More Empire-Building from Mary Woo: Massive Expansion of a Provincial Commission Could Delay Legitimate Grievances [Proposals for Change to the BC Human Rights Commission]." *British Columbia Report* 9, 22: 16.

de la Cadena, Marisol, and Orin Starn, eds. 2007. *Indigenous Experience Today*. Oxford: Berg.

Edinborough, Kevan, Marko Porčić, Andrew Martindale, Thomas Jay Brown, Kisha Supernant, and Kenneth M. Ames. 2017. "A Radiocarbon Test for Demographic Events in Written and Oral History." *Proceedings of the National Academy of Sciences* 114, 47: 12436–41. https://doi.org/10.1073/pnas.1713012114.

Eliadis, Pearl. 2014. *Speaking Out on Human Rights: Debating Canada's Human Rights System*. Montreal/Kingston: McGill-Queen's University Press.

—. 2015. Review of *Equality Deferred: Sex Discrimination and British Columbia's Human Rights State, 1953–84,* by Dominique Clément. *Canadian Journal of Law and Society* 30, 3: 491–92.

Eltringham, Nigel. 2012. "Spectators to the Spectacle of Law: The Formation of a 'Validating Public' at the International Criminal Tribunal for Rwanda." *Ethnos* 77: 3, 425–45. https://doi.org/10.1080/00141844.2011.620131.

–. 2013. "'Illuminating the Broader Context:' Anthropological and Historical Knowledge at the International Criminal Tribunal for Rwanda." *Journal of the Royal Anthropological Institute* 19, 2: 338–55.

Engel, David. 2012. "Vertical and Horizontal Perspectives on Rights Consciousness." *Indiana Journal of Global Legal Studies* 19, 2: 423–55. https://www.jstor.org/stable/10.2979/indjglolegstu.19.2.423.

Englund, Harri. 2012. "Cutting Human Rights Down to Size." In *Human Rights at the Crossroads,* edited by Mark Goodale, 198–209. New York: Oxford University Press.

Ewick, Patricia, and Susan S. Silbey. 1998. *The Common Place of Law: Stories from Everyday Life.* Chicago: University of Chicago Press.

First Nations Child and Family Caring Society of Canada. n.d. "I am a Witness." Accessed December 16, 2016. https://fncaringsociety.com/i-am-witness.

Foucault, Michel. 1979. *Discipline and Punish: The Birth of the Prison.* New York: Vintage Books.

–. 1980. "Two Lectures." In *Power/Knowledge: Selected Interviews and Other Writings 1972–1977,* edited by Colin Gordon, 78–108. New York: Pantheon Books.

Freckelton, Ian, and Hugh Selby. 2009. *Expert Evidence: Law, Practice, Procedure and Advocacy.* 4th ed. Sydney, Australia: Lawbook Company.

Fromme, Joan. 2007. "Restorative Justice and Human Rights." Master's thesis, Royal Roads University.

Furniss, Elizabeth. 1999. *The Burden of History: Colonialism and the Frontier Myth in a Rural Canadian Community.* Vancouver: UBC Press.

Geertz, Clifford. 1983. *Local Knowledge: Further Essays in Interpretive Anthropology.* New York: Basic Books.

Goffman, Erving. 1959. *Presentation of Self in Everyday Life.* New York: Doubleday.

Goodale, Mark. 2017. *Anthropology and Law: A Critical Introduction.* New York: New York University Press.

Green, Joyce, ed. 2014. *Indivisible: Indigenous Human Rights.* Halifax and Winnipeg: Fernwood Publishing.

Haack, Susan. 2008. "Of Truth, in Science and in Law." *Brooklyn Law Review* 73, 3: 985–1008. https://brooklynworks.brooklaw.edu/cgi/viewcontent.cgi?referer=https://www.google.com/&httpsredir=1&article=1315&context=blr.

Hastrup, Kirsten. 2003. "Violence, Suffering and Human Rights: Anthropological Reflections." *Anthropological Theory* 3, 3: 309–23.

Henderson, James Sákéj Youngblood. 2002. "Postcolonial Indigenous Legal Consciousness." *Indigenous Law Journal* 1: 1–56.

Hillebrecht, Courtney. 2014. "The Power of Human Rights Tribunals: Compliance with the European Court of Human Rights and Domestic Policy Change." *European Journal of International Relations* 20 (4): 1100–1123. https://doi.org/10.1177/1354066113508591.

Howe, R. Brian, and David Johnson. 2000. *Restraining Equality: Human Rights Commissions in Canada.* Toronto: University of Toronto Press.

Human Organization. 1951. "Code of Ethics of the Society for Applied Anthropology." *Human Organization* 10, 4: 4.

Hutchins, Peter W. 2011. "Holding the Mirror Up to Nature: Law, Social Science, and Professor Arthur Ray." In *Telling It to the Judge: Taking Native History to Court*, by Arthur J. Ray, xxiii–xxxv. Montreal/Kingston: McGill-Queen's University Press.

Isa, Felipe Gómez. 2014. "Cultural Diversity, Legal Pluralism, and Human Rights from an Indigenous Perspective: The Approach by the Colombian Constitutional Court and the Inter-American Court of Human Rights." *Human Rights Quarterly* 36, 4: 722–55.

Jacobs, Beverley, Yvonne Johnson, and Joey Twins. 2021. "Decolonizing Corrections." In *Decolonizing Law: Indigenous, Third World, and Settler Perspectives*, edited by Sujith Xavier, Beverley Jacobs, Valarie Waboose, Jeffery G. Hewitt, and Amar Bhatia, 239–59. New York: Routledge.

Jacobs, Sue-Ellen. n.d. "Cases and Solutions." In *Handbook of Ethical Issues in Anthropology*, edited by Joan Cassell and Sue-Ellen Jacobs, n.p. American Anthropology Association. https://www.americananthro.org/LearnAndTeach/Content.aspx?Item Number=1942.

Janzen, John M. 2016. "Ethnography in the Service of Understanding Human Conflict." *Psychosociological Issues in Human Resource Management* 4, 2: 75–103.

Jensen, Stephen L.B. 2019. "Decolonization: The Black Box of Human Rights?" *Human Rights Quarterly* 41, 1: 200–3.

Johnston, Darlene. Discussant. 2012. "Aboriginal Oral Histories in the Courtroom: More Than a Matter of Evidence." Panel Discussion, Liu Institute for Global Issues, UBC Press, February 8, 2012.

Kahlon, Ravi. n.d. *A Human Rights Commission for the 21st Century: British Columbians Talk about Human Rights*. Victoria: Government of British Columbia. Accessed June 15, 2020. https://engage.gov.bc.ca/app/uploads/sites/121/2017/12/HRC-Final -Report.pdf.

Kallen, Evelyn. 1995. *Ethnicity and Human Rights in Canada*. 2nd ed. Toronto: Oxford University Press.

Kandel, Randy Frances, ed. 1992a. *Double Vision: Anthropologists at Law*. NAPA Bulletin 11. Washington, DC: American Anthropological Association.

–. 1992b. "How Lawyers and Anthropologists Think Differently." In *Double Vision: Anthropologists at Law*, edited by Randy Frances Kandel, 1–4. NAPA Bulletin 11. Washington, DC: American Anthropological Association.

–. 1992c. "A Legal Field Guide for the Expert Anthropologist." In *Double Vision: Anthropologists at Law*, edited by Randy Frances Kandel, 53–76. NAPA Bulletin 11. Washington, DC: American Anthropological Association.

Kleinman, Arthur, Veena Das, and Margaret Lock. 1998. *Social Suffering*. Berkeley: University of California Press.

Kuper, Adam. 2003. "The Return of the Native." *Current Anthropology* 44, 3: 389–402.

LaForme, Justice Harry S. 2005. "The Justice System in Canada: Does It Work for Aboriginal People?" *Indigenous Law Journal* 4: 1–17.

Langer, Rosanna L. 2007. *Defining Rights and Wrongs: Bureaucracy, Human Rights, and Public Accountability*. Vancouver: UBC Press.

Lurie, Nancy Oestreich. 1955. "Anthropology and Indian Claims Litigation: Problems, Opportunities, and Recommendations." *Ethnohistory* 2: 357.

—. 1956. "A Reply to 'Land Claims Cases: Anthropologists in Conflict.'" *Ethnohistory* 3: 72–81.

Madron, Nathan, and Amarilys Estrelle. 2019. Session Abstract, American Anthropological Association Annual Meetings. Vancouver.

Martin, Carol Muree, and Harsha Walia. 2019. *Red Women Rising: Indigenous Women Survivors in Vancouver's Downtown Eastside*. Vancouver: Downtown Eastside Women's Centre.

Martindale, Andrew. 2014. "Archaeology Taken to Court: Unraveling the Epistemology of Cultural Tradition in the Context of Aboriginal Title Cases." In *From the Margins: The Archaeology of the Colonized and Its Contribution to Global Archaeological Theory*, edited by Neal Ferris and Rodney Harrison, 397–422. Oxford: Oxford University Press.

Mawani, Renisa. 2009. *Colonial Proximities: Crossracial Encounters and Juridical Truths in British Columbia, 1871–1921*. Vancouver: UBC Press.

McAllister, Maeve. 2020. "Indigenous Women in a Colonial Legal Framework: An Intersectional Analysis of the British Columbia Human Rights Tribunal." Paper written for Anthropology 471, University of British Columbia. Copy in possession of author.

McCall, Sophie. 2011. *First Person Plural: Aboriginal Storytelling and the Ethics of Collaborative Authorship*. Vancouver: UBC Press.

McCallum, Myrna. 2020, October 12. "Practicing Cultural Humility in Human Rights Advocacy: A Debrief Session with Amber Prince." In The Trauma-Informed Lawyer, hosted by Myrna McCallum, podcast. https://thetraumainformedlawyer. simplecast.com/episodes/practising-cultural-humility-in-human-rights-advocacy -a-debrief-session-with-amber-prince.

McCormack, Fiona. 2016. "Indigenous Claims: Hearings, Settlements, and Neoliberal Silencing." *Polar: Political and Legal Anthropology Review* 39, 2: 226–42.

McGranahan, Carole. 2016. "Theorizing Refusal: An Introduction." *Cultural Anthropology* 31, 3: 319–25.

"Memorandum of Affiliation." n.d. Accessed May 21, 2020. https://indigenous.ubc.ca/ files/2011/01/UBC-Musqueam-MOA-signed1.pdf.

Mendeloff, David. 2009. "Trauma and Vengeance: Assessing the Psychological and Emotional Effects of Post-Conflict Justice." *Human Rights Quarterly* 31: 592–623.

Merchant, Peter. 2020. "As Far as the Eye Can See: The Shíshálh in Their Territory, 1791–1920." PhD diss., University of British Columbia.

Merry, Sally Engle. 1990. *Getting Justice and Getting Even: Legal Consciousness among Working-Class Americans*. Chicago: University of Chicago Press.

—. 2006. *Human Rights and Gender Violence: Translating International Law into Local Justice*. Chicago: University of Chicago Press.

—. 2006b. "Transnational Human Rights and Local Activism: Mapping the Middle." *American Anthropologist* 108, 1: 38–51.

—. 2009. "Relating to the Subjects of Human Rights: The Culture of Agency in Human Rights Discourse." In *Law and Anthropology: Current Legal Issues 2008*, vol. 12, edited by Michael Freeman and David Napier, 385–407. Oxford: Oxford University Press.

Metge, Joan. 1998. "Kia Tupato! Anthropologist at Work." *Oceania: Anthropology, Maori Tradition and Colonial Process* 69, 1: 47–60.

Miller, Bruce Granville, ed.. 1992a. "Anthropology and History in the Courts," special issue, *BC Studies* 95.

Miller, Bruce Granville. 1992b. "Common Sense and Plain Language." In "Anthropology and History in the Courts," edited by Bruce G. Miller, special issue, *BC Studies* 95: 55–65.

–. 1995. Consultant to Mr. Zool Suleman, Barrister and Solicitor acting in *Watt v Liebelt et al.*

–. 1999. "Culture as Cultural Defense: A Sacred Site in Court." *American Indian Quarterly* 22, 1: 83–97.

–. 2001. *The Problem of Justice: Tradition and Law in the Coast Salish World*. Lincoln: University of Nebraska Press.

–. 2004. *Invisible Indigenes: The Politics of Non-Recognition*. Lincoln: University of Nebraska Press.

–. 2006. "Bringing Culture In: Community Responses to Apology, Reconciliation, and Reparations." *American Indian Culture and Research Journal* 30, 4: 1–17.

–. 2010. "Oral History in Courts." Invited speaker at Indigenous Bar Association Elders' Gathering on Oral History Evidence, Turtle Lodge, Manitoba, March 29–31.

–. 2011a. *Oral History on Trial: Recognizing Aboriginal Narratives in the Courts*. Vancouver: UBC Press.

–. 2011b. "Report to the Missing Women Commission of Inquiry Concerning Discrimination and Racism." Prepared for the Missing Women Commission of Inquiry.

–. 2012a. Invited panelist. "Aboriginal Oral Histories in the Courtroom: More Than a Matter of Evidence." Panel Discussion, Liu Institute for Global Issues, UBC Press, February 8, 2012.

–. 2012b. "Life on the Hardened Border." *American Indian Culture and Research Journal* 36, 2: 23–46.

–. 2012c. *Expert Report affidavit concerning Coast Salish Social and Cultural Systems*. For Project Tallio of the UBC Law Innocence Project, October.

–. Panelist. 2013. "Missing Women Commission of Inquiry: Unpacked and Revisited." Hosted by the Centre for Policy Research on Culture and Community, Simon Fraser University, First Nations Studies, SFU, and the Social Justice Centre, Kwantlen Polytechnic University, Harbour Centre, Vancouver. July 9.

–. 2014. "An Ethnographic View of Legal Entanglements on the Salish Sea Borderlands." *UBC Law Review* 47, 3: 991–1024.

–. 2016a. "Sur la frontiére: les Salish du littoral et l'érosion de la souveraineté [Coast Salish Borderlands and the Erosion of Sovereignty]. In "Pluralismes Juridiques et Interculturalités," edited by Geneviève Motard, Emmanuelle Piccoli, and Christoph Eberhard, special issue, *Anthropologie et Sociétés* 40, 2: 155–76.

–. 2016b. "The Oral and the Written in Understanding Treaties." In *The Contemporary Coast Salish: Essays by Bruce Granville Miller,* memoir 12, co-edited by Bruce Granville Miller and Darby C. Stapp, 326–37. Richland, WA: Northwest Anthropology.

–. 2018a. *Report to BC Human Rights Tribunal re: Clara Menzies* [name changed] *v. Vancouver Police Department.*

–. 2018b. *Response to Dr. von Gernet's Report "Approach to Oral Histories and Traditions: and Suggested Applications to Matters Relating to Certain Treaty No. 4 Reserves."* Concerning T-2155–00 and T-2153–00, in the Province of Saskatchewan.

–. n.d. fieldnotes, Radek, McCue, Menzies. Notes; analysis of cases 1997–2015. In possession of author.

Miller, Bruce Granville and Bill Angelbeck. 2006. *Traditional Cultural Properties Study of the Ross Lake and Vicinity.* Submitted to Seattle City Light, Skagit Hydroelectric Project and Skagit Systems Tribes.

Miller, Bruce Granville, Bill Angelbeck, Molly Sue Malone, Robert R. Mierendorf, and Jan Perrier. 2021. *Upper Skagit Indian Tribe Historical Atlas.* Sedro-Woolley, WA: Upper Skagit Indian Tribe.

Miller, Bruce Granville, and Daniel Boxberger. 1989. *Snohomish Social Organization, 1934–1950s. Report for Snohomish Tribal Council.*

Miller, Bruce Granville, and Gustavo Menezes. 2015. "Anthropological Experts and the Legal System: Brazil and Canada." *American Indian Quarterly* 39, 4: 391–430.

Million, Dian. 2013. *Therapeutic Nations: Healing in an Age of Indigenous Human Rights.* Tucson: University of Arizona Press.

Mills, Aaron. 2010. "Aki, Anishinaabek, kaye tahsh Crown." *Indigenous Law Review* 9, 1: 107–66.

Mills, Antonia. 1994. *Eagle Down Is Our Law: Witsuwit'in Laws, Feasts, and Land Claims.* Vancouver: UBC Press.

–. 1996. "Problems of Establishing Authority in Testifying on Behalf of the Witsuwit'in." *Political and Legal Anthropology Review* 19: 39– 51.

–, ed. 2005. *'Hang Onto These Words': Johnny David's Delgamuukw Evidence.* Toronto: University of Toronto Press.

Milstead, Mary. 2010. "Profile: Amber Prince ('05)." *UBC Law Alumni Magazine,* Winter: 22–25.

Milward, David. 2012. *Aboriginal Justice and the Charter: Realizing a Culturally Sensitive Interpretation of Legal Rights.* Vancouver: UBC Press.

Monture-Angus, Patricia. (1998) 2015. "Standing against Canadian Law: Naming Omissions of Race, Culture and Gender." *New Zealand Yearbook of New Zealand Jurisprudence* 7. http://www.nzlii.org/nz/journals/NZYbkNZJur/1998/2.html.

Moore, Sally Falk. 2001. "Certainties Undone: Fifty Turbulent Years of Legal Anthropology, 1949–1999." *Journal of the Royal Anthropological Institute* 7, 1: 95–116.

Mullings, Delores V. 2009. "The Paradox of Exclusion within Equity: Interrogating Discourse at the Canadian Human Rights Tribunal." PhD diss., Wilfrid Laurier University.

Nadasdy, Paul. 2017. *Sovereignty's Entailments: First Nations State Formation in the Yukon.* Toronto: University of Toronto Press.

Napoleon, Val. 2013. *Mikomosis and the Wetiko.* Victoria, BC: University of Victoria, Indigenous Law Research Unit.

–. 2019. "Did I Break It? Recording Indigenous (Customary) Law." *Potchefstroom Electronic Law Journal* 22: 1–35. http://dx.doi.org/10.17159/1727–3781/2019/v22 i0a7588.

Narine, Shari. 2012. "Court Hears Complaint against Rights Tribunal Decision." *Windspeaker* 29, 12: 10.

National Association for the Practice of Anthropology. n.d. "Guidelines for Ethical Practice 2018." Accessed May 11, 2020. https://www.practicinganthropology.org/practice/ethics/.

Native Women's Association of Canada. 2011. "Report of the Native Women's Association of Canada." In *A Report to Parliament on the Readiness of First Nations Communities and Organizations to Comply with the Canadian Human Rights Act*, by Minister of the Department of Indian Affairs and Northern Development, 61–82.

Nitsan, Tal. 2014. "From Left to Rights: Guatemalan Women's Struggle for Justice." PhD diss., University of British Columbia.

O'Neill, Terry. 1999. "Guilty of Sexual Thought: A Case against a BC Professor Sparks Demands to Trash the Human Rights Industry." *Report Newsmagazine* 26, 42: 24.

Pablo, Carlito. 2009. "Bright Lights: Gladys Radek."*Georgia Straight,* September 23. https://www.straight.com/article-258851/bright-lights-gladys-radek.

Paine, Robert. 1996. "In Chief Justice McEachern's Shoes: Anthropology's Ineffectiveness in Court." *PoLAR: Political and Legal Anthropology Review* 19, 2: 59–70.

Palmer, Andie Diane. 2000. "Evidence 'Not in a Form Familiar to Common Law Courts': Assessing Oral Histories in Land Claims Testimony after *Delgamuukw v B.C.*" *Alberta Law Review* 38: 1040–50.

Peetush, Ashwani K. 2009. "Indigenizing Human Rights: First Nations, Self-Determination, and Cultural Identity." In *Indigenous Identity and Activism*, edited by Priti Singh, 190–204. Delhi, India: Shipra Press.

Philbrick, Nathaniel. 2006. *Mayflower: A Story of Courage, Community, and War*. New York: Penguin.

Povinelli, Elizabeth A. 2002. *The Cunning of Recognition: Indigenous Alterities and the Making of Australian Multiculturalism*. Durham, NC: Duke University Press.

Prince, Amber. 2020. Virtual lecture to Anthropology 471, University of British Columbia, November 26. Unrecorded.

Queen's Bench Rules, n.d. Foundational Rules. Part 5: Disclosure of Information, Part 3: Experts and Expert Reports, 23. https://pubsaskdev.blob.core.windows.net/pubsask-prod/81637/25QBRules-Parts1-18.pdf.

Radke, Amelia Jayne. 2018. "Murri Courts: An Ethnography of Indigenous Sentencing Courts in Southeast Queensland, Australia." PhD diss., The University of Queensland.

Ralph, Laurence. 2020. "Police Violence in Chicago." Lecture to the Department of Anthropology Seminar Series, University of British Columbia, December 8.

Ray, Arthur J. 2004. Title Unknown. Talk given to Department of Justice session on Expert Witnessing, February 2. Vancouver: University of British Columbia.

–. 2011. *Telling It to the Judge: Taking Native History to Court*. Montreal/Kingston: McGill-Queen's University Press.

–. 2016. *Aboriginal Rights Claims and the Making and Remaking of History*. Montreal/Kingston: McGill-Queens University Press.

Razack, Sherene H. 1998. *Looking White People in the Eye: Gender, Race, and Culture in Courtrooms and Classrooms*. Toronto: University of Toronto Press.

–. 2016. *Dying from Improvement: Inquests and Inquiries into Indigenous Deaths in Custody.* Toronto: University of Toronto Press.

Reilly, John. 2019. *Bad Law: Rethinking Justice for a Postcolonial Canada.* Calgary, AB: Rocky Mountain Books.

Richland, Justin. 2008. *Arguing with Tradition: The Language of Law in Hopi Tribal Court.* Chicago: University of Chicago Press.

Ridington, Robin. 1992. "Fieldwork in Court 53: A Witness to *Delgamuukw v. B.C.*" In "Anthropology and History in the Courts," edited by Bruce Miller, special issue, *BC Studies* 95: 12–24.

Rigby, Peter, and Peter Severeid. 1992. "Lawyers, Anthropologists and the Knowledge of Facts." In *Double Vision: Anthropologists at Law,* edited by Randy Frances Kandel, 5–21. NAPA Bulletin 11. Washington, DC: American Anthropological Association.

Rodriguez, Leila. 2020. *Culture as Judicial Evidence Expert Testimony in Latin America.* Cincinnati, OH: University of Cincinnati Press.

Rosen, Lawrence. 1977. "The Anthropologist as Expert Witness." *American Anthropologist* 79: 555–78.

–. 1979. "Response to Stewart." *American Anthropologist* 8: 111–12

Royal Commission on Aboriginal Peoples. 1991. Report of the Royal Commission on Aboriginal Peoples, Vol. 1, *Looking Forward, Looking Back.* Ottawa: Royal Commission on Aboriginal Peoples.

–. 1996. *Bridging the Cultural Divide: A Report on Aboriginal People and Criminal Justice in Canada.* Ottawa: Royal Commission on Aboriginal Peoples.

Sarris, Greg. 1993. *Keeping Slug Woman Alive: A Holistic Approach to American Indian Texts.* Berkeley: University of California Press.

Schweitzer, Marjorie, ed. 1999. *American Indian Grandmothers: Traditions and Transitions.* Norman: University of Oklahoma Press.

Scott, James C. 1985. *Weapons of the Weak: Everyday Forms of Peasant Resistance.* New Haven, CT: Yale University Press.

Sikkink, Kathyrn, and Carrie Booth Walling. 2007. "The Impact of Human Rights Trials in Latin America." In "Special Issue on Protecting Human Rights," *Journal of Peace Research* 44, 4: 427–45.

Simpson, Audra. 2007. "Ethnographic Refusal: Indigeneity, 'Voice' and Colonial Citizenship." *Junctures* 9: 67–80.

–. 2014. *Mohawk Interruptus: Political Life across the Borders of the Settler State.* Durham, NC: Duke University Press.

Stephen, Lynn. 2017. "Bearing Witness: Testimony in Latin American Anthropology and Related Fields." *Journal of Latin American and Caribbean Anthropology* 22, 1: 85–109.

Steward, Julian. 1955. "Theory and Application in Social Sciences." *Ethnohistory* 2: 292–302.

Stewart, Omer C. 1973. "Anthropologists as Expert Witnesses for Indians: Claims and Peyote Cases." In *A Report of the Symposium on Anthropology and the American Indian at the Meetings of the American Anthropological Association, San Diego, California, November 20, 1970,* 35–42. San Francisco: Indian Historian Press.

–. 1979. "An Expert Answers Rosen." *American Anthropologist* 81: 108–11.

Teeple, Gary, 2005. *The Riddle of Human Rights*. Amherst, NY: Humanity.

Teillet, Jean. 2011. "Foreword." In *Telling It to the Judge: Taking Native History to Court*, by Arthur J. Ray, xix-xxi. Montreal/Kingston: McGill-Queen's University Press.

Timmer, Alexandra. 2011. "Toward an Anti-Stereotyping Approach for the European Court of Human Rights." *Human Rights Law Review* 11, 4: 707–38.

–. 2011. "Anthropology Pure and Profane: The Politics of Applied Research in Aboriginal Australia." *Journal of Social Anthropology and Comparative Sociology* 21, 3: 233–55.

United Nations Commission on Human Rights. 2005. *Advancing the Rights of Indigenous Peoples: A Critical Challenge*. https://publications.gc.ca/collections/Collection/E84-10-2005E.pdf.

Venetis, Penny M. 2013. "Enforcing Human Rights in the United States: Which Tribunals Are Best Suited to Adjudicate Treaty-Based Human Rights Claims?" *Review of Law and Social Justice* 23, 2: 121–93.

Venne, Sharon Helen. 1998. *Our Elders Understand Our Rights: Evolving International Law regarding Indigenous People*. Syilx territory on the Penticton Indian Reserve in British Columbia: Theytus Books.

von Gernet, Alexander. 2018. *Approaches to Oral History and Traditions and Suggested Applications to Matters Relating to Certain Treaty No. 4 Reserves*. Report prepared for Attorney General of Canada in relation to *Watson et al. v. HMTQ* (Federal Court TD T-2153–00) and *Bear et al. v. HMTQ* (Federal Court TD T-2155–00).

Waldram, James E. 2004. *Revenge of the Windigo: The Construction of the Mind and Mental Health of North American Aboriginal Peoples*. Toronto: University of Toronto Press.

Walkem, Ardith. 2020. *Expanding Our Vision: Cultural Equality and Indigenous Peoples' Human Rights*. British Columbia Human Rights Tribunal. http://www.bchrt.bc.ca/shareddocs/indigenous/expanding-our-vision.pdf.

Washington State Administrative Office of the Courts. n.d. "Testimony by Experts." Washington State Court Rules. Accessed May 9, 2020. https://www.courts.wa.gov/court_rules/pdf/ER/GA_ER_07_02_00.pdf.

Weiss, Joseph. 2007. "Eliding Experience to Fit the Rules: The Transformation of Experience Inherent in the B.C. Human Rights Tribunal Process." In "Humans: Anthropological Perspectives on Holism," Anthropology Graduate Student Conference Proceedings, University of British Columbia, 2007. Copy in possession of author.

–. 2018. *Shaping the Future on Haida Gwaii: Life beyond Settler Colonialism*. Vancouver: UBC Press.

West-Newman, Catherine. 2005. "Feeling for Justice? Rights, Laws, and Cultural Contexts." *Law and Social Inquiry* 3, 2: 305–35.

Wiget, Andrew. 1982. "Truth and the Hopi: An Historiographic Study of Documented Oral Tradition concerning the Coming of the Spanish." *Ethnohistory* 29, 3: 181–99.

–. 1995. "Recovering the Remembered Past: Folklore and Oral History in the Zuni Land Trust Damages Case." In *Zuni and the Courts: A Struggle for Sovereign Land Rights*, edited by E. Richard Hart, 172–87. Lawrence: University Press of Kansas.

–. 1996. "Father Juan Greyrobe: Reconstructing Tradition Histories, and the Reliability and Validity of Uncorroborated Oral Tradition." *Ethnohistory* 43, 3: 459–82

Wilson, Richard Ashby. 2006. Afterword to "'Anthropology and Human Rights in a New Key': The Social Life of Human Rights." *American Anthropologist* 108, 1: 77–83.

Yirish, Craig. 1997. "A Modern-Day Star Chamber [Procedural Irregularities in Human Rights Cases in BC]." *British Columbia Report* 8, 46: 18.

Index

Note: Page numbers with (t) refer to tables. BCHRT refers to British Columbia Human Rights Tribunal.

Aboriginal, as term, 8. *See also* Indigenous peoples
academic scholarship: in expert reports, 75–76; hierarchy of knowledge, 40–41, 77–78; Indigenous legal scholars, 28–30; Indigenous oral research, 127, 128, 136, 142–43, 147–55, 157–59; literature review in reports, 75, 95; litigation's influences on anthropology, 76–78; publications as expert qualifications, 75–77; in tenure process, 158–59. *See also* expert-witnesses, qualifications; expert-witnesses, reports; *McCue v University of British Columbia* (2018) BCHRT
academic scholarship, peer-review: about, 75–76; gray literature, 76; Indigenous vs Western concepts, 147–50, 152–54, 157–59; publications as expert qualifications, 75–77; reports by expert-witnesses, 45; tenure process, 135
accommodations. *See* human rights, accommodations
adversarial colleagues. *See* expert-witnesses, relations with colleagues

Agarwal, Ranjan, 95
age as discrimination grounds, 65, 102, 108, 108(t). *See also* BCHRT, discrimination grounds for complaints
Allen, Lori A., 34
alternative dispute resolution, 105, 106, 191. *See also* BCHRT, mediation and settlement
American Anthropological Association (AAA), 42, 86–88
American Indians, as term, 14. *See also* United States, Native Americans
American Society for Ethnohistory, 34–35
ancestry as discrimination grounds, 4–5, 102, 108, 108(t). *See also* BCHRT, discrimination grounds for complaints
Angelbeck, Bill, 155
anthropologists as expert-witnesses. *See* expert-witnesses
anthropology: about, 5–6, 79; "accepted in the field," 93–94, 96, 180; concepts as debatable, 79, 93–95; ethics, 84, 86–90, 179; ethnohistory, 34–35; fact and truth, 79, 93–96, 179; fieldnotes, 35, 86–88; fieldwork, 35, 79, 83, 86;

208

hierarchy of knowledge, 40, 77–78; holism, 37, 83, 96; Indigenous scholars, 28–30; inferences, 4, 85, 95, 129; legal vs anthropological language, 75, 83, 91–95, 179; litigation's influences on, 76–78; medical anthropology, 62; methods, 35, 79, 86; negative stereotypes of, 38; non-experimental, 79; participant observation, 35, 86; qualitative data, 79; role in litigation, 5–6, 79–81, 191–92; schematization of social action, 55, 183; sociocultural anthropology, 79; soft vs hard sciences, 79; transformation of oral into written story, 5, 119–20, 179–80, 188–89. *See also* expert-witnesses; Miller, Bruce

"Anthropology and History in the Courts" (Miller), 19

appeals courts, 5, 75, 147, 185, 188. *See also* courts

Archibald, Jo-Ann, 128

Atleo, Shawn, 28, 111–12

Australia: court guidelines, 81; discrediting of expert qualifications, 47; experts as adversaries, 72; Indigenous culture in courtrooms, 130–31; *Mabo* case, 47; panel of experts (hot-tubbing), 81, 180; spiritual sites, 66–67

Bailey, F.G., 192

Baines, Stephen, 88

bands, as term, 8. *See also* Indigenous peoples

Battiste, Marie, 128

BCHR Commission (British Columbia Human Rights Commission): closure and reestablishment, 4, 102, 105–6, 118, 130, 185; mandate, 4; mediation, 105–6, 109–10; public education mandate, 114, 130

BCHRT (British Columbia Human Rights Tribunal): about, 4–5, 99–109, 119–25, 185–92; access and inquiries, 4–5, 101, 105–7, 113–14; appeals to courts, 5, 147, 185, 188; complainants and witnesses, 4–5; confidentiality, 128; critiques of tribunals, 109–18, 192;

discrimination grounds, 102, 108, 108(t); effectiveness, 99; historical background, 102–9; Indigenous-based programs or hiring, 105; influence on senior courts, 120, 184; jurisdiction, 107, 147; mandates and values, 102–4, 190; media coverage, 112–13, 120; motivation for complaints, 109–10, 160; procedures, 4–5, 105, 107, 113–14, 140; public education on, 114, 130; public hearings, 130, 190; recommendations for reforms, 99, 185–92; report on *(Expanding Our Vision)*, 100–101; screening of complaints, 102, 106, 114; setting for hearings, 5, 129–31, 186, 190; tribunal members, 119, 131–33, 140; UNDRIP implementation, 164–65, 185; visibility/invisibility, 112–14, 117–18; website, 101, 113. *See also* BCHRT, decisions and compensation; BCHRT, discrimination grounds for complaints; BCHRT, Indigenous complainants; BCHRT, mediation and settlement; BCHRT, research projects; BCHRT, self-represented complainants; *Expanding Our Vision 2020* (Walkem); expert-witnesses; human rights; human rights tribunals

BCHRT, decisions and compensation: about, 101, 122–25; compensation, 119, 122–25, 123(t), 124(t), 125(t), 181–82; complaints against Indigenous institutions, 108–9, 108(t); equity in judgments, 122–25, 123(t), 124(t), 125(t), 181–82; Indigenous complainants, 108–9, 108(t); jurisdiction, 105, 107; preliminary decisions, 105–7; statistics, 101, 106–7, 108(t); success rates, 122–25, 123(t), 124(t), 125(t), 181–82; tribunal member's powers, 131

BCHRT, discrimination grounds for complaints: about, 4–5, 102, 122–25, 123(t), 124(t), 125(t), 181–82; anti-stereotyping approach, 112, 114–15; areas of discrimination, 108, 108(t); complaints against institutions, 104–5, 107, 108–9, 181; discrimination categories, 4–5, 102, 108, 108(t), 122–25, 123(t), 124(t), 125(t), 181–82; evidence, 33, 128–29; *Human Rights Code,* 4, 102, 129; inferences, 129; motivation for discrimination, 129; personal characteristics, 108, 108(t); principles in *Radek,* 129; recommendations for reforms, 186–87

BCHRT, Indigenous complainants: about, 4–5, 100–101, 107–9, 108(t), 181; anti-stereotyping approach, 114–15; complaints against Indigenous institutions, 104–5, 108–9, 108(t); discrimination grounds, 102, 108, 108(t), 122–25, 123(t), 124(t), 125(t), 181–82, 186–87; equity in judgments, 122–25, 123(t), 124(t), 125(t), 181–82; gender/sex, 23, 108, 108(t), 181–82; human rights as useful frame, 7, 104, 110–11, 114; legal representation, 101, 113, 127, 160, 188; mediation, 101, 105–6; Miller as expert-witness and ethnographer, 24–26, 101; motivation for complaints, 109–10, 160; personal qualities of, 156, 189–90; personal transformative power of processes, 84, 120–21, 184; public awareness of BCHRT, 101, 113–14, 182; recommendations for reforms, 186–92; report on *(Expanding Our Vision),* 100–101; screening of complaints, 102, 106, 114; temporal patterns, 108(t). *See also* BCHRT, decisions and compensation; BCHRT, research projects; BCHRT, self-represented complainants; courts and tribunals, Indigenous cultural traditions; *Expanding Our Vision 2020* (Walkem); Indigenous peoples, trauma in legal processes; McCue, June; Menzies, Clara; Radek, Gladys

BCHRT, Indigenous complainants, difficulties: about, 113, 119–20; colonial courtroom, 132; emotional costs, 119–21, 181; failure to file complaints, reasons for, 113, 190; fears, 101, 120, 181, 184, 187–88; lack of Indigenous traditions in courts, 154; power relations, 101, 131, 181; recommendations

for reforms, 186–92; rights vs humanistic aspects of law, 34, 180, 186; time limits, 107; transformation of oral into legal story, 5, 113, 119–20, 179–80, 188–89. *See also* BCHRT, Indigenous complainants, diminution of

BCHRT, Indigenous complainants, diminution of: about, 5, 27–34, 180–81, 189–90; challenges to Indigenous status, 20, 143–46, 159, 189; colonialism, 27, 112; credibility attacks, 27, 34; demeaning comments, 119–20, 132; grounds for cases, 27; interruptions, 132, 140, 158; lack of recognition, 181; in legal processes, 5, 27; long cases, 27, 33; symbolic violence, 6, 30–34, 159, 161, 178, 180–85; women complainants, 23. *See also* Indigenous peoples, trauma in legal processes

BCHRT, mediation and settlement: about, 105–6, 181, 191; BCHR models, 105–6; BCHRT procedures, 102, 182; case settlement, 24–25; failures, 161; Indigenous complainants, 24–25, 182; mandatory mediation, 109–10; power relations, 105, 181; recommendations for change, 186, 191; statistics, 106, 110

BCHRT, research projects: about, 99–101, 107–8, 181–82; abandonment of complaints, 113, 181; access to justice, 100–101; cases against Indigenous institutions, 104–5, 108–9, 108(t), 181; compensation, 122–25, 123(t), 124(t), 125(t), 181–82, 190; complaints, statistics, 113–14; decisions, 101, 107–9, 108(t); discrimination grounds, 102, 107–8, 108(t), 181; equity in judgments, 122–25, 123(t), 124(t), 125(t), 181–82; gender/sex, 108, 108(t), 181–82; Indigenous-based programs or hiring, 105; mediation, 105–6, 181; methodology and findings, 100–101; preliminary decisions, 107; quantitative analysis, 101, 107–9, 108(t); research questions, 99; research time period (1997 to 2020), 108–9, 108(t), 181; researchers, 100; success rates, 122–25, 123(t), 124(t),

210 INDEX

125(t), 181–82; women as complainants, 23, 108, 181–82. See also *Expanding Our Vision 2020* (Walkem)

BCHRT, self-represented complainants: about, 151, 189–90; difficulties, 127, 133, 151, 182; Indigenous complainants, 127, 133, 145, 151, 156–57, 189–90; personal qualities, 156, 189–90; power relations, 127, 145, 156–57, 189–90; symbolic violence, 189–90. See also McCue, June

Beals, Ralph, 80

Bertoncini, Riley, 28, 100, 112, 122–25, 181–82

birthplace, discrimination grounds, 4–5

Black, William, 105–6, 109–10

Blackjack, Cynthia (inquest), 56, 58, 59–61

Blackjack, Cynthia (mother of Cynthia), 61–62

Blackjack inquest (2018) Yukon: about, 56–63; community letters, 57–58, 60–62; coroner's notes and recommendations, 58–59, 61–62; demeaning language, 65; health services, 57–60, 69; jury's questions to Miller, 69–70; letter to Blackjack's mother, 61–62; Miller as expert-witness, 56–63, 65, 69–71, 91–92; Miller's expert qualifications, discrediting, 56–57, 62–63, 65; Miller's expert report, 57–63; stereotypes and discrimination, 58–61; systemic racism, 56–61, 62–63, 69–70; unexpected events, 69–71, 186; *voir dire*, 56–57

Bombardier, Quebec v (2015) [Latif], 95

border litigation (Canada/US), 19–20, 47–48, 68

Borrows, John, 28, 29, 152

Bourdieu, Pierre, 36, 192

Boutilier, Lalaini, 95

Boxberger, Dan, 8, 76–77, 79–80

Brazil, 35, 38, 39, 88

British Columbia: history of anthropologists as witnesses, 72; land title cases, 33, 35; Missing Women Commission of Inquiry, 39, 165, 175; treaties, 14; *Tsilhqot'in* (2014), 33, 35;

UNDRIP legislation, 115, 185. See also Coast Salish peoples (BC, WA, OR)

British Columbia, human rights, 4–5. *See also* BCHR Commission (British Columbia Human Rights Commission); BCHRT (British Columbia Human Rights Tribunal); *Human Rights Code* (1967) (BC)

British Columbia Supreme Court, 120. See also *Delgamuukw v BC* (1997)

British Empire. *See* colonialism

Browne, Annette J., 61

Bryden, Philip, 105–6, 109–10

Bullock, Narida, 45, 79

Burke, Paul: advocacy by experts, 85–86; anthropology as non-experimental, 79; cross-examination of experts, 64; expert reports, 75; experts as adversaries, 72; legal suspicion of intellectual, 36, 38; overstepping expert roles, 91–92; panel of experts (hot-tubbing), 81; symbolic violence, 36; thinning the evidence, 47; transformation of anthropology into legal form, 36, 38, 180; vertical power, 40

Calder v British Columbia (1973) *[Nisga'a]*, 72

Canada: historical background, 13–16; state, as term, 9. *See also* Indigenous peoples, Canada

Canada, Department of Justice: *Constitution Act, 1982*, 14, 35, 78; court rules, 45–46, 81–82; as Crown, 9; *Delgamuukw*, 19; panels of experts, 81–82; session on expert witnesses (2004), 80

Canadian Anthropology Society (CASCA), 88

Canadian Human Rights Act: complaints against institutions, 104–5, 107, 108–9

Canadian Human Rights Commission (CHRC), 115

Canadian Human Rights Tribunal (CHRT), 104, 109, 111–12

Carlson, Keith, 78

Chotalia, Shirish, 111–12

Christie, Gordon, 116
CHRT (Canadian Human Rights Tribunal), 104, 109, 111–12
CILS (Centre for Indigenous Legal Studies), 139–40, 148
Citizens to Preserve Nookachamps Valley et al. v Skagit County, et al., 65–67
Clément, Dominique, 117
Coast Salish peoples (BC, WA, OR): border litigation, 19–20, 47–48, 68; child protection, 22; Indigenous legal practices, 191; legal recognition, 20–22; litigation's influences on anthropology, 76–78; Miller as anthropologist-expert, 17–21, 65; oral tradition, 155; spindle whorl, 139–40, 156; spiritual traditions and workers, 67, 163, 181. *See also* Musqueam Nation; United States, Native Americans; Upper Skagit Tribe of Indians (WA)
code, human rights. See *Human Rights Code* (1967) (BC)
code of ethics, 84, 86–90, 179
colleagues of experts. *See* expert-witnesses, relations with colleagues
colonialism: evolutionist anthropological models, 37–38, 78; failure to recognize, 39; gendered violence, 24; historical background, 13–16; vs human rights, 41, 110–11, 116; lack of recognition of Indigenous status, 20–22; legal systems, 13–16, 29–33, 112, 114; spatial segregation, 116; universalization of Western ideals, 110, 115–17, 118. *See also* decolonization
Comack, Elizabeth, 55
common law, 4, 13, 19, 38. *See also* legal systems
compensation, BCHRT. *See* BCHRT, decisions and compensation
complainants, 4–5, 119, 180. *See also* BCHRT (British Columbia Human Rights Tribunal); BCHRT, Indigenous complainants; BCHRT, Indigenous complainants, diminution of; BCHRT, self-represented complainants
confidentiality, 88, 128

Conley, John M., 158
Constitution Act, 1982: Aboriginal rights (s. 35), 14, 35, 78
counsel. *See* expert-witnesses, relations with lawyers; lawyers; lawyers, Indigenous
courtrooms: alternatives for BCHRT hearings, 186, 190; BCHRT hearings, 5, 129–31; Bourdieu's field of power, 36; Indigenous culture (AU), 131; power relations, 40, 131; vertical force field, 40. *See also* courts and tribunals, Indigenous cultural traditions
courts: about, 5–6; appeals courts, 5, 75, 147, 185, 188; BCHRT's influence on senior courts, 120, 184; common law, 4, 13, 19, 38; enforcement of tribunal orders, 5; international criminal courts, 41; limitations on tribunals, 185; physical settings, 131; power relations, 40, 131; state's sovereignty, 9. *See also* courts and tribunals, Indigenous cultural traditions; expert-witnesses; Indigenous peoples, trauma in legal processes; judges; juries; lawyers; lawyers, Indigenous; legal systems; oral and written evidence in legal processes; Supreme Court of Canada; thinning of evidence
courts, unexpected events: about, 69, 92; challenge to Indigenous status, 143–45; experts and Indigenous clients, 84; experts and lawyers, 84, 92, 179; jury questions for experts, 69–71
courts and tribunals, Indigenous cultural traditions: cultural resurgence, 27–30, 167; eagle feathers, 133, 161, 162, 163, 165–66, 167, 185; elders in attendance, 132, 133, 154, 161, 163, 165; land acknowledgments, 164; Maori spaces, 110; personal transformative power of, 184; prayers, 28, 133, 154, 161, 162, 163; recommendations for reforms, 186; smudging ceremonies, 132, 162, 163, 173, 186
Cousineau, Devyn, 163, 165–67, 170, 176–77, 188

Cree people, 63, 73, 171
criminal law: gendered criminalization, 24; *Gladue* (1999), 39; international criminal courts, 41; offender's background, 24, 39; sentencing, 39, 191
cross-examination: about, 64; on expert qualifications, 46, 47–48, 49, 64–65; of experts, 64, 70–71; open-ended questions, 70–71; preparation using experts, 73; by self-represented complainants, 127, 137–42, 151, 158; symbolic violence, 36; of witnesses, 140
Crown, as term, 9
Cruikshank, Julie, 37, 38, 73, 94–95, 152

Daly, Richard, 32–33, 35–36, 38, 40, 90, 192
Darien-Smith, Eve, 30
Daum, Robert, 155
Day, Shelagh, 118, 185
decisions, BCHRT. *See* BCHRT, decisions and compensation
decolonization: cultural resurgence, 16, 27–30; culturally safe settings, 186, 190; diversity as value, 116–17; human rights as useful, 114–16; Indigenous culture in courts (AU), 130–31; Indigenous legal scholars, 28–30; of legal systems, 27–30; recommendations for BCHRT reforms, 186–87; self-rule, 115–17; of Western liberal ideals, 115–17. *See also* courts and tribunals, Indigenous cultural traditions
Delgamuukw v BC (1997): about, 19, 35–36; evolutionist anthropological models, 35–36, 37, 78; legal setting, 190; oral evidence in written processes, 157; symbolic violence, 32–33, 35–36
Department of Justice. *See* Canada, Department of Justice
diminution of expert-witnesses. *See* expert-witnesses, diminution of
diminution of Indigenous peoples, 27–34. *See also* BCHRT, Indigenous complainants, diminution of
disability, mental and physical: BCHRT discrimination grounds, 102, 108, 108(t), 109. *See also* BCHRT, discrimination grounds for complaints
discrediting of experts. *See* expert-witnesses, qualifications; thinning of evidence
discrimination: anti-stereotyping approach, 114–15; popular culture and stereotypes, 65; stereotypes, 48, 58–61, 65, 112, 114–15; as term, 30. *See also* BCHRT, discrimination grounds for complaints; racism, systemic; racism and racial discrimination
dispute resolution, 105, 106, 191. *See also* BCHRT, mediation and settlement
DTES. *See* Vancouver, Downtown Eastside (DTES)
Duff, Wilson, 72
Duwamish tribe (WA), 21

elders. *See* Indigenous peoples, elders
Elders' Gathering on Oral History Evidence (2010), 29
Eliadis, Pearl, 102, 117, 184–85
Eltringham, Nigel, 41, 129–30
employment discrimination: discrimination grounds, 102, 108, 108(t); *McCue*, 127–29; Yukon case (2008), 25, 68. *See also* BCHRT, discrimination grounds for complaints; *McCue v University of British Columbia* (2018) BCHRT
epistemologies: alienation of Western legal education, 31–32; fact and truth models, 95–96, 179; hierarchy of knowledge, 40, 77–78; Indigenous resurgence, 27
equity in judgments, 122–25, 123(t), 124(t), 125(t), 181–82. *See also* BCHRT, decisions and compensation; BCHRT, Indigenous complainants
ethics, 84, 86–90, 179
ethnography, 7–8, 17–22, 85, 111, 180
ethnohistory, 34–35, 81, 85
European Court of Human Rights, 114, 115
evidence: corporate knowledge of research teams, 80; for BCHRT discrimination grounds, 33, 128–29;

INDEX 213

inferences, 4, 85, 95, 129; "invention of anthropology," 37; judges as overwhelmed by, 63; limited pool of experts, 6, 79–82, 180; of racism, 39; recordings of oral evidence, 85; trick questions by counsel, 76. *See also* BCHRT, discrimination grounds for complaints; oral and written evidence in legal processes; thinning of evidence

evolutionist anthropological models, 35–36, 37–38, 78

Ewick, Patricia, 23, 41, 119

Expanding Our Vision 2020 (Walkem): about, 100–101, 186–92; dispute resolution, 191; public awareness of BCHRT, 182; racializing behavior in tribunals, 111, 132; recommendations, 101, 186–87, 190–91; as a result of *Menzies*, 100, 161; survey findings, 100–101, 190; visibility/invisibility of BCHRT, 113

expert-witnesses: about, 4–6, 18, 34–40, 43–46, 74, 179–80; advocacy, 85–86; anthropologists as, 5–6, 18, 34–40; continuing obligations, 44; contract work, 90, 92; court as "strange classroom," 36–37, 180; court rules, 43–46, 81–82; criminal tribunals, 41; duties and roles, 4, 18, 43–45, 74, 79–80, 192; ethics, 84, 86–90, 179; ethnohistory, 34–35; Expert Witness Retention Agreement (SK), 43–45; for claimants vs respondents, 71; for Indigenous people vs the state, 79–81; friend of the court, 80; hierarchy of knowledge, 40, 77–78; historical background, 34–35, 72; identities at trial, 78–82; inferences, 4, 85, 95, 129; as a legal term, 83; limited pool, 79–82, 180; Master as agreed, 80, 180; objectivity, 79–80, 82, 89; overstepping of roles, 62–63, 91–92; panel of experts, 81–82, 180; recommendations for reforms, 186–92; research teams, 80; testimony, 74; transformation of oral into legal story, 5, 113, 119–20, 179–80, 188–89; truthfulness, 44–45; unexpected events, 69;

weight of testimony, 131. *See also* courts, unexpected events; expert-witnesses, relations with colleagues; thinning of evidence

expert-witnesses, diminution of: about, 63–64, 71; accusations of overstepping of roles, 62–63, 91–92; badgering by lawyers, 68, 71; credibility, 27, 34; demeaning comments, 63–68, 71; discrediting qualifications, 46–49, 55–56, 62–65, 71, 75–76, 131; lack of information on duties and roles, 71; misquotations, 74. *See also* thinning of evidence

expert-witnesses, qualifications: about, 45–46, 64–65, 71; BCHRT statements, 131; court rules, 43–46; cross-examination on, 46, 47–48, 64–65; description and c.v. in reports, 45–46, 71; discrediting, 46–49, 55–56, 62–65, 71; peer-reviewed publications, 75–76, 77; thinning of evidence, 46. *See also* thinning of evidence

expert-witnesses, relations with colleagues: about, 72–82; academic publications, 75–76; audience for reports, 75; cases without opposing expert, 72; collaboration, 80–82; colleagues' critiques of reports, 73–76; critiques of evolutionist models, 78; discrediting qualifications, 75–76; extreme positions, 72–73; hired gun, 80; limited pool of experts, 79–82, 180; litigation's influences on anthropology, 76–78; misquotations, 74; objectivity, 78–80, 82, 89; panel of experts, 81–82, 180; recommendations for cooperation, 80–82

expert-witnesses, relations with Indigenous clients: about, 83–84; ownership of data, 86–88; personal transformative power of processes, 84, 184. *See also* BCHRT, Indigenous complainants

expert-witnesses, relations with lawyers: about, 83–96, 178–80; "accepted in the field," 93–94, 96, 180; case theory

shared, 83, 85–86, 90–92, 179–80; ethics, 84, 86–90, 179; fieldnotes, ownership of, 86–88; inferences, 4, 85, 95, 129; language, legal vs anthropological meanings, 83, 91–95, 179; lawyers as protectors, 91; overlap in reasoning, 95–96; overstepping expert roles, 62–63, 91–92; qualifications review, 46, 71; recommendations for change, 83, 90–92; scheduling proceedings, 92, 179; team vs team-like, 83–85, 90–91; truth and fact, 85, 93–96, 179; unexpected events, 84, 92, 179. *See also* courts, unexpected events; expert-witnesses, diminution of; thinning of evidence
expert-witnesses, reports: about, 45–46, 75; advocacy, 85–86; in appeals courts, 75; audiences, 75; colleagues' critiques of reports, 73–76; confidentiality, 128; court rules, 43–46, 81–82; critique of reports, 40–41; deliberate omissions, 39; evidence preservation, 44; hierarchy of knowledge, 40, 77–78; joint reports, 81; literature review in, 75, 95; ownership of data, 86–88; peer review of reports, 45; plain language vs complexity, 75, 77; power relations, 39–40; qualifications, 45–46, 71; revisions for lawyers, 85

facts: "accepted in the field," 93–94, 96, 180; concepts of fact and truth, 93–96, 179; inferences, 4, 85, 95, 129; schematization of social action, 96, 183; skeletonization of facts in law, 96
family and marital status: BCHRT discrimination grounds, 102, 108, 108(t). *See also* BCHRT, discrimination grounds for complaints
fears and legal processes. *See* BCHRT, Indigenous complainants, difficulties
fieldnotes, 35, 86–88
fieldwork, 35, 79, 83, 86
First Nation Child and Family Caring Society and Assembly of First Nations (2016) (CHRT), 111–12

First Nations: as term, 8. *See also* BCHRT, Indigenous complainants; Indigenous peoples
fishing rights: cross-border fishing, 20, 47–48, 68; fishing rights *(US v. Washington)*, 76, 93–94; thinning of evidence, 47–48; *Van der Peet* (1996), 37–38, 78
Fiske, Jo-Anne, 61
Foucault, Michel, 40
Fromme, Joan, 121–22
Furniss, Elizabeth, 55

A Gathering of Wisdoms (Clarke, ed.), 28, 31
Geertz, Clifford, 95–96
gender/sex: BCHRT discrimination grounds, 23–24, 102, 108, 108(t); identity or orientation, 102; trans men and women as complainants, 122–25, 123(t), 124(t), 125(t), 181–82. *See also* BCHRT, discrimination grounds for complaints; Indigenous peoples, women; women
Gitxsan and Wet'suwet'en peoples, 28, 35. See also *Delgamuukw v BC* (1997)
Gladue, R v (1999), 39
Goffman, Erving, 78
Goodale, Mark, 40, 185–86
gray literature, 76. *See also* academic scholarship, peer-review
Green, Joyce, 114, 117

Harris, Douglas, 80
Hastrup, Kirsten, 34
healing discourses, 33. *See also* Indigenous peoples, trauma in legal processes
health care, Indigenous peoples, 56–61. See also *Blackjack* inquest (2018) Yukon
Heerspink, Insurance Corp. of BC v. (1982), 117–18
Henderson, James (Sákéj) Youngblood, 28, 29
Henry, Frances, 128
Highway of Tears, 175
Howe, R. Brian, 118

HRT. *See* BCHRT (British Columbia Human Rights Tribunal); human rights tribunals

human rights: about, 4, 40–42, 109–18; anti-stereotyping approach, 114–15; concepts of humanness, 42; critiques of, 34, 40–42, 109–18; ethnographic approach, 40–42; as fundamental law, 110, 112, 118; harmful discourses, 42; as imperialism, 116; individual rights built on, 116; as legal rights, 104, 109–10, 112, 118; liberal ideals, 116–17; in mediation, 109–10; neoliberalism, 110; of non-human entities, 22, 116, 191; rights vs humanistic aspects of law, 34, 180, 186; state-centered, 118, 180; three-tiered system, 104; universalization, 110, 115–17, 118; Western discourses, 109–12, 115–18, 180

human rights, accommodations: BCHRT discrimination grounds, 102, 108–9, 108(t); of Indigenous thought, 19, 117–18, 135–36, 149, 154; of oral evidence, 19. *See also* BCHRT, discrimination grounds for complaints

human rights, Indigenous peoples: about, 40–42, 180–81; alienation due to process, 180–81; anthropological approaches, 40–42; complainants to tribunals, 4–5, 119–20, 180; concept as useful frame, 7, 104, 110–11, 114–16, 180–81; emotional costs, 181, 182; frozen rights, 39; healing and trauma discourses, 33; identity, 186–87; power relations, 40–41, 181; reconciliation and rights, 90, 114, 117, 118; resistance, 185–86; rights as weapon of the weak, 40–42; rights vs humanistic aspects of law, 34, 180, 186; self-rule, 110, 115–17; as Trojan Horse for Western values, 116–17, 118; UNDRIP rights, 27–28, 115, 164–65, 185; vs Western frameworks, 109–12, 115–18. *See also* BCHRT, decisions and compensation; BCHRT, discrimination grounds for complaints; BCHRT, Indigenous complainants;

BCHRT, Indigenous complainants, diminution of

Human Rights Code (1967) (BC): about, 4, 102–4, 186–87; amendments (2002), 105; BCHRT created under, 102, 104; critique of, 183; discrimination grounds, 4, 102, 186–87; historical background, 102–5; Indigenous identity, 186–87; mediation, 110; recommendations for reforms, 186–87. *See also* BCHRT (British Columbia Human Rights Tribunal); human rights

Human Rights Commission. *See* BCHR Commission (British Columbia Human Rights Commission)

Human Rights Council (BC), 4

Human Rights Tribunal (BC). *See* BCHRT (British Columbia Human Rights Tribunal)

human rights tribunals: about, 23–26, 102, 109–18, 185; cases without opposing experts, 72; complainants, 4–5; critiques of, 34, 109–18, 192; diminution of Indigenous complainants, 5; discrimination grounds, 102; human rights as legal rights, 104, 109–10, 112, 118; humanity in human rights, 34; international tribunals, 114–15; limitations by higher courts, 185; media coverage, 112–13, 114–15, 120; racism, 111–12, 114; real vs ideal, 116–17; recent trends, 115, 118; rights vs humanistic aspects of law, 34, 180, 186; state-centered rights, 118, 180; as stimulus for reform, 115; symbolic violence, 159, 178, 180–85; transformation of oral into legal story, 5, 113, 119–20, 179–80, 188–89; tribunal members, 7; visibility, 112–15, 117–18; women as complainants, 23. *See also* BCHRT (British Columbia Human Rights Tribunal); BCHRT, Indigenous complainants; BCHRT, Indigenous complainants, diminution of; human rights, Indigenous peoples; Indigenous peoples, trauma in legal processes; Yukon Human Rights Commission

Hutchins, Peter, 37, 38, 90–91
Hwlitsum First Nation (BC), 21

Indian, Status, as term, 9, 13, 14. *See also*
Indigenous peoples, Canada
Indian Act (1876), 9, 14
Indian Claims Commission (US), 34–35,
90–91
Indigenous peoples: assimilation, 37;
border litigation (Canada/US), 19–20,
47–48, 68; colonialism, 13–16, 37–38;
cultural resurgence, 16, 27–30; gendered violence, 24; legal recognition,
20–22; terminology, 8–9; UNDRIP
rights, 27–28, 115, 164–65, 185. *See also*
Australia; Coast Salish peoples (BC,
WA, OR); colonialism; human rights;
human rights, Indigenous peoples;
United States, Native Americans
Indigenous peoples, Canada: about, 8–9,
13–14; border litigation (Canada/US),
19–20, 47–48, 68; colonial history,
13–14, 16; constitutional rights (s. 35),
14, 35, 78; *Indian Act* (1876), 9, 14;
Indigenous legal scholars, 28–30; land
claims, 14; legal recognition, 9, 14, 20–
22; Royal Proclamation of 1763, 14–15;
seven dimensions of well-being, 115;
spatial segregation, 116; Status Indians,
9, 13, 14; stereotypes, 48, 58–61, 65, 112,
114–15; terminology, 8–9; treaties, 14;
well-being, dimensions of, 115. *See also*
Coast Salish peoples (BC, WA, OR);
colonialism; human rights, Indigenous
peoples; Indigenous peoples; Métis
Indigenous peoples, complaints to
human right tribunals: about, 4–5, 27–
28, 107–8, 108(t). *See also* BCHRT,
Indigenous complainants; BCHRT,
Indigenous complainants, difficulties;
BCHRT, Indigenous complainants,
diminution of; human rights tribunals; Indigenous peoples, trauma in
legal processes
Indigenous peoples, elders: attendance at
courts and tribunals, 132, 133, 154, 161,
163, 165; as witnesses, 27, 32–34, 73

Indigenous peoples, legal traditions:
about, 13; Indigenous legal scholars,
28–30; nonhuman entities, rights, 22,
116, 191; protocols for research, 149–
50; resurgence of, 28–30, 191; sentencing phase, 191; spiritual teachings, 117.
See also courts and tribunals, Indigenous cultural traditions
Indigenous peoples, oral tradition:
about, 73; open-ended system, 73;
oral research in tenure processes, 127,
128, 136, 142–43, 147–55, 157–59; in
past and present, 73; recordings as
evidence, 85; sacred sites, 65–67; Snake
and Beaver story, 66; as theatre, 95;
and Western knowledge, 152–57.
See also *Delgamuukw v BC* (1997);
Indigenous peoples, elders; Indigenous peoples, spiritual traditions
Indigenous peoples, spiritual traditions:
about, 117; generational training, 67;
legal recognition of, 22, 66–68; in
legal traditions, 117; rights of non-
human entities, 22, 116, 191; sacred
sites, 66–68. *See also* courts and tribunals, Indigenous cultural traditions;
Indigenous peoples, oral tradition
Indigenous peoples, trauma in legal
processes: about, 6, 27–28, 30–34, 178–
85, 187–88; complex systems, 31; critique of trauma narratives, 33–34, 41;
distrust of lawyers, 31; double trauma,
30; elders as witnesses, 27, 32–34, 73;
emotional costs, 33–34, 41, 119–21, 159,
181, 182; financial costs, 31, 184; healing
discourses, 33; human rights tribunals,
178; Indigenous legal experts, 28–30;
lateral violence, 54–55; law school
trauma, 31–32; missing women inquiries, 22, 39, 164, 165; perpetuation
of trauma, 6; recommendations for
reforms, 185–92; relational vs rules-
based view, 41–42, 182–83, 191; self-
represented complainants, 127, 151,
189–90; symbolic violence, 30–34, 159,
178; terminology, 30, 33; testimony at
inquiries, 22; transformation of oral

into legal story, 113, 188–89; trauma-informed lawyering, 28, 30–31, 161, 188. *See also* courts and tribunals, Indigenous cultural traditions; thinning of evidence

Indigenous peoples, ways of knowing: Indigenous studies as emerging field of knowledge, 152–53; peer review concept, Indigenous vs Western, 147–50, 152–54, 157–59; vs Western knowledge, 152. *See also* Indigenous peoples, oral tradition; oral and written evidence in legal processes

Indigenous peoples, women: about, 23, 181; BCHRT complainants, 23, 108(t), 120–25, 123(t), 124(t), 125(t), 181–82; as community protectors, 23, 121; criminalization of, 24; diminution at inquiries, 22; *A Gathering of Wisdoms,* 31; gendered violence, 24; Highway of Tears, 175; human rights tribunal complainants, 181; inquiry into missing and murdered women, national, 22, 164, 168; inquiry into missing women, BC, 39, 165, 175; intergenerational trauma, 24; interruptions in court, 132, 140, 158; power relations, 22–23, 164; *Red Women Rising* report, 28, 164–65, 172, 174; VPD relations, 28, 164, 172, 174, 175–76

inquests. See *Blackjack* inquest (2018) Yukon

Inuit, 8, 13, 14

Invisible Indigenes (Miller), 9, 21, 144

Jacobs, Beverley, 24, 28
Jacobs, Sue-Ellen, 86–87
Janzen, John, 34, 41
Jay Treaty (1794), 47–48, 68
Jensen, Stephen L.B., 110–11
JIBC (Justice Institute of BC), 122, 167, 173
Johnson, David, 118
Johnson, Yvonne, 24
Johnson v M'Intosh (1823) (US), 15
Johnston, Darlene, 28, 29–30
judges: as amateur anthropologists,

37–38, 47–48, 66–67; audience for reports, 75; bias for high profile experts, 77; control over anthropology, 36–37; demeaning comments to experts, 66–68; evolutionist anthropological models, 5, 37–38, 78; "invention of anthropology," 37; knowledge of legal vs anthropological terms, 92–93; overstepping by experts, 62–63, 91–92; overwhelmed by evidence, 63; in a "strange classroom," 36–37, 180

juries: audience for reports, 75; direct questioning of experts, 69–71; not in BCHRT, 131; overstepping by experts, 62–63, 91–92

Justice Institute of BC (JIBC), 122, 167, 173

Kandel, Randy Frances, 37, 83, 91, 96, 178–79

Knucwentwecw Society Human Rights Complaint (2006) BCHRT, 24–25

Kroeber, Alfred, 90–91

Laforme, Harry, 28, 29
Lake Babine First Nation, 144. *See also* McCue, June
Lalani, Faiz, 95
Lamarche, Lucie, 118, 185
land titles: constitutional rights (s. 35), 35; *Tsilhqot'in* (2014), 33, 35. See also *Delgamuukw v BC* (1997)
Lane, Barbara, 76, 80
Langer, Rosanna, 117
language: ancestral names, use of, 163, 166, 169–70, 175, 184; complexity vs plain language, 18, 75, 77; duelling epistemologies, 95–96; legal vs social science meanings, 46, 83, 92–95, 179
Latif case (Bombardier) (2015), 95
law schools. *See* legal education; UBC, Allard School of Law
Law's Anthropology (Burke), 8, 36, 47, 90, 180. *See also* Burke, Paul
lawyers: demeaning comments by, 119–20; and expert-witnesses, 83; financial costs in complaints, 127; support for

Indigenous complainants, 121; transformation of oral into legal story, 5, 119–20, 179–80, 188–89; views on process difficulties, 119–20. *See also* expert-witnesses, relations with lawyers; oral and written evidence in legal processes; thinning of evidence

lawyers, Indigenous: Indigenous scholars, 28–31; obligation to live by Indigenous teachings, 31–32; personal transformative power of legal processes, 184; trauma of law school, 31–32; trauma-informed lawyering, 30–31, 161, 188. *See also* expert-witnesses, relations with lawyers; McCallum, Myrna; McCue, June; Prince, Amber

legal education: trauma of Indigenous students, 31–32. *See also* academic scholarship; expert-witnesses, qualifications; UBC, Allard School of Law

legal systems: about, 2, 9, 29–34, 185–86; "accepted in the field," 93–94, 96, 180; alternatives to adversarial practices, 191; border litigation (Canada/US), 19–20, 47–48, 68; civil law, 38; colonialism, 13–16, 29–33, 112, 114; common law, 4, 13, 19, 38; decolonization of, 29–30; epistemologies, 95–96; fact and truth concepts, 93–96, 179; hierarchy of knowledge, 40, 77–78; human rights as fundamental law, 110, 112, 118; law as regulator of social life, 185–86; law as story, 5, 40, 96, 179–80, 188–89; legal pluralism and anthropology, 77; liberal ideals, 116–17; litigation's influences on anthropology, 76–78; political interference, 21; positivism, 41; relational vs rules-based views, 41, 182–83, 191; rights vs humanistic aspects of law, 34, 180, 186; skeletonization of facts, 96; social science entanglements, 17; state's sovereignty, 9; tool of oppression, 31–32; transformation of oral into legal story, 5, 113, 119–20, 179–80, 188–89. *See also* courts; expert-witnesses; human rights tribunals; judges; lawyers; oral

and written evidence in legal processes; witnesses

legal systems and Indigenous people: colonialism, 13–16, 29–33, 112; Indigenous legal scholars, 28–30; influence on Western systems, 30; legal recognition, 20–22; symbolic violence, 30–34, 159, 180–85. *See also* BCHRT, Indigenous complainants; BCHRT, Indigenous complainants, diminution of; courts and tribunals, Indigenous cultural traditions; Indigenous peoples, legal traditions; Indigenous peoples, trauma in legal processes; oral and written evidence in legal processes

Les Carpenter v Faro (2008, 2010) Yukon, 25, 68

LGBTQ. *See* gender/sex

literature, academic. *See* academic scholarship

Little Salmon Carmacks First Nation, 56–59. See also *Blackjack* inquest (2018) Yukon

Lurie, Nancy, 35

Lyster, Lindsay, 119

Malloway, Frank (Siyémches), 17

Malone, Molly, 81

Mandell, Louise, 84

Marshall Trilogy (US), 15

Martin, Carol Muree, 28, 164, 172, 174

Mashpee Wampanoag tribe (MA), 21

Master as agreed, 80, 180

Mawani, Renisa, 116

McAllister, Maeve, 100, 104

McCall, Sophie, 29

McCallum, Myrna: Indigenous lawyer, 28; lawyer for *Menzies*, 161–62, 171–72, 184, 188; trauma-informed lawyering, 30–31, 161, 188

McCormack, Fiona, 110

McCue, June: about, 127, 158–59; challenges to her Indigenous status, 20, 143–46, 159, 189; denial of tenure and promotion, 127–29, 158–59; human costs, 25–26, 159, 183; ill treatment by law students, 134, 141; Indigenous studies as emerging field, 134–35; legal scholar, 28, 127, 134, 158; personal qualities, 23, 156, 158, 189; self-representation, 25, 127, 133, 145–46, 151, 153, 156–58; symbolic violence of legal processes, 159

McCue v University of British Columbia (2018) BCHRT: about, 25, 126–59; analysis, 151–59; community letters of support, 134, 157–58; community work as scholarly work, 127, 128, 134–35, 138–39, 147–52, 157–58; decisions, 127–29, 158; employment discrimination grounds, 127–29; expert witness reports, 128, 144; Indigenous studies as emerging field, 152–53; McCue's Indigenous status, challenges to, 143–46, 159, 189; Miller's ethnography, 25–26; Miller's narrative, 101, 126, 129–59; oral research as scholarly work, 127, 128, 136, 142–43, 147–55, 157–59; peer review concept, Indigenous vs Western, 147–50, 152–54, 157–58; power relations, 140; preliminary decision, 127–28; SAC (senior appointments committee), 134, 146–51; tenure process, 136, 142–43, 146–51, 153–54, 158–59; UBC collective agreement, 136, 146–48, 150, 153; UBC's relations with Musqueam people, 155–56; unexpected events, 143–45; written final submissions, 151, 157

McCue v University of British Columbia (2018) BCHRT hearing (2016): about, 129–51; as colonial courtroom, 132; Dean's testimony (former Dean), 135–42, 153, 155–57; diminution strategies, 132, 140–42, 149–50, 158, 189; faculty witnesses, 142–46; lack of Indigenous protocol, 154; McCue's cross-examinations, 134–35, 137–42, 147–51; physical setting, 129–31; public attendance, 130, 132, 145–46; time limits, 142, 154; Toope's testimony (former UBC president), 133–36, 149, 152, 154, 158; tribunal member, 132–35, 137, 140–43, 145–51, 157; UBC lawyers, 132, 135, 137–38, 142, 148–49, 151

McLay, Eric, 155

media coverage of tribunals, 112–13, 120

mediation. *See* BCHRT, mediation and settlement

medical anthropology, 62–63, 70

men: BCHRT complainants, 102, 108, 122–25, 123(t), 124(t), 125(t), 181–82. *See also* BCHRT, discrimination grounds for complaints; gender/sex

Mendeloff, David, 41

Menezes, Gustavo, 16, 35, 37, 38, 39, 77, 88

Menzies, Clara: about, 7, 23, 49–56, 160–77; ancestral names, use of, 163, 166, 169–70, 175, 184; on colonialism, 50–51, 54–55, 109, 188; diminution, 27; DTES as Indigenous space, 50–51, 53–55; her fear of police retaliation, 56, 170, 176, 187–88; human costs, 50–51, 54–56, 122, 161, 176–77; influence on case law, 184; length of proceedings, 27; motherhood, 50–54, 166; personal qualities, 23, 122, 161, 189; pseudonym, 122; symbolic violence, 161, 188–89; visible minority, 54

Menzies v Vancouver Police Board (2019) BCHRT: about, 7, 49–56, 160–77; analysis, 53–56, 176–77; decision and compensation, 122, 161–62, 176–77, 190; evidence not included, 166; exclusion from *voir dire,* 49, 55–56; McCallum as Menzies's lawyer, 161–62, 171–72, 184, 188; mediation failures, 161, 162; Menzies's interview by Miller, 154; Miller as expert witness, 25–26, 160, 162, 165; Miller's expert report, 49–56, 160; Miller's interview of Menzies, 50–56; Miller's qualifications, discrediting, 49, 55–56; Prince as Menzies's lawyer, 160–63, 166–71, 188; racialized policing, 49–52, 55–56, 165, 170, 176; redacted police notes, 50, 55–56; as resistance, 122, 186; VPD cultural training, 53, 161, 167–68, 170, 173–75, 189; Walkem's report as response to, 100, 161

Menzies v Vancouver Police Board (2019)
BCHRT hearing (2019): about, 162–
77; ancestral names, use of, 163, 166,
169–70, 175, 184; Cousineau (tribunal
member), 133, 161, 163, 165–67, 170,
176–77, 188; Indigenous traditions,
132–33, 154, 161, 162, 163, 165–67;
intervener (Union of BC Indian
Chiefs), 162, 164–65; Menzies's lawyers, 162–63, 166–72, 184; Menzies's
testimony, 165–67; Miller as expert
witness, 165, 166–67; Miller's narrative, 101, 126, 162–76; physical setting,
129–31, 162; public attendance, 154,
163–65; VPD constables, 7, 167–71,
174–75, 189; VPD Indigenous liaison,
171–74, 176; VPD lawyer, 162, 165, 167,
170, 174
Merry, Sally Engle, 23, 41
Metge, Joan, 43, 74, 81, 85–86
Métis: BCHRT complainants, 102, 107,
108; legal experts, 112; legal recognition, 14, 137; legal scholars, 28–30, 37,
137; as term, 8, 107; VPD protocol
officer, 171. *See also* Indigenous peoples
Michalson, Laraine, 60
Miller, Bruce: about, 4–5, 16–22; as
anthropologist-ethnographer, 7–8, 17–
22, 79, 85, 111, 126, 132–33, 180, 186; as
anthropologist-expert, 4–6, 17–22, 79;
legal entanglements, 17; legal recognition of Indigenous peoples, 20–22;
litigation, 5, 18–22; medical anthropology, 62–63, 70; methods, 79; oral
evidence in written processes, 19, 119;
qualifications for legal processes, 64–
65, 71; reports and studies, 17–22;
rights tribunals, 17–18, 24–26; social
position, 17, 18; thinning of evidence,
191–92. *See also* BCHRT, research
projects
Miller, Bruce Granville, works: "Anthropology and History in the Courts,"
19; *Invisible Indigenes,* 9, 21, 144; *Oral
History on Trial,* 19, 29, 63, 155;
"Report to the Missing Women
Commission of Inquiry," 39, 165;

*Upper Skagit Indian Tribe Historical
Atlas,* 18
Million, Dian, 24, 28, 33, 110
Mills, Aaron, 28, 29
Mills, Antonia, 35
Milward, David, 28, 29
Missing Women Commission of
Inquiry (BC), 39, 165, 175. *See also*
National Inquiry into Missing and
Murdered Indigenous Women and
Girls
monetary compensation. *See* BCHRT,
decisions and compensation
Monture-Angus, Patricia, 28, 31–32
Moore, Sally Falk, 41
Moore v BC (2012), 129, 185
Mullings, Dolores V., 111, 114
Murri Court (AU), 130–31
Musqueam Nation: ancestral names, use
of, 163, 166, 169–70, 175, 184; elders,
28, 163; UBC relations, 137, 139–40,
155–56; unceded territory, 137, 156,
164; VPD police liaison, 172. *See also*
Menzies, Clara

Nadasdy, Paul, 118
Napoleon, Val, 28, 29
Narine, Sahri, 112
National Association for the Practice of
Anthropology (NAPA), 89
National Inquiry into Missing and
Murdered Indigenous Women and
Girls, 22, 164, 168. *See also* Indigenous
peoples, women
nations, as term, 9. *See also* Indigenous
peoples
Native Americans. *See* United States,
Native Americans
Native Women's Association of Canada
(NWAC), 24, 28, 112
New Zealand, 74, 85–86, 110
Nisga'a case *(Calder)* (1973), 72
Nitsan, Tal, 41
nonhuman entities, rights, 22, 116, 191
Nookachamps Rock, 65–67
Nooksack tribe, 20, 28
Norman, Ken, 118, 185

INDEX   221

O'Barr, William M., 158
oral and written evidence in legal processes: about, 113, 119–20; concepts as debatable, 94–95; emotional costs, 119–21; law as story, 5, 96, 113, 119–20, 179–80, 188–89, 192; Miller's role, 19, 29, 79, 133; privileging of written over oral, 157; sacred sites, 65–67; truth and fact, 94–95. See also *Delgamuukw v BC* (1997); Indigenous peoples, oral tradition; Indigenous peoples, ways of knowing; legal systems; *McCue v University of British Columbia* (2018) BCHRT
Oral History on Trial (Miller), 19, 29, 63, 155
oral tradition. *See* Indigenous peoples, oral tradition

Palestinians, 34, 41
panels of experts, 81–82
participant observation, 35, 86
peer review. *See* academic scholarship, peer-review
Peetush, Ashwani, 115–17, 185
Pender Harbour First Nation (BC), 21
Pivot Legal Society v. Downtown Ambassadors (2012) BCHRT, 120
police and policing: racialized policing, 49–51, 55, 164; systemic racism evidence, 39. See also *Menzies v Vancouver Police Board* (2019) BCHRT
popular culture and discrimination, 65. *See also* discrimination
power relations in legal processes: Bourdieu's fields, 36; courtrooms, 32, 36, 131; Foucauldian capillaries, 40; hierarchy of knowledge, 40, 77–78; human rights as challenge to power, 40–41; Indigenous claimants, 164, 180–81; mediation, 105; physical settings, 131, 186, 190; reenactment of trauma, 22; state's sovereignty, 9; symbolic violence, 30–36, 159, 178, 182–85; vertical power in government, 40, 131; women, 23, 158, 164. *See also* BCHRT, self-represented complainants;

Indigenous peoples, trauma in legal processes
Price, Roberta, 28, 163
Prince, Amber: barriers for Indigenous complainants, 182; career as Indigenous lawyer, 28, 84, 131, 160; on importance of *Menzies,* 100, 160–62, 184; lawyer for Menzies, 119, 160–62, 187, 188; trauma-informed lawyering, 30–31, 161, 188

qualifications of experts. *See* expert-witnesses, qualifications

racism, systemic: about, 181; health services *(Blackjack),* 56–60, 62–63, 69–70; ineffectiveness of tribunals, 190; policing *(Menzies),* 161, 165, 170, 176; reports on evidence, 39
racism and racial discrimination: BCHRT discrimination grounds, 4–5, 102, 108, 108(t); common-sense racism, 55; emotional costs of testimony, 33–34, 51, 119–21; lateral violence, 54–55; omission of evidence in reports, 39, 165; schema for negative actions, 55; stereotypes, 48, 58–61, 65, 112, 114–15, 129; Western liberal rights discourses, 110, 118. *See also* BCHRT, discrimination grounds for complaints; oral and written evidence in legal processes
Radek, Gladys: about, 120–21; human costs, 119–20; personal qualities, 23, 121, 189; personal transformative power of legal processes, 120–21, 184; views on racism, 121
Radek v Henderson Development (2005) BCHRT: about, 24, 120–22; decision and compensation, 120–22, 190; diminution of Radek, 119; discrimination grounds, 129; expert report, 48–49; influence on case law, 120, 184; media coverage, 120; Miller's qualifications, 46, 49, 131; as resistance, 121, 186; security industry training, 122; thinning of evidence, 46, 48–49, 131; Timberg as counsel, 119, 121

222 INDEX

Radke, Amelia Jayne, 130–31
Ralph, Laurence, 30
Ray, Arthur: colleagues' critiques of reports, 73–74; court as "strange classroom," 36–37, 180; courtroom as physical setting, 131; discrediting of expert qualifications, 47–48; expert reports, 75, 95; experts as adversaries, 72–74; experts as colleagues, 8; hostilities in legal processes, 37, 38; scholarly publications as qualifications, 76; shared theory of the case, 90–92; unexpected events, 69, 92
Razack, Sherene, 145
recognition of Indigenous peoples, 20–22. *See also* Indigenous peoples
Red Women Rising (Martin and Walia), 28, 164, 172, 174
Reilly, John, 30
relational vs rules-based law, 41–42, 182–83, 191. *See also* legal systems
religion and spirituality: BCHRT discrimination grounds, 4–5, 102, 108, 108(t). *See also* BCHRT, discrimination grounds for complaints; courts and tribunals, Indigenous cultural traditions; Indigenous peoples, spiritual traditions
Report on Equality Rights of Aboriginal People (CHRC), 115
"Report to the Missing Women Commission of Inquiry" (Miller), 39, 165
reports. *See* expert-witnesses, reports
research on BC tribunals. *See* BCHRT, research projects
reservations and reserves, as terms, 9. *See also* Indigenous peoples
residential schools, 168, 171–72, 173
resurgence, Indigenous, 16, 27–30, 191. *See also* courts and tribunals, Indigenous cultural traditions; decolonization
Richland, Justin, 179
Ridington, Robin, 37, 38
rights. *See* human rights; human rights, Indigenous peoples
rights tribunals. *See* BCHRT (British Columbia Human Rights Tribunal);

human rights tribunals; Yukon Human Rights Commission
Rodriguez, Leila, 5
Rosen, Lawrence, 80
Royal Commission on Aboriginal Peoples, 28, 31–32
Royal Proclamation (1763), 14–15
Rush, Stuart, 84

Salish people. *See* Coast Salish peoples (BC, WA, OR)
Samish tribe (WA), 21
Sarris, Greg, 152
Saskatchewan, expert witness agreements, 43–46
schematization of facts, 55, 96, 121, 183
scholarship. *See* academic scholarship; anthropology; legal education; social sciences
Scott, James C., 41
security industry. *See* police and policing; *Radek v Henderson Development* (2005) BCHRT
security industry training, 122, 190
self-represented claimants. *See* BCHRT, self-represented complainants
sentencing, 39, 191. *See also* criminal law
settlements, BCHRT. *See* BCHRT, decisions and compensation; BCHRT, mediation and settlement
sexuality. *See* gender/sex
Silbey, Susan S., 23, 41–42, 119
Silverfox, Tanya, 28, 62
Simpson, Audra, 28, 117
Sister Watch, Vancouver, 171, 172
Skagit, Upper. *See* Upper Skagit Tribe of Indians (WA)
Skagit County, et al., Citizens to Preserve Nookachamps Valley et al. v, 65–67
skeletonization of facts, 96
Snake and Beaver story, 66
Snohomish tribe (WA), 21
social sciences: "accepted in the field," 93–94, 96, 180; adversaries in court, 72–74; concepts as debatable, 79; language, legal vs anthropological meanings, 46, 83, 92–95, 179; legal

entanglements, 17. *See also* academic scholarship; anthropology; expert-witnesses, relations with colleagues

Society for Applied Anthropology (SFAA), 89

spindle whorl, Musqueam, 139–40, 156

spirituality. *See* courts and tribunals, Indigenous cultural traditions; Indigenous peoples, spiritual traditions; religion and spirituality

Starlight Tours, 164

state, as term, 9

state-centered human rights, 118, 180

Status Indian, as term, 9, 13, 14. *See also* Indigenous peoples, Canada

Steilacoom tribe (WA), 20–21

Stephen, Lynn, 40, 41

stereotypes, Indigenous, 48, 58–61, 65, 112, 114–15, 129

Steward, Julian, 78, 80

Stogan, Vince, 163

Stó:lō Nation, 17, 38, 78

Stonechild Inquiry, 163–64

story, law as, 5, 96, 113, 119–20, 179–80, 188–89, 192. *See also* legal systems

success rates, BCHRT. *See* BCHRT, research projects

Supreme Court of British Columbia. *See* British Columbia Supreme Court

Supreme Court of Canada: *Gladue,* 39; *Heerspink,* 117–18; *Latif,* 95; limitations on tribunals, 185; *Moore,* 129, 185; *Tsilhqot'in,* 33, 35. See also *Delgamuukw v BC* (1997)

Swinomish tribe (WA), 28, 31

symbolic violence, as term, 30. *See also* Indigenous peoples, trauma in legal processes

systemic racism. *See* racism, systemic

Taylor, Herbert, 77

team approach to litigation, 80, 83–85, 90–91. *See also* expert-witnesses, relations with colleagues; expert-witnesses, relations with lawyers

Teillet, Jean, 28, 37, 38

Telling It to the Judge (Ray), 47–48. *See also* Ray, Arthur

Tewalt Rock, 65–67

thinning of evidence: about, 6, 46–48, 191–92; demeaning comments, 63–68; disinformation, 63–64; forms of, 46–49, 64, 66–68; incorrect inferences, 63, 95; judges and lawyers as amateur anthropologists, 66–67; legal vs social science terminology, 46; Miller as ethnographer, 8; omissions, 39; oral evidence in legal processes, 19; recommendations for reform, 191–92; of systemic racism, 39; *voir dire,* 45–46, 56, 192. *See also* expert-witnesses, diminution of; expert-witnesses, qualifications; expert-witnesses, relations with lawyers

Thompson, E.P., 186

Timberg, Tim, 119, 121

Tinseltown Mall, Vancouver, 48–49, 120–21. See also *Radek v Henderson Development* (2005) BCHRT

Toope, Stephen, 133–36, 149, 152, 154, 158

trans men and women, BCHRT complainants, 122–25, 123(t), 124(t), 125(t), 181–82

transformative power of legal processes, 84, 120–21, 184

tribal councils, as term, 8. *See also* Indigenous peoples

tribunals. *See* BCHRT (British Columbia Human Rights Tribunal); human rights tribunals; Yukon Human Rights Commission

truth: fact and truth concepts, 93–96, 179; inferences, 4, 85, 95, 129; postmodernists, 79; truthfulness of expert-witnesses, 44–45. *See also* facts

Truth and Reconciliation Commission (TRC), 168, 175

Tsawwassen First Nation, 68

Tseil-Waututh First Nation, 163, 164

Tsilhqot'in Nation v BC (2014), 33, 35

Twins, Joey, 24

twists and turns in courts. *See* courts, unexpected events

224 INDEX

two-spirit Indigenous people, 108. *See also* gender/sex

UBC (University of British Columbia): collective agreement, 136, 146–48, 150, 153; Indigenous-based programs or hiring, 105; Musqueam relations, 137, 139–40, 155–56; oral teaching methods, 155

UBC, Allard School of Law: CILS (Centre for Indigenous Legal Studies), 139–40, 148; display of Coast Salish culture, 139–40, 156; display of Musqueam/UBC documents, 140, 156; First Nations Law School program, 137, 138–39; First Nations Legal Studies Plan (2000), 139; Indigenous tenured faculty, 137; SAC (Senior Appointments Committee), 134, 146–51. See also *McCue v University of British Columbia* (2018) BCHRT

UNDHR (UN Universal Declaration of Human Rights) (1948), 102, 104

UNDRIP (UN Declaration of the Rights of Indigenous Peoples), 27–28, 115, 164–65, 185

unexpected events. *See* courts, unexpected events

Union of BC Indian Chiefs, 162, 164–65

United Nations Commission on Human Rights, 115

United States: American Revolution, 14; gender and legal actions, 23; state, as term, 9

United States, Native Americans: about, 14–16; anthropologists as expert-witnesses, 34–35; assimilation, 15–16; bill of rights, 16; border litigation (Canada/US), 19–20, 47–48, 68; colonial history, 13–16; ethnohistory, 34–35; federal recognition, 14–16, 20–22; fishing rights, 76, 93–94; gendered violence, 24; human rights tribunals, 114; Indian Claims Commission, 34–35, 90–91; *Johnson v M'Intosh*, 15; land claims, 15; legal experts, 28–30; Miller as anthropologist-expert, 17–22;

politics in legal processes, 21; symbolic violence, 178; terminology, 9, 14; treaties, 15, 47–48, 68, 76, 93–94, 114; tribal courts, 16, 67–68, 179, 191; *US v. Washington* (fishing rights), 76, 93–94

United States v Washington (1974), 76, 93–94

University of British Columbia. *See* UBC (University of British Columbia); UBC, Allard School of Law

unlikelihood of winning a case. *See* BCHRT, decisions and compensation

Upper Skagit Indian Tribe Historical Atlas (Miller), 18

Upper Skagit Tribe of Indians (WA), 17–18, 28, 62, 65–67, 93–94

Van der Peet, R v (1996), 37–38, 78

Vancouver: BCHRT hearings, 5, 129–31. *See also* BCHRT (British Columbia Human Rights Tribunal); UBC (University of British Columbia)

Vancouver, Downtown Eastside (DTES): demographics, 48–49; as Indigenous space, 48–49, 53; *Red Women Rising* report, 28, 164–65, 172, 174; Sister Watch program, 171, 172; Tinseltown Mall (International Village), 48–49, 120–21. See also *Menzies v Vancouver Police Board* (2019) BCHRT; *Radek v Henderson Development* (2005) BCHRT

Vancouver Police Department (VPD): complainants' fear of, 56, 170, 176, 184, 187–88; cultural training, 53, 161, 167–69, 170, 173–75; Indigenous liaison officer, 171–74 176; Indigenous women's reluctance to call, 164, 172, 175–76; racialized policing, 49–51, 55, 164; *Red Women Rising* report, 28, 164, 172, 174; retaliation against complainants, 170, 176, 187–88; statistics on officers, 172. See also *Menzies v Vancouver Police Board* (2019) BCHRT

VANDU (*Vancouver Area Network of Drug Users) v. DVBIA* (2014) BCHRT, 188

VANDU (*Vancouver Area Network of Drug Users*) *v. DVBIA* (2014) BCHRT, 188

Venne-Manyfingers, Sharon, ix–xi, 29

vertical power, 40. *See also* power relations in legal processes

violence, symbolic, as term, 30. *See also* Indigenous peoples, trauma in legal processes

voir dire (preliminary hearing), 45–46, 49, 55–56, 192

Von Gernet, Alexander, 73, 79

VPD. *See* Vancouver Police Department (VPD)

Waitangi Tribunal (AU), 74, 110

Walia, Harsha, 28, 164, 172, 174

Walkem, Ardith Walpetko We'dalx, 28, 100. See also *Expanding Our Vision 2020* (Walkem)

Walter, Bernd, 119

War of 1812, 14

Washington: expert testimony, 74; sacred sites (*Nookachamps Valley et al. v Skagit County, et al.*), 65–67; treaty fishing rights (*US v. Washington*), 76, 93–94. *See also* Upper Skagit Tribe of Indians (WA)

ways of knowing. *See* Indigenous peoples, ways of knowing

Weiss, Joseph, 100, 104, 121, 182–83, 190

Wet'suwet'en and Gitxsan peoples, 28, 35

William, Roger, 28, 33

Williams, Alice, 28, 66

Williams, Robert C., 143–46

Wilson, Richard A., 40

witnesses: about, 4; elders, 27, 32–34, 73; emotional costs, 41, 119–21; fear of giving testimony, 101, 120, 184; ill health from legal processes, 33–34; lay witnesses, 27, 74. *See also* BCHRT, Indigenous complainants; expert-witnesses; Indigenous peoples, trauma in legal processes

women: BCHRT complainants, 23, 122–25, 123(t), 124(t), 125(t), 181–82; women's studies, 153. *See also* Indigenous peoples, women

written final submissions to tribunals, 151, 157

written vs oral knowledge. *See* oral and written evidence in legal processes

Yeqwyeqw:ws First Nation, 17

Yukon, Supreme Court of, 56

Yukon Human Rights Commission: hiring discrimination (2008), 25, 68. See also *Blackjack* inquest (2018) Yukon